TESTIMONIALS

"We are all experts in our own lives and Jodee is an expert who has much to say to others who find themselves stumbling hand-in-hand along the dark passageways of addiction."

-Dr. Gerry Fewster Author, *Don't Let Your Kids Be Normal*

"Truth hurts. And truth heals. The breath-taking honesty of Jodee Prouse's powerful story is like a barrage of blows to the gut, as she tells of the unrelenting assault of addiction on the wounded body and soul of her family. Yet, it is that same brutal truth-telling that helped her recover from the hurt, not unscarred, but alive and at peace. This beautifully written memoir proves that there is the power to heal in not remaining silent in the face of our most stigmatized of diseases. I highly recommend *The Sun Is Gone* for the intimate and moving way it explores both sides of truth – the darkness and the light."

-Bud Mikhitarian, filmmaker and author of *Many Faces One Voice, Secrets of The Anonymous People*

I just finished the last page of your book and all I can say is....."wow." LOVE what you are doing for people who think they are in it alone. It's way more common than people seem to think. I think your story should become a movie someday to let people see what living with an addiction like that is REALLY like. It is hell on earth for all involved.

-Athena Bass, entertainer Femme Fatale, Actress Ex-Wives of Rock

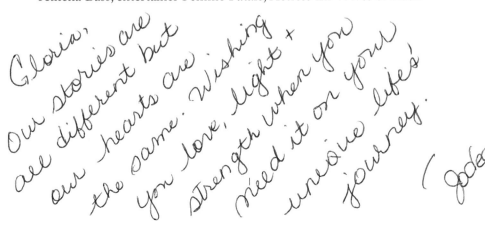

Gloria,
Our stories are all different but our hearts are the same. Wishing you love, light + strength when you need it on your life's unique journey.

Jodee

THE SUN IS GONE

A Sister Lost in Secrets, Shame, and Addiction,
and How I Broke Free

JODEE PROUSE

First Published in Canada Feb, 2017 by Hope & Humility Inc.
ISBN: 9780995890503

Editor: Nina Shoroplova
Typeset: Greg Salisbury

DISCLAIMER: This is a work of non-fiction and certain names have been changed. The author has been faithful to her memory and experiences.

CONTENTS

Everything I did yesterday, I do today, and my hope for tomorrow is because of the love I have for four men. Jim. Rick. Ryan. And Brett

And for the families that love someone addicted to drugs or alcohol.

You are not alone.

"Addiction is a family disease that stresses the family to the breaking point, impacts the stability of the home, the family's unity, mental health, physical health, finances, and overall family dynamics.

"Living with addiction can put family members under unusual stress. Normal routines are constantly being interrupted by unexpected or even frightening kinds of experiences that are part of living with alcohol and drug use. What is being said often doesn't match up with what family members sense, feel beneath the surface or see right in front of their eyes. The alcohol or drug user as well as family members may bend, manipulate and deny reality in their attempt to maintain a family order that they experience as gradually slipping away. The entire system becomes absorbed by a problem that is slowly spinning out of control. Little things become big and big things get minimized as pain is denied and slips out sideways.

"Without help, active addiction can totally disrupt family life and cause harmful effects that can last a lifetime."

Reprinted with permission from the National Council on Alcoholism and Drug Dependence, Inc. (NCADD) www.ncadd.org

INTRODUCTION

I have known what the word "alcoholic" means since I was five years old. Not because anyone told me; families keep secrets and my family is no different. Or should I say they think they keep secrets, but even as little children we figure things out very quickly. By the time I was six, I had already set my life's plan in motion, my feet planted firmly on the ground. This alcohol-fueled life my parents had was never going to be mine, never. I could not have been more wrong.

No one teaches you how to be a sister; you just become one. You enter the world in a particular birth order, which you didn't choose, but it often defines who you are and the role you take on in the world. My brother would become an addict and I a sister of an addict. It is a job that came with a lifetime's contract but no one gave me the skills to complete the assignment.

My brother, a fine, young man innocently took that first sip of alcohol in high school. That sip eventually led to a bottle, which took him down a path of destruction few could fathom. And I was along for the ride. From the time we are little people we are taught lessons, no different from learning to tie our shoelaces, only some of these lessons are not said out loud.

Things that we absorb, our interpretation of events, even one's that aren't traumatic, all shape our lives. We aren't supposed to say these things about someone that we love. For some, saying someone else is an alcoholic is a negative, disparaging statement. "It will ruin their reputation." How dare I? But perhaps, that is their judgment, not mine.

I am not ashamed. I know all too well how secrets and shame keep families hiding and our loved ones sick.

Our parents didn't beat my brother and me, but the scars remained. I see now that we missed the danger signs and perhaps they set the stage for what was to come. Those drunken Friday nights would change who we would be forever. They would make me strong, stoic, loud, and able to take on the world. The quiet little boy with the big heart would become scared, fearful, lacking in confidence, and riddled with anxiety. My love and sense of responsibility for him and his dependence on me would last us a lifetime and almost destroy us both.

This is the *whole* story of addiction, not a partial glimpse. You will hear this many times in recovery circles and it is my hope for all of you since I do not know all the answers.

"TAKE WHAT YOU WANT AND LEAVE THE REST."

PROLOGUE

My mother and I sat for about an hour, waiting for Brett to be seen. His leg rattled with anxiety until he was brought into a private emergency room. We explained to the nurse, not that we needed to as it was very clear by his scruffy appearance and glassy eyes, that Brett was severely intoxicated and needed help to safely withdrawal off the alcohol. And she began to take his vitals.

It wasn't the nurse's cold, disassociated approach while taking my brother's blood pressure, pricking his arm with a needle, or asking him how much he had had to drink that made my blood boil. It was the fact that it was obvious she absolutely *loathed* him. For the first time ever, I felt what my brother felt like a bolt of electricity running through my veins. I felt judgment. Pure unadulterated judgment. As she left the room, I scampered quickly behind her catching up in front of the nurse's station.

"Excuse me," I said. She didn't hear me so I repeated myself. She turned around to look at me. "Hi. Listen, I don't mean to be rude. I completely understand and appreciate how hard your job is and how many different things you must see. I even get that on some level maybe to you my brother isn't sick in the same way as most of the people here, and that you believe this may be purely self-induced. What I need to remind you is that he is a human being."

She didn't blink.

I continued, "Now I don't care what you did yesterday or how you are tomorrow. All I care about is that for right now, when you come into *that* room, you show a little compassion as that is a person in there. A person! That is someone's brother, someone's son. And despite what you very obviously perceive as completely disgusting, someone loves him. Do you think you can do that?"

I didn't give her time to answer.

"'Cause if you can't, then what I suggest is that for the next hour or so you FAKE IT!"

I walked away, so I didn't have to look at her stony expression for another second. I caught my breath as I was so overwhelmingly pissed off, before stepping through the door to sit quietly in the corner of my brother's room.

I understand and appreciate how hard nurses work—after all, our mother is a nurse—and I can imagine that they see all sorts of things. But that's their job, a job that they choose. To treat someone very obviously, whatever their circumstance, like they are below dirt I cannot take. As I looked at my brother at his worst, just as I had done so many times before, all I thought was *he is in there*.

The doctor arrived a short time later. I knew the drill; it seemed like I had heard this a thousand times before. They couldn't keep Brett overnight as all the beds were full, although I appreciate the doctor did give him a shot of Valium. At least I think it was Valium, which by then I knew belongs to the class of medications called benzodiazepines. It is used for the short-term relief of symptoms of mild to moderate anxiety and for alcohol withdrawal. Mom and I knew that at least it would help Brett get through the night and the suggestion the doctor offered was for us to head back to the detox center in the morning. Although severe alcoholics can actually *die* from the effects of withdrawal, there was nothing more the doctor could do.

It seemed like a completely different nurse came into the room, yet it wasn't. She was kind, compassionate, and caring, and as we left, she said to my brother, "Take care of yourself, Brett."

I whispered "Thank you" to her as we walked out the door, and I hope she knew how much I meant it.

It didn't matter how many times I had been in these situations, every minute of every day was consumed with some disaster, all of which led us to some health care professional or institution, more often than not the hospital. I promised myself, for my own wellbeing and the sake of my sons, that I wasn't going to get involved; yet I did it again, sacrificing my own children for the brother I loved.

Just a few hours earlier, I had arrived at the arena for Rick & Ryan's weekend lacrosse tournament. We had stayed for only an hour. I didn't say anything at first, but soon told my husband Jim that we were leaving to get

Brett. The thing is he knew anyway, even before I found the courage to tell him. After all, my mother being there with me was a dead giveaway. She never attends her grandsons' activities—not karate, nor their sporting events, nor their band concerts. Meanwhile, the sun rises and sets on my nieces. For reasons only our mother can explain, she has never shown any interest in my children. So, Jim knew that, after fourteen years, Mom wasn't going to all of a sudden be compelled to watch them play lacrosse. He may not have said anything directly to me, but trust me, I knew he was not pleased.

Mom and I pulled up next to the seedy motel on Macleod Trail about an hour and a half later. We called Brett on his cell from the parking lot, to tell him we'd found him, and he immediately gave us his room number. Walking up the ten or so steps, we opened the unlocked door to my brother's room. It was a sight I had seen so many times. Absolute filth, musty, empty vodka bottles piled up everywhere with an overturned mattress covering the window to block out the light.

Brett was sitting silently with his head up against the headboard, looking innocent, like he was saying, "What do I do now?"

He wanted us to come up and get him, although I am not sure it was really a matter of *want*. The more likely reason was that once he ran out of money, he had no further options and therefore he welcomed the rescue.

Mom and I had grabbed all of his things and stuffed them into a small garbage bag. We knew he would have to go through withdrawal after being almost three weeks in that hell hole. We worked together and got him in the car and swiftly drove to the detox center.

I returned to the car and spoke quietly to our mother, explaining what I had feared: they were full to capacity and couldn't help us. They apologized and suggested that we come back early the next morning. We both knew he couldn't wait until tomorrow without having something to drink, so we had headed to our only other option—the emergency room.

As we left the hospital, we realized that hadn't worked either so we quickly needed to figure out another plan.

We decided to get a hotel for the night and then head straight back to detox first thing in the morning. They have a limited number of beds, but we were going to take our chances since people leave every day, usually bright and early. We needed to get him sober again, and that required medical assistance.

By now, my brother wasn't stumbling drunk. To an outsider, it might have appeared he wasn't drunk at all, but I knew better. Based on the amount of liquid he could consume; he was "off the charts wasted."

Mom checked us into the hotel then came back to us in the waiting car.

As we walked through the main entrance of the hotel, someone made eye contact with Brett. "What the fuck are you looking at?" he barked.

The innocent guy, minding his own business, was taken by surprise.

"Gosh, I am so sorry … he has Tourette's," I quickly lied to the man.

When he was sober, Brett would never talk to someone like that, let alone a stranger. That was what alcohol did to my brother; he became a different person. Here was a guy who was so kind and passive that he struggled to open up in individual therapy as he believed he was betraying people and gossiping if he spilt details about others' past mistakes and possible causes for his drinking. Quite honestly, I had no idea where this tight-lipped attitude came from or why he would believe that. I had never in my life heard him speak harshly about anyone, in fact. Of course, that is a huge problem since talking about issues, feelings, and people one lives with and associates with is the core premise behind how and why counseling works.

Navigating the rest of the lobby with our fingers crossed that nobody else would look in our direction, we lead Brett into the elevator, along the hall, and into our room. It was quite a contrast from where he had been sleeping—it looked like the penthouse at the Four Seasons compared to the dump we had just come from.

That evening, we were all completely exhausted. Brett's clothes were a mess so I had no choice but to throw him a pair of my pajama bottoms as he went to shower and clean up. As he exited the bathroom, it was one of the funniest things I had ever seen, although I realize none of this is funny at all.

One of my favorite things about my brother has always been his quick-witted, dry sense of humor. Even when he didn't say anything.

He came out of the bathroom, showered and ready for bed, and smelling like a cheap bar of soap. Brett is very hairy, not gross hairy, but hairy with the beginnings of a belly. My white, fluffy pajama bottoms were too short and skin tight. As tight as a leotard. And I couldn't help but laugh out loud.

"Fuck you, Jodee," he said, only in his loving way and he gave a little smirk. He thought it was funny too.

He held out his hand and Mom grabbed a few sleeping pills from her leather Baby Phat purse. He tilted his head back, took a sip of water, swallowed, and crawled under the fresh sheets of the queen beds. I nestled in beside our mother and settled down for the night.

At 6 a.m., we arrived back at the detox center, but there were still no beds available. By now, Brett was feeling the effects of withdrawal, and when I came back to the car to tell him and Mom the news, there was instant terror in his eyes. It had been more than twelve hours without him having something to drink and we all knew what that meant.

"I don't want to have a seizure! Please, I don't want to have a seizure," he started to cry.

Although he had never had one, it is a real possibility for an alcoholic to have a seizure in withdrawal and they know it. Besides the excruciating pain of withdrawal, they will do *anything* to stop all this from happening. He was in sheer panic mode, shaking like a lit firecracker in the backseat of the car. So, we quickly headed towards Calgary, where Mom lived, to try another center. We knew it was either that or stop at the nearest liquor store. It was a three-hour drive south, and she made an important detour halfway through the trip to drop me off. I had to get home to my own family.

And my brother entered the gates of detox once more.

I try hard to remember the happy times but they became farther and farther apart. We were all living in an impossible reality. How did our beautiful, loving family get here?

It was our past that I tried to forget, but I remember it because it is where it all began.

"D-I-V-O-R-C-E"

We were an average, everyday, normal family.

Before my younger sister Nicole came along, we had had the same babysitter for years, Mrs. Judson. Both our parents had to work since we were hardly rich. My little brother Brett and I were both very young at the time I'm remembering, probably two and six. My brother would follow me everywhere at Mrs. Judson's house. Even when I went to the bathroom, there he would be. He couldn't bear for us to be apart even for a second. When our mom Annie worked the late shift at the hospital, our dad Peter would pick us up after work at five o'clock, which was when the babysitter's closed.

Well, that was what was supposed to happen anyway.

On many occasions, too many to count, I would overhear Mrs. Judson on the phone.

"It's okay, Annie, the kids are fine. I will see you later."

I didn't know what was happening really; I just knew it wasn't right. When everyone, including her own kids, went to bed, she would neatly tuck Brett and me under the itchy brown-and-tan handmade afghan on the couch. Brett, too young to know or remember what was going on, was just content as we snuggled together on the sofa watching *Sonny & Cher* on television until his little eyelids got too heavy to stay open.

Our mom would hurry to come and get us after 11 p.m. when her shift ended. Thankfully, there are some amazing people in this world, ones who go over and above what they need to. She didn't need to make sure we were safe and well looked after. I suspect most babysitters would have told my mother to find a new babysitter, but that is not what Mrs. Judson did. This was an example of a tremendous act of kindness and a powerful lesson I learned early on, looking out for others even if you don't completely understand.

I always knew where my dad was when he didn't pick us up—at the Arlington. That name I always overheard. The Arlington. It doesn't take a person long, even as a young kid, to figure out that it was a bar. Children start to understand lots of things that they shouldn't. They put together the puzzle pieces. Children have naturally curious minds, absorbing everything like little sponges. Evaluating and interpreting, trying to figure out why things are the way they are. Like around the same time when I told Mom that Dad was bringing a girl home when Mom was at work. Of course, I didn't know what it meant then, but I most certainly do now.

I don't remember the exact conversation since I was just a little girl. I do, however, remember very clearly telling Mom that the girl was coming home with Dad and Mom's response was firm. Although I was only six or so, the next time I saw Daddy's lady friend, I relayed the message my mother asked me to give her, "My mommy said you are not allowed to come to our house ever again!"

Brett and I sat silently in the backseat of Dad's car while he and that woman both leaned over the hood, clearly having a huge argument over what I had just said. And I never saw that girl again.

Memories are strange. None of us remembers everything that happens throughout our lives. It is obvious why some things stay with us forever and how these experiences affect us all differently. Other things are more complicated; it takes much more work and self-reflection to understand them.

I remember a day with no special significance. It was over thirty-five years ago and I can still feel the hot sun on my cheeks. I can hear the rumbling tires of a big wheel going up and down the concrete sidewalk when I close my eyes. My little brother loved his big wheel, his little legs moving frenetically on the black pedals. I was on the front lawn; playing Barbie and hopscotch with my girlfriend, like most nine-year-olds did. He was surrounded by neighborhood kids, whipping back and forth, laughing and screaming as they did little jumps in the air off the pieces of wood that they found in our backyard. Innocent little boys; rambunctious, invincible, and testing their limits without a care in the world.

We lived in a modest new home, covered in white swirly concrete that Mom and Dad had built in a great family community across town. I looked up to the large bay window and standing there doe-eyed was my baby sister

Nicole, not yet walking, hanging on with dear life to the wooden frame and looking out intently at her older brother and sister. My sister was the cutest baby girl I had ever seen. White blonde hair, a fair complexion, and huge, piercing blue eyes. I knew she wanted to come out and play but she was just too young at the time.

Soon the happy laughter was replaced with cries of hurt. "Jodee, Jodee," my brother wailed as I dropped my Ken doll and ran from my blue blanket on the grass. Brett had slipped off his big wheel and was already running in my direction when I got to him. His elbows were skinned and bleeding with some little pebbles stuck in the red liquid dripping down his knees. I ran for our mom, who was an emergency room nurse. She knew instantly this minor accident wasn't life threatening as she lifted his little body onto the bathroom countertop. She lovingly wiped away the blood with the facecloth, like all good moms do, and bandaged the cuts as he continued to cry. "It hurts, Jodee, it hurts," is all I remember him saying until the tears finally subsided.

I was my brother's safe haven and that started long ago.

You see, the nights were different from the days. I would be cozy and warm, sound asleep in my bed, dreaming of once-upon-a-time and frog princes, but that peace and serenity didn't last long as something familiar always woke me up. I could hear screaming coming from my parents' bedroom. It was Friday night and I knew what was going to happen next because this seemed to always happen on Friday nights. Our dad had come home drunk again.

Our mother would not be impressed to say the least, and I could literally hear the wails, him crying out her name, "Annie, Annie." She didn't like him when he was like that, sneaking in late then trying to give her very wet, slobbery kisses, wanting the only thing on his mind. She always got up and tried to go sleep on the couch, which of course pissed him off.

I am not sure if that is how it started on this particular night, but I always knew how it would end. I would pull the covers over my head and try to block out the sounds, try to hide, escape, pretend it was not happening, but I knew it was only going to get worse. I was just a little girl, tired, frightened; I just wanted to go back to sleep and forget. Brett was going to wake up soon, like he always did, so I made sure I was quiet as I snuck down to the bunk bed below, got under that gaudy seventies comforter and crawled in beside him.

The bright moon peeked through the curtains just enough so I could see he was squirming and slowly opening his eyes. My little brother was only five years old and he looked so cute when he was sleepy, with his short brown hair, little chubby cheeks, and round face. He smiled gently when he saw that I was there as he was too young to comprehend what was going on around him. I knew he could hear them too, so I squeezed him close, and I could feel the pounding of his heart as I gently rubbed his hair. I whispered in his right ear, promising him, "It's okay, Brett. It's okay."

When he was safely sleeping again, I slipped out of bed and went into the living room to tell our parents to stop fighting. Our dad was screaming obscenities and Mom was crying hysterically. He shoved and pushed her a couple of times and I thought he was going to hurt her. "Leave her alone!!" I yelled at him at the top of my lungs as I stood in our hallway.

Instantly, he was mad at me and he quickly turned around and hollered, "Get back to bed!!" His breath was horrible and warm and he didn't even look like Daddy. Instinctively, Mom grabbed me by the hand, but she didn't have to say anything because I already knew what to do next. After all, this wasn't the first time, the second, or the third.

I hurried into my bedroom as fast as I could and found Brett was awake again, but frightened, crying so hard that he could hardly breathe. Our mom was in the other room getting Nicole and we were getting the hell out of there.

We were in a hurry, of course, so I grabbed Brett's little blue coat and beloved brown cowboy boots by the backdoor because it was all that I could find through the commotion and in the dark. As I struggled to put his little arms into the holes, I tried wiping away his tears with my other hand while he continued to sob my name.

I promised him, "Everything is going to be alright."

Even as I said it I never believed it myself, after all, it was impossible to believe since Mom and baby Nickie were crying too. I used to cry; well, I think I did; it wouldn't have been normal if I hadn't. But the truth is I don't know. All I really recall is that I felt, if I cried, my little brother would be even more terrified, and all I wanted was for him not to be scared.

The four of us headed out the front door in the middle of the night, leaving behind our little white house in Anders Park. We ran down the path to Mom's red Pontiac car with our father in hot pursuit. Since no drunk person stays coordinated, he was stumbling and struggling to get down the path, screaming at us not to go.

After we all got in the car, Mom quickly reached over and locked the door on the passenger side, but our father wouldn't let go of the handles. He was crying too and begging us to stay, but we zoomed away, hearing the shrill squeal of our mother's tires on the quiet street in the middle of the night.

Some nights when this had happened, we would wake Nana, Mom's mom, who lived just around the corner and up the street. She wouldn't say anything, when she came to the door rubbing her eyes, her eyes locked with our mother's, cementing her distaste for our dad. On other nights, as I lay my head back on the seat I would see the bright lights of an old hotel. People at the desk would try their best to act like this was a normal occurrence, a dishevelled lady in the middle of the night, struggling with three children. A hotel was not a luxury we could afford and our mom was visibly embarrassed as she fumbled to find enough money in her purse.

I don't remember where we stayed this particular night, whether we hid the car in the alley at my grandmother's so our daddy couldn't find it if he came looking. Or whether another stranger at a front desk looked at us with piercing judgmental eyes, and sent us to a dingy room. Either way we came back home on Saturday as usual, still wearing our same clothes. Our dad was usually sleeping on the couch, looking shitty and hungover. But that day was different. As I walked in the front door, ahead of our mom, my brother, and my sister, and up the five or six stairs into the living room, he wasn't there.

I continued into the kitchen and saw a note on the table in Dad's handwriting. His gold wedding ring was sitting on top.

I just stood there, paralyzed. I didn't want to hear what our father had to say and to this day I have no idea what that one-page note said, except I saw the "All my love forever, Peter" in his squiggly handwriting that I had seen many times before. But I knew what the letter and the ring meant. Daddy was gone and he wasn't coming back. I didn't move, the nine-year-old girl not saying a word, comprehending, analyzing.

And I felt a sense of peace as I stood there, silently, thinking, "Today is the best day of my life."

"KEY LARGO"

For a short time after our dad left, it was just the four of us: me, Mom, Brett, and Nicole. Since Mom was a nurse, which required long hours and erratic shift work, I took on a lot of the family responsibilities. I spent most of my time babysitting my siblings, while Mom was busy trying to make ends meet.

Brett and I spent countless hours playing in our unfinished basement with friends, listening to music on our huge stereo unit filled with records. We loved jumping around and singing along to Shaun Cassidy's "Da Doo Ron Ron" or John Travolta's "Greased Lightning." We played school or tumbled on our green shag carpet doing gymnastics, Brett in his tight blue underwear. Although there was a four-year difference between the two of us, from the very beginning we were the closest of friends. At eight years younger than me, Nicole was too young to play with us, but she was content sitting in the corner playing with her dolls.

We were all happy, healthy, well-adjusted children and the divorce didn't seem to affect us at all. My brother did suffer from severe, piercing headaches and occasional sleepwalking when he was a little boy; it went on for years. One episode terrified me when I was babysitting Brett and Nicole. I will never forget it. A little girl doesn't know what to do when it's late at night and her brother comes down the hall in a daze, eyes wide open, mumbling things that don't make sense, then bolts out the front door into the dead of night. Of course there were no cell phones back then, so I couldn't call my mother who was out on a date. So I dialed the number of a neighbor to come and help.

Brett seemed to outgrow this as he got older, so there was no mention of it ever again.

Our lives changed again when Mom brought home a fireman she'd been dating. I was a little uncomfortable (okay, a lot uncomfortable, I hated it), which I suppose was a normal reaction for any young child. When it didn't work out, she dated another fireman. Then another, but that time she fell madly, deeply in love. His name was Ron Joel.

Ron was much younger than my mom. He was only twenty-six at the time, and she was thirty-one with three kids in tow. It was a huge gap. Our mother was exceptionally beautiful, so she was hard to resist. So gorgeous, in fact, that guys would stop and stare. She had a petite frame, long brown hair with some blonde highlights, and she always wore full makeup. She always liked the attention, it was obvious. Ron was just as handsome as she was beautiful with a tall, athletic build. They not only looked perfect together, they were perfect together, inside and out.

Life felt perfect for us kids, too, as Ron loved us like we were his own. He and Mom got married even after she made it clear she would never have any more children. So, he made the ultimate sacrifice and built a life with the four of us.

My brother and Ron instantly formed a special bond. Ron would pull up to the house on many occasions in the fire department's huge red fire truck to take Brett for a ride. Brett always ran out the front door with a huge smile and eyes as big as saucers, knowing Ron was there just for him. I am sure he felt like the coolest kid on our block—after all, no other boy's Dad did that.

Our summers were filled with fun, family vacations. Although we never had the money to go to Disneyland or on a tropical vacation, for us it was just as exciting going one province away to Kelowna, British Columbia. Mom and Ron would pack the station wagon with everything we needed and leave at midnight with the three of us sleeping under a pile of blankets in the back. We would wake up early and see a beautiful lake and begin our vacation first thing in the morning. To this day, my favorite place to be is on or near the water. And these were what my brother would call later, the "Golden Years," our true bliss.

The happiness of hanging out with the family didn't end after the summer. Our winters were filled with ski trips to the mountains in Banff and so many of Brett's hockey tournaments that I lost count. Then Christmas time, which included time with Nana, was filled with singing and laughing.

Our nana still lived a block or so away so we saw her often. She too had been an emergency room nurse, the head nurse in fact, though she had since retired. We never had a sleepover at her house (our middle of the night encounters do not count). Not once. She wasn't that type of grandma. Like our own mother, she wasn't mushy or touchy-feely, but a little cold and distant. Even so, we always knew in our hearts that she loved us very much. It was the little things that Nana did, whether taking us and her dog Benji out for soft ice cream, picking me up from work at Burger Village when I got older and I needed a ride, or just driving by daily with the honk-honk-honk-honk of her little GMC Acadian car as she whizzed by. She showed us love in different ways.

Nana was divorced from our Grandfather Papa, who lived in a modest apartment he rented in Calgary. Papa was everything our nana wasn't. He was sweet, soft-spoken, kind, sensitive, and gave hugs and kisses often. Papa was also an alcoholic, although I didn't really know that when I was a kid. Even now really, his problems are a well-kept, guarded family secret.

Our dad lived less than an hour away from us in a small town. We continued to see Dad on occasional weekends back then. He had remarried but that marriage didn't last. Same story; different page.

Our life with Ron worked, partly because of Ron's commitment to helping our mother. Since they both worked hard, they shared all responsibilities. He was always vacuuming, cooking, doing whatever needed to be done. That was not the norm back then, even now it isn't in some homes. From this, I developed a sense of total equality between a man and a woman, and for that I am eternally grateful.

What was missing, compared to our early years, was that alcohol was not a factor. I don't ever recall seeing Mom or Ron drunk. Sure, they would have occasional cocktails with friends, or enjoy drinks while on vacation, but nothing more than that. Our mom never did hold her liquor well; her eyes would go instantly glassy and she would act a little stupidly when tipsy, so I was always glad she never indulged past a couple of glasses. There was never more than a normal argument. No chaos or dysfunction. Such a complete and utterly happy, mundane, average, normal life for my brother, sister, and me.

I would be lying if I said that I always got along with Ron. I didn't. I became a know-it-all teenager and we butted heads often.

Neither Ron nor my mother had any idea that when I was fourteen and in grade nine, I would sneak out of my bedroom window at night, and run around town with friends, hanging out at Mac's Convenience Store to play Pac Man, then sneaking back home just before dawn. We were already into underage drinking, getting drunk on bottles of Strawberry Angel on more than a few occasions.

Soon I began working at the local burger bar. That's one thing about me—I always loved to work, so I spent a lot of time there. The cooks, who were a few years older, invited me to parties with a room full of smoke and joints being passed around. That was my introduction to drugs. We would get high on hash oil on a regular basis during our shifts at work or at parties at night. By fifteen, I looked the legal drinking age of eighteen, so I could get into the liquor store and bars. I was very responsible in other ways, continuing to work hard thus being able to buy my prized possession, a Turbo Trans Am. All through high school, I was partying hard, skipping school, driving drunk (or high) in my sports car, and having the time of my life. So much so, that the partying got in the way of my studies and I did not graduate from high school, which remains one of my few life's regrets.

I never got arrested and I never ever got caught. Not once. If you told any of these things to my mother, it would come as a huge surprise and I doubt she would believe it. But that does not make it any less true.

Ron and I argued all the time, but for stupid, less meaningful reasons. As an adult we see things completely differently; he was just trying to set some boundaries and rules. I wasn't used to that and I hated it. And what I see now was that he gave us safety, stability, and nothing but love.

I left home early, shortly after my seventeenth birthday. Our mom called me soon after to see if I would move in and care for my nana who had been diagnosed with what they thought at the time was Alzheimer's. Without any conscious thought of what this would entail, that's exactly what I did. I had a full-time job, but I would do all the cooking and cleaning, take her on errands, and make sure she was well looked after. I was paid five hundred dollars a month and managed as well as any teenager could, until it was obvious she needed round-the-clock medical attention, which is when she went to live in a nursing home.

At nineteen, I couldn't get out of Red Deer fast enough. Nothing exciting ever happened there, so off I went to the big city in search of a new life. I moved to Edmonton, an hour and a half away.

I had been there for less than a year when I applied for a job working as a waitress for an upscale restaurant. During the interview, I was introduced to one of the kitchen workers and I couldn't help but stare at him—he was the best looking guy I had ever seen.

On our first shift together, we exchanged smiles and quick conversations as I grabbed the plates from under the heat lamp. Just being around him—his crisp white shirt, checkered black-and-white pants, thick mustache, mullet, and bright blue eyes—I felt butterflies. Even though I had known him for only five hours, I went home that very night and told my roommate that I was going to marry the head chef. I am sure she shrugged her shoulders, suggesting she thought that was highly unlikely. His name was Jim.

But my butterfly instincts were right. Within a few short weeks I was head over heels in love and I needed to tell someone. Naturally, the first person I wanted to share this news with was my brother, my closest confidant. I excitedly picked up the phone. "Brett, honestly, I am in love. I can't wait for you to meet him."

"Has he told you he loves you?" Brett asked me point blank.

"No."

"Did you tell him?"

"No, not yet."

"Jodee. Do not ever, ever be first to tell a guy you love him."

"Okay."

"I am serious!" Brett said, driving home his point, so confident and full of knowledge for a sixteen-year-old kid. "Never. He will feel obligated to say it back."

"Okay, I hear ya."

My brother always makes me smile. We'd had a similarly serious conversation just months before when he'd told me he had lost his virginity. I made him promise, swear actually, that he would never trust a girl just because she said she was on the pill and to always wear protection.

"I got it, Jode!" he had said loudly, when I repeated it twice.

Brett and I were close, very close. Being separated by four years and being the opposite sex didn't matter—we saw life the same way and we were dedicated to each other.

So, I took my little brother's advice. I waited and Jim did tell me he loved me first. Our romance intensified very quickly and we got engaged in March, just six months after we'd met. We were both much older than our years, ready to settle down, and we wanted the same things out of life. Although we were not yet married, those same things included wanting to start a family immediately. We were ecstatic to find out that I was pregnant after just one month of trying to conceive. We were thrilled with the news that our first baby was going to be a boy.

At twenty-one, on June 30, 1990, I married the man of my dreams. A small church ceremony was followed by a barbecue in our backyard. We were surrounded by about seventy family members and close friends.

Dad was there with his new girlfriend Leona and Mom and Ron were at our wedding together too, although they had been separated for a while. I knew they had been having problems for quite some time. Ron had been spending more and more time with friends, golfing, and drinking, and not coming home. I knew these specifics as our mother always had a habit of sharing with me, however inappropriately, what was going on in her life. I had come home to visit them months earlier, and she needed my advice. With her at the wheel, we drove down the road eventually arriving at the golf course, circling the parking lot, her head moving back and forth like a bobblehead. Then we came to a dead stop, me almost hitting my head on the windshield.

"See, look."

I looked up and saw Ron's little truck. She pointed her finger in its direction like she was trying to substantiate her facts.

"What do I do?" she asked.

I wanted to say, "Mom, how the hell would I know? I am twenty years old!"

But I didn't. Instead, I tried my best to make her feel better, not really giving her advice at all. Besides, our mother would not want to hear what I really thought; that maybe she should be talking to him instead of to me; that he had always tried to make her happy but that she was difficult at times, so he always failed just slightly. I knew that even back then, but I didn't want to hurt my mother.

Even though I was young and not yet full of life's experiences, I was already very aware of the many factors that complicate lives. I knew that it wouldn't have been easy for Ron; Nana had recently passed away and I knew how excruciatingly painful that was. Watching someone deteriorate slowly into a shell of who they once were was hard for each of us, and it wasn't even right under my nose. I felt for Ron. This added stress and responsibility, combined with the fact they had two teenagers at home, would be hard for him.

Being older now, I have a clearer understanding of why someone begins to indulge more and more into alcohol; self-medicating to eliminate the problems. And of course that works, for a while. I didn't know all the details of what had gone on for the last three or four years since I'd left home. Only they knew the reality of that, and of course Brett and Nicole would have witnessed it as well. Was alcohol getting in the way of a happy marriage? Yes. Was it the only reason? Of course not, but I have no doubt it was the only reason in our mother's mind.

Soon the lives of everyone in the little white house in Anders Park was about to change as Mom and Ron did decide to divorce. I always felt so badly for my siblings, my brother in particular, as this would be the second loss of a father figure for him. There would be no weekend visits, eventually seeing Ron less and less. The man Brett and Nickie absolutely adored was practically gone from their lives.

However, I had my own life to celebrate, my new family with Jim was only just beginning. On January 19, 1991, Jim and I welcomed Ricky Thomas James Prouse into the world.

"SOMETHING TO BELIEVE IN"

I couldn't concentrate fully on my own life and family. Mom called me in the summer of 1991 asking me to help with my sister. Brett was leaving home to go to trade school and Mom said she was having a hard time with Nicole. I had known that was going on for a while. Nicole had been struggling ever since Ron had left the year before. She had just turned fifteen and had become increasingly hard for my mother to handle, in fact getting way out of hand.

Then I got the call. "Please, Jodee, would you and Jim be able to take Nickie in for this school year?" she pleaded.

My family has always depended on me, calling me to their rescue when they need something. Our mom, my sister, and my brother. And I took on that duty like a soldier protecting her country. That job had been bestowed on me when I was just a little girl. I would never deny one of them when they needed help; I just never understood then how deep my sense of responsibility was for them. It wasn't that I couldn't say no. The God's honest truth is, as I came to understand years later, I didn't know I could.

Without hesitation, and probably a five-minute discussion between Jim and me, we agreed that Nicole could come to live with us. Two young parents, twenty-two and twenty-three, with a seven-month-old baby, would now have the additional responsibility of looking after a rebellious teenager.

The high school agreed Nickie would be able to enroll in grade ten even though she had failed grade nine and would be behind in many classes. Mom was happy for her to continue onto high school, but I disagreed as she would learn no lesson in that. Since I was now the guardian, the choice was mine. I would have Nicole repeat grade nine.

Problems with Nicole began from the get-go, with constant visits to the principal's office for one reason or another. Either she was skipping classes, not doing homework, or having a horrible attitude with teachers. Jim and I had a very stable and loving home and we tried our best to be a great influence over Nickie, but we had rules and my sister did not like the word "no."

There were small moments of peace and calm, but they were few and far between. She was great with little Ricky and showed much love for her nephew back then. I tried to teach her how to cook, but she got frustrated and annoyed at the simplest thing like peeling a potato, so she had no interest in that. She broke curfews, got fired from her first job for stealing, and continually ended up on Jasper Avenue, Edmonton, not the place for a young girl.

Nicole ran away one night, with suitcase in hand. She called me about an hour later.

"Um, I am just wondering, would I be able to get my allowance?" she asked.

Without skipping a beat, I replied calmly, "No, I'm sorry, Nickie, when you live on your own you don't get an allowance."

She was back a couple of hours later.

Another time, we thought she was safely sleeping at a girlfriend's, when we got a call in the wee hours of the morning. Nicole was with her friend at the hospital who was getting drugs pumped out of her stomach.

By the next June, she was finishing her repeated grade nine school year and I was pregnant with our second child. Jim and I had already made the decision that she would move back with Mom, but then my heart took over. The year of all those stresses and problems somehow seemed to fade in my memory when I thought how it might hurt a young girl by telling her she couldn't live with us any longer. Without even asking Jim, I told Mom that Nicole could stay with us for another school year.

My husband's brain wasn't clouded by emotion and extended family obligations, however, so we ended up in a huge screaming match in the kitchen. Rip-roaring yelling at the tops of our lungs. It ended with Jim throwing his full dinner plate into the sink—the red spaghetti sauce and noodles flew into the air and stuck on the kitchen's flowery wallpaper border. Nicole wasn't home, and we continued our loud screams into the backyard. What I wasn't expecting was that he was so furious he took a quick few steps back into the house and locked the door behind him.

Through the small window in the top of the door, I could see him calling someone. I knew who.

"She goes or I go!" he said loudly to his mother-in-law.

He knew this was too much for our family. And he was right. And my little sister went back to live with Mom.

Our mother had put me and Jim in the parental role with Nicole, and it changed our sister-sister dynamic forever. It makes me incredibly sad to realize this, and I don't think my sister has any idea. But we have never recovered.

"SMELLS LIKE TEEN SPIRIT"

I was more than ready to give birth to my second child. My doctor scheduled me to be induced when I was about a week overdue and weighing just over 200 lbs. (unfortunately ass, not water). By late in the afternoon on February 12, 1993, I had already been at the hospital for a few hours. My best friend Kim was with me as well as Jim. I was lying patiently waiting for contractions to start and the baby to be born. The bag of clear liquid had been in my arm for a while, and with the exception of the slight twinge in my gut, not much was happening.

Brett stopped by the hospital for a quick visit to see how I was doing. Even while all of us laughed and talked, I was getting very impatient. By dinnertime, the doctor decided this was going a little too slowly and she would break my water. She pulled the curtain to give us some privacy, and lifted a small tool that to me looked a lot like a knitting needle. I felt absolutely nothing at all, then instantly the warmth of water.

She pulled back the drapes, walked to the doorway, and began putting on her jacket.

"Jodee, I am going for dinner. I will be back later to check on you," she said.

Her second arm was barely in the sleeve of her jacket when the jolt of lightning in my abdomen made me scream out, "The baby is coming!"

My loud screech panicked everyone in the room, except the doctor who calmly walked back over to me. This wasn't a contraction type of yell. I knew the baby was coming, NOW!

Of course, I looked to my doctor for safety and reassurance, and when her eyes got as big as saucers as she checked me, my panic really set in. I had felt nothing a second earlier and now a baby was on its way down the birth canal.

"Hold her leg!" the doctor yelled to Brett who was wondering what the hell was happening as he frantically tried to make his way out the door, but he was too late to escape.

I had had no medication, so the nurse brought in a big cylinder with some kind of gas and tried to place it over my mouth. The smell was foul and unbearable. I grabbed the clear mask and threw it off my face. This was not the peaceful, easy delivery that I'd had with Ricky. This time, I was panicked and flailing, and the baby was crowning in what seemed like a couple of minutes!

My girlfriend offered support in my right ear, reminding me to breathe. My husband was on my left, and my then twenty-year-old brother stood in plain view and held my leg as instructed. Brett witnessed a miracle on that day: the birth of his youngest nephew, Ryan Joel Prouse. Named after our step-father, Ron Joel.

As my proud husband cut the umbilical cord, tears of happiness fell from his and Brett's eyes; I still remember that today.

Soon after, Brett joined us in Edmonton and lived with us for almost a year while he looked for work and got settled. Once again Jim accepted my sibling with open arms; and never complained. Besides, he truly enjoyed my brother's company and so Jim was also glad he was there. Although our house was small and the basement wasn't finished, we all pitched in and made a make-shift bedroom in the basement for Brett.

Then without warning, Jim, who had always worked full time, had his hours cut to four hours a week. I was on maternity leave with Ryan, just a newborn on formula and a two-year-old barely out of diapers, and soon Jim and I were flat broke. It was a struggle for a while even to find enough to pay our mortgage. Once a week the five of us would go to dinner at the only Kentucky Fried Chicken I had ever seen that had a buffet. Brett, Jim and I would leave giggling and laughing at the greasy chicken legs and thighs overflowing from Ryan's diaper bag. I am not proud of that memory, but the truth is sometimes you do what you have to do. What was never in short supply was an abundance of love. I often watched my brother with his nephews and I could see in his eyes and playful gestures that he was filled with pride. He loved Ricky and Ryan deeply, and they loved him too.

By 1994, Brett too had found happiness and the woman of his dreams. When I met Bobbie for the first time, I could see the attraction. She had expressive, dark brown eyes, exotic-looking dark skin, and large, curvy breasts. My brother would never be attracted to the typical blonde haired, blue eyed beauty. Bobbie was "hot," as he would say. And he was right. She had a very young son, Joshua, from a previous relationship. That might scare off a typical twenty-one-year-old man, but not Brett.

Girls flocked to my brother—like a magnet—they always had. And not just because of his good looks. He respected women. His soft-spoken nature and sweet sensitivity made him all the more attractive to the opposite sex. He was, as some might say, the full package: a handsome guy with a huge heart and a kind and caring demeanor that people in general, not just women, gravitated towards. He was also a guy's guy, and shared deep friendships with everyone in his life. I don't think you could find anyone that would say an unkind word. Everyone , absolutely everyone he met, loved Brett.

But, seeing him with Bobbie, I knew all those other girls could forget it. I knew my brother. She was the one, and he was deeply, madly in love.

Bobbie and Brett started living together, building their life as a young couple. Brett was working at an appliance company, which was a very physically demanding job that didn't pay very much. Bobbie eventually got a job at a high-end beauty salon downtown. They were renting an adorable older, character home in a quiet street about ten minutes from us. The street was lined with trees as though it had been taken right out of the country. Brett loved the country and the outdoors. Of course, he got that from our father. Brett and Bobbie were happy in their cottage-like home that truly had everything, even the picket fence.

Since Joshua was close in age to Ricky and Ryan—our boys—Jim and I spent tons of time with Brett and Bobbie, doing family things. Life got busy, with everyone working full-time, but we still shared a tremendous amount of time together. As I watched Brett with little Josh, my heart melted. The little squeals of "Daddy Brett! Daddy Brett!" filled the house with joy.

I had seen this before. I said nothing, but it reminded me of the excited little boy whose face lit up when he saw Ron pull the red fire truck up to our house when we were kids. I just smiled.

By March 1995, the man I loved and I were not as happy as I had thought. Jim and I suffered through a catastrophic, drunken event that included a 911 call. We came close to losing all I have ever wanted: to be married to the same man forever and to live in a stable and loving home with him and my children. That evening cemented my distaste for alcohol. That nothing good ever came out of it.

Through this hell, which included a six-month separation and a new understanding of who we were, we began to acknowledge other problems in ourselves and in each other. We were honest, painfully honest, and we listened to the therapist we had hired to help us. We did the work and we changed. My husband and I became different people from that split second of horror. We both decided never to have a drink again. We had always wanted to give our sons a different life from the ones we came from, but we almost lost our way.

Very few people know what we went through and what really happened. We knew there would be enormous stigma and judgment attached. Shame was never my motivating factor for staying silent but my husband was crippled with guilt. And I know people can be very judgmental and unforgiving even when it has nothing to do with them. No one who has met us in the last twenty years knows the secret we have never shared—not friends, neighbors, co-workers, and not even some members of our own family.

Jim and I made a pact we would keep it a secret forever, even from our now-adult sons. Of course, they have recollection of the separation. They just don't know all the unimaginable specifics. We agreed, unless something unforeseen were to happen, we would never tell anyone including our boys.

After all, there was no reason to share. It was a grave mistake and we were no longer those people.

Christmas soon arrived and it was our dad's turn to host the annual Boxing Day Celebration. Ever since we were little children, the whole Tisdale side of the family was very tightknit. My Grandma Tisdale made sure of that. So tightknit in fact that our cousin Kelly also happens to be Brett's best friend.

We had spent lots of time at Grandma's farm when we were children—close cousins, playing in the sandpit she owned and sliding down the hill to the creek for hours on our toboggans through brutal Alberta winters. I remember the sleepovers at Grandma Tisdale's house vividly, long before Nicole was born. She would tuck Brett and me into her old-fashioned steel bed, pull over the covers, and then in a quiet tone read chapters of the bible to us for what seemed like hours. My eyes popped open when she stopped reading. I am not religious; I am more spiritual; I just loved the sound of her voice.

Of course, over the years, the family had continued to grow in size. Each year the siblings—Uncle Les, Auntie Mary, Auntie Myrna, and Dad—would take turns hosting the Boxing Day celebrations, their spouses and all of us cousins getting together. These gatherings continued to grow with the next generation as we began having kids of our own.

Our dad still lived not too far away and was now married to Leona. Since they were hosting the annual gathering, we all packed into his old farmhouse. It was small, but seemed like a mansion compared to his childhood home with Grandma, and we made it work as we were all happy to be together. There were so many of us that there always seemed to be some kind of special event to celebrate, whether it was a wedding, a baby shower, an anniversary, or this Christmas get-together. Everyone made an effort to come. With my perspective now it seems that life was so much simpler back then.

That year, one very important family member was missing.

As the story goes, just before Grandpa Tisdale passed away when I was four or five, he told my grandmother to look after their eldest son, Uncle Ed. She took that literally.

I have no idea how or when Uncle Ed's drinking started—I was too young to know or understand—but I knew Uncle Ed was an alcoholic. He lived just steps behind Grandma's little farmhouse in a mobile home that she bought for him. For as long as I knew him, he never had a job and never left the security of that trailer. He drank, every day, all day, and Grandma paid his bills. When she passed away, the siblings took over responsibility for their brother. Although I didn't know the details back then, what I saw was shocking to me as a little girl. It was not how we or anyone I knew lived.

Dad would take us as kids to visit our Uncle Ed once in a while. I remember vividly the small, chain-link-fenced yard with overgrown weeds, a swing set, and a big tire sandbox left by my aunt and uncle who had owned the lot before him, now camouflaging what went on inside. Even now, it's impossible to forget. Years, decades really, of not cleaning were evident when you walked through the front door. The musty odor burned my nostrils; the old furniture and the disgusting bathroom that had never been cleaned would make me cringe. Boxes and boxes of empty beer bottles were stacked high in the front porch. What seemed like hundreds of bottles of various shapes and sizes were scattered on countertops. A stale loaf of bread in the empty fridge or the occasional girlfriend each visit were the only signs that someone could possibly live there.

At Christmas, Dad would arrive with a clean set of clothes and would have to actually force Uncle Ed to shower and clean up, so he could join us all for the annual Tisdale dinner. He was thin and frail, seemingly happy, and would sit on a chair in the corner, cocktail in hand, as all of us little cousins laughed and played and joked with him.

I have seen pictures of Uncle Ed when he was younger. He was an extremely handsome young man. His striking features remind me of his sister Myrna's kids, my twin cousins Trent and Trevor. He was a popular teenager and was married briefly. He had a daughter whom none of us have ever seen since the day his wife left. What I always knew, with absolute certainty, was that he was loved deeply by everyone in our family.

Now, all these years later, I can step back and feel so much empathy, understanding, and heartbreak for our father, my aunts, and my uncle. How lost and alone they must have felt. After all that was the seventies; they did not have the help or tools to know how to support their brother in a healthy way. They did the best they knew with the knowledge they had at the time. We, however, are blessed to have those tools, that is if ALL involved are willing to listen and understand that our part in the process can affect the outcome. I didn't know then how someone, with so much potential for an amazing life, could fall so far. I would spend much of my life trying to figure that out.

Uncle Ed died on December 5, 1995 from lifestyle complications a few weeks before that year's family gathering. He was fifty-one. As Brett would say "…in the skin of an eighty-two-year-old man."

And to this very day, if I smell the sweet stench of Pilsner beer I instantly feel like I am twelve years old.

"ANEURYSM"

Brett loved Bobbie, but they began to face challenges in their relationship. After all, they had been together for quite a while and while Brett still loved her beyond measure, their "real life" had set in. Although there was nothing we didn't tell one another, the truth is my brother was a little reserved. His deep feelings were always trapped just below the surface so he had a problem communicating them. I am sure that was a struggle for Bobbie. It wasn't just that he had a quiet nature—with me, he wasn't *quiet* at all—but usually when he started getting deeper emotions, he shut down and preferred to change the subject. We were never encouraged to open up and discuss our feelings in our family, let alone to deal with issues. Perhaps we were raised this way because if you don't talk about them then they aren't issues, they don't exist. That's a flawed philosophy, for sure. And one that I never adopted.

When Brett told me that Bobbie had cheated on him, we sat on the teal green sofa in my living room and talked for the longest time. I had never seen him look so sad, and it broke my heart to see him in such pain. He was heartbroken and confused, and rightfully so. But he still loved her. She still loved him too, and she was so sorry. I am not sure what he thought I would say.

"Brett, people make all sorts of mistakes and sex is just one of them. If you stay together, both of you will have to do a ton of work to repair your relationship. Only *you* can decide if you can forgive and if you can then work on all the issues," I told him.

And I meant it, with no hatred or bitterness. None of us is perfect, and Bobbie is no exception. I had already learned many of life's lessons, not only about the power of love but about forgiveness and, most importantly, about change. Besides, it was his life. Whatever choice he made, it had to be his. My resenting Bobbie would only complicate my life if they made it work. Hating her would force my brother to choose and I would never do that. His priority should always be what was best for him and his family, which was Bobbie and Joshua. He loved her and so that's all I needed to know.

I reminded him that I would always be there for him, leaned over, and kissed him on the cheek.

"I love you."

"I love you, too," he replied.

They decided to stay together, sorting through life's challenges as a young couple.

Meanwhile, our mother had moved from Red Deer as she had left her emergency room job a few years earlier and had been working at a gas plant in their Health Services Department. She was then offered a huge promotion at their head office in Calgary, about three hours away from Brett and me. Nicole, then nineteen and all grown up, had decided to join us all in Edmonton. Brett and Bobbie welcomed her with open arms to stay with them for a while. Some months back, they had moved into an apartment, just a couple of blocks away from Jim and me. The fact that it was only a two-bedroom apartment and they already had little Josh didn't matter; they made it work.

I loved Bobbie, we got along really well. But I knew she and Brett had more in common sometimes with my younger sister than with Jim and me, since we didn't drink alcohol any longer. The three of them enjoyed going out to bars on the occasional Friday or Saturday night. Bobbie and Brett's occasional weekend out wasn't any more frequent than any other young couple in their early twenties. Perhaps that helps explain the enormous shock.

I was always excited when my brother stopped by, for one reason or another or for no reason at all. That fall day was no different, except this time he had a favor to ask. Brett needed me to go somewhere with him and he wouldn't let me ask him where or why. I was in the kitchen getting dinner ready and Jim had taken the boys to the park, so I grabbed a notepad from the drawer and scribbled a quick note:

Ran with Brett for a quick sec, won't be long, xo.

I was a little apprehensive until Brett promised me things were fine. After all, we did favors for each other all the time, so this wasn't out of the ordinary.

My heart began to beat a little faster, both worried and excited at the same time, wondering *What's the surprise?*

We drove for about five minutes through our Mill Woods neighborhood until we reached a small brick building. There wasn't a sign outside, so I had no clue where we were after he carefully parallel parked and turned off the ignition. Brett stepped out silently and I followed close behind, walking around the back and entering through an open door.

As we walked up the eight or nine steps and entered a room full of strangers, I was feeling confused and uneasy. They were talking among themselves, sipping coffee, and munching on a table of snacks. They all seemed to know each other so I felt uncomfortable, like an outsider. I had absolutely no idea whatsoever where we were or what we were doing there. That is still hard for me to imagine, even today, as I am far from naïve.

Within a couple of minutes, the fifteen or twenty people began taking their seats, so we followed their lead. One by one, they introduced themselves by name. And then they got to my brother.

"Hi, my name is Brett and I am an alcoholic."

My head began to spin. My heart was broken. No one else said a word, just staring at me intently. I was completely unable to move or speak; just the sound of a stranger shaking and gasping for breath. Everything became fuzzy as my worst fear was realized.

I just sat in my chair and cried. And cried. And cried.

"KRYPTONITE"

Jim and I had wanted to move to Sylvan Lake for years, but it seemed like an impossible dream with bills, jobs, and commitments. Sylvan Lake was just twenty minutes west of my childhood home of Red Deer. It had a magnificent lake for the boys to enjoy and a breathtaking view of the Rocky Mountains just a forty-five minute drive away. Its natural beauty inspired us—the cold crisp air, rippling creeks, pine trees as far as we could see, and majestic snow-covered peaks (even in the summer).

We always have loved the mountains. Driving there through winding roads, we almost always saw some form of wildlife: moose, mountain sheep, coyotes, deer, and, if it was an extraordinary day, perhaps a bear with her cubs. Nothing in this world could make me feel smaller and yet also part of something bigger than the epic scale of the Rockies and the many different creatures running wild and free who call it home.

We yearned for a small-town family life that felt safe, calm, and quiet. Ironically, all the things I had hated about Red Deer when I was a teenager were now exactly what I wanted for my own family. In April 2000, we decided to take a huge risk: Jim quit his job and I relocated my candle company, a business I had started five years earlier.

We also loved that many of my family members, including aunts, uncles, and cousins, lived around Sylvan Lake too. Our mom was still in Calgary, but even that was only about an hour and a half away. Her job was very demanding, so we saw her less and less as time went by. Nicole had moved back to Red Deer, and although she was not married, she had recently given birth to my beautiful niece Payton in 1998. We didn't see Nicole very often either. The truth is she had always been more invested in friends than in family. What was happening in the life of my family—and that included her nephews—was not a priority to my sister. She was rarely present at any of the family gatherings. I tried my best to make excuses for her so my sons' feelings wouldn't get hurt, but I never did understand.

At seven and nine, Ricky and Ryan had already grown into handsome, thoughtful young boys. We were positive that they would enjoy the simpler life at the lake. We didn't have much money, but we always managed to save up for things like camping trips, skiing, soccer and baseball uniforms, and even a boat. I was realistic enough to know that one day my two sons would also appreciate the "bikini babes" at the local beach, too, and the open farmer's field next to our two-storey house. That would be ideal for snowmobiling in the winter months. Yes, they were going to love it there.

My own family was blissfully happy, but deep in my heart I knew something was wrong with someone else I loved; I had known it for a while. I called Brett, but he didn't answer. I wasn't surprised; I rarely saw or heard from my brother those days. We were still close. I didn't think that could ever change, but things were definitely different.

It had been a couple of years since he and Bobbie had eventually broken up. He took that alone time to get his ticket in power engineering and worked at a nearby gas plant.

I never asked who ended the relationship; after all, as close as we were, I didn't insert myself completely into his love life. I felt there were boundaries, and we are brother and sister after all, not best girlfriends who might have talked about things in more detail. So, he had never talked about it and I accepted that as meaning he was alright. All I know is that Bobbie and Josh moved away to Vancouver in British Columbia and Brett did not ever see them again. He never whispered about the heartbreak and pain he must have felt deep inside, losing a little boy he loved as though he was his own son. But what I did know was that he still loved Bobbie. For him, she was still "the one."

I left a message for Brett. The phone rang a few hours later. It was Brett calling back and I got right to the point, as I normally did when I had something important on my mind. I let him know that I was really worried. I believed that he was drinking too much, and that living less than fifteen minutes from our father was not good for his wellbeing.

There wasn't a blazing sign that my brother's life might be heading toward complete and utter disaster. How different things could have been if we could have all seen that in advance. All it took for me was noticing a small personality change. My little brother, who had always prioritized me and my family, had been coming around less and less over these last years. He would never, under any circumstances, miss one of our birthdays or a special occasion, and he used to just pop by for no reason at all. Now, when he did show up, he pounded back a few drinks and he had no problem drinking and driving.

I never told anyone about the Alcoholics Anonymous (AA) meeting that Brett took me to five years earlier, except Jim, and of course, our mom. After that day so long ago, Brett never mentioned or acknowledged a problem with alcohol, not even once. Neither did our mother. All I knew was that he didn't believe he had a problem any longer. But that is not how I saw things. Jim also shared my worry and as usual, with nothing but love and support, agreed with me that it would be a good idea if Brett moved in with us for a few months.

Whether my brother wanted my guidance or not, if it was something I felt was important, I gave him my advice. And he always listened. He sat silently on the other end of the line, didn't agree or disagree, but promised to drop by when he was on his days off.

He arrived a few days later, the sun barely up, with a coffee in hand. We sat together on the porch and talked for a couple of hours. We always had something to say to each other. I'm not saying that we always agreed or shared the same opinions, but we respected each other's point of view.

Brett insisted that there was nothing to worry about as he really wasn't drinking very much. I didn't argue, but I knew that was not the case. He had a deep bond with our dad; in fact, at this time in Brett's life he considered our dad as one of his best friends. But all these fun times between father and son—fishing, camping, snowmobiling, and their new passion of quading in the mountains out west—had always revolved around the same thing: *alcohol*. And to drive those powerful toys, drinking was not just accepted, it was encouraged, almost required.

I love my father, but my adult relationship with him was a constant struggle. We were hot and cold. Off and on. One of the things I couldn't handle or ignore were his phone calls, which he only dared to make when he was plastered out of his mind. They had always bothered and upset me, and so instead of getting in a fight, which is not my style, I would just hang up the phone.

There was only one good thing that ever came out of Dad's telephone rants and drunken stupors. It was when the phone had rung a few years earlier. Clearly, my father was enraged that particular evening because I had a relationship with my mother while mine and his had begun to sour. So, completely unprovoked and out of the blue, he yelled down the line at me: "If your mom is so Goddamn perfect, Jodee, then where the hell is your older sister!"

My first thought was *Okay, this man has finally lost his fucking mind* and I casually hung up the phone. My older sister? What a ludicrous thing to say. So absolutely bizarre, crazy that I told my mother about this conversation. Her instant discomfort told the story. *Holy shit.* He hadn't lost his mind after all; he was actually telling the truth. My parents had gotten pregnant in 1963 when my mother was only fifteen. She had given the baby up for adoption. Brett, Nicole, and I had a full-on sister out there somewhere. Of course, my aunts and uncles and even some of my cousins knew the truth. This had been the best-kept family secret so far.

Within a few weeks, without talking to anyone except my husband, I put in a request to find our older sister. It didn't take long for the adoption agency to make the connection; she had been looking for us, too. I was so excited when, shortly thereafter, Jim and I took our young sons for a weekend getaway to beautiful British Columbia to meet our older sister Jane and her family.

And my relationship with my dad continued to create a constant conflict in my heart.

Brett opened up and admitted that something was going on. Even though he always had tons of friends, many of whom he'd had since childhood and still played hockey with, he was beginning to feel more anxious than usual.

34

He confessed that he was having trouble playing hockey because he became so agitated about seeing his hockey buddies that he would have to arrive an hour early just to calm himself down sufficiently to face them.

Until he said this, I had had absolutely no idea that Brett suffered from anxiety; I just thought he got quiet and uncomfortable sometimes because he was shy. Nor did he know that I had anxiety challenges, too.

It's hard to explain. But that's the thing about anxiety—it doesn't make logical sense.

We talked about our blushing. It was embarrassing to both of us that, for no reason at all, our faces could often turn bright red in mundane situations, usually only involving people we know well. Which when it was happening made us even more self-conscious and uncomfortable. Our hearts pound and we want to run a mile from whatever situations we are in, whether it was when we went to school, or bumped into someone at the mall or the movie theater. The feeling of discomfort and slight panic attacks would happen out of the blue at illogical times. The little voice in both our heads would say, "Calm down, calm down."

I was shocked at first that this had never come up before, in all those years, through all the things we had shared with each other. But, why would it? We didn't even understand it was happening. I had no choice but to confront the reality that I had anxiety because my little Ryan had it too.

Ry had been just six years old. It was a regular school day. We woke up, he got dressed, did his hair, munched on some cereal, then brushed his teeth like every other day. We then drove the five minutes it took to get him to his school. When we pulled up to the brick building, he grabbed my neck. Like a scared cat, he started scratching, clawing, and screaming, begging me not to make him get out of the car.

"Please, Mom! Pleeeeaaase. I don't feel so good!" Ryan screamed in fear.

I took him home, tucked him into bed, and he was fine. This same scene played out the next day. And the next. Ultimately this turned into weeks and started affecting his life in sports as well. He was fine warming up at karate, but as soon as the classes began, then "boom"—severe panic and crying.

Jim and I did everything humanly possible to find out what was happening with Ryan. Poking, prodding, countless blood tests, and medical exams. Doctors kept telling us nothing was wrong with him physically.

With no other explanation or advice or whisper of any kind from any member of my family that it might be a non-obvious kind of illness that maybe ran in our family, I was convinced that he must have been sexually abused at school. I was so relieved when I found out that I was wrong.

Ryan had always been quiet, sweet, and sensitive, like his great grandfather, Papa, and like his Uncle Brett. We just didn't know how sensitive. Soon, Ryan was on Zoloft®, a medication for anxiety and depression. And my sweet little son, with the good home we provided, certainly had nothing to be depressed about. We combined the medication with the talks we arranged twice a week with a psychiatrist—yes, a child in grade one talking about his feelings with a psychiatrist. That made all the difference.

We continued to try to wean him off the medication every few months, but his panic and tears resurfaced almost instantly and it took a couple of years before he could go med free.

When Ryan was having his problems, I would never have relied on just a physician or just medication as the ultimate answer. As his mother, if I had been doing anything to contribute to what was going on, I wanted to know what that was and I would take responsibility for that. I look at physicians and medications together as tools we use to help us through diseases and life's problems. My husband and I could have just used medications as the possible cure, rather than also arranging for Ryan's talk therapy to get to the bottom of his anxiety. I am not saying medications are not important or are not needed in some cases, because of course they are. But I think we are breeding a society that is heavily overmedicated. People buy into the illusion that medication is the sole solution, which takes away personal responsibility. And of course, if meds don't cure the problem right away, people take more and more. What begins innocently enough sometimes becomes an addiction, even to prescription medications.

The whole experience with Ryan helped solidify Jim's and my belief in always being honest about our individual feelings. We recognized that Ryan's social anxiety will probably last forever, so he will need to be aware of that, especially as he grows older. And most importantly, since anxiety is considered a mental illness, there is *nothing* to be ashamed of.

So, on that day on my porch, my advice to my brother was to challenge his feeling of panic and face his fears. I told him avoiding them wasn't the answer. And neither was drinking alcohol as a way to cope, as that would just make his problems, and his anxiety, much worse.

I left him with an offer—he was welcome to live with us, rent free. We would help him to save by asking for five hundred dollars from each of his two-week paychecks. I would return all the money to him when he had enough for a down payment on a house. Although we are not perfect, seeing how happy and healthy our family was—a sober home—I thought would be a good influence on him. I wanted him to see that there is a completely different way to live. I admit a part of me was also thinking he was twenty-eight years old, so it was time for him to grow up, have adult responsibilities, and focus less on just having a good time. But I didn't share that with him. And besides, Brett could deny that drinking was a problem all he wanted. I knew deep down in my soul that my brother was in trouble.

A week later, after sitting on things for a while, Brett called to tell me he had given notice to his landlord and would be moving in with us. A girl he had been seeing had broken up with him to get back together with an old boyfriend, so it was a good time to "get the hell out of here."

Brett's job at the gas plant was about a forty-five-minute drive from our place. Power engineering, especially in Alberta, allows for two things: a substantial hourly wage and, due to twelve-hour shifts, many days off. What was called a "compressed work schedule" equated to fifteen days off a month, and with every five weeks worked, he got another full week off (and none of this was included in his holidays). Although Brett was working extremely hard, he had lots of spare time on his hands. He took off in his truck with his quad in the back, and he would be out of contact for days at a time, almost always with our father. When he was home, he did a horrible job of convincing me he wasn't drinking on his days off. If I'm being honest, he wasn't trying to convince me at all. So my misguided, mastermind plan had gone to shit in a matter of weeks.

I wasn't used to fighting with my brother. In fact, we had never had so much as an argument in our lives, so it was difficult taking him to task every two weeks over five hundred bucks. We didn't ask him to pitch in for food or even rent, so it frustrated the hell out of me that it was an issue for him to put money aside—money that ironically he'd eventually get back. I finally demanded that he showed me his bills to see where his wages were disappearing.

It turned out that Brett was hugely in debt with his credit card companies and was into an overdraft at the bank. Even with making a great deal of money, he had nothing substantial to show for it. I just didn't understand what he could possibly be spending it on. I suppose I underestimated how much alcohol really costs.

When he was out late at night, I lay awake in bed, worrying and seething. He often returned home in the early hours of the morning, intoxicated and hungry, with no concern or concept at all of being quiet. Banging around in the kitchen, he woke everyone up, kids included. It was like having a teenager—a drunken teenager—living in the basement.

Despite the resistance, Brett's savings eventually added up to about $8,000. Together, he and I spent a few weeks looking for the perfect place for him to buy. Typically, we didn't have the same taste, but he ended up choosing a home that even I loved: it was a brand new, bi-level house, perfect for a single guy, not too big, yet with huge potential.

I helped explain to Brett practical things about his finances so that he could manage the mortgage himself. Although our childhood was filled with love, we were never taught many of life's skills. Being the oldest, I had figured them out. He relied on me to show him how all that worked, details like the term for the mortgage and the interest rates. I felt comforted that the mortgage payments on the $135,000 house were totally within his budget, since he was making well over $80,000 a year.

Jim and I, along with our cousin Kelly, helped Brett move in on a bright sunny day in July. Jim and I gave him some of our old furniture that we were no longer using. Brett proudly showed me the other things he'd found. While my taste was more *House & Home* magazine, he preferred one-of-a kind objects he picked up at pawn shops and used furniture stores. My brother would never go to Sears for a kitchen table and perfectly matching chairs—*never*.

To celebrate his new home, Mom bought him a top-of-the-line front-load washer and dryer for $2,000, which she paid to have delivered. I couldn't help but think, just for a quick instant, that when Jim and I purchased our new home she got us a plant.

"STAY AWAY"

The house was a mistake. I had known it for a long time but now it just couldn't be ignored. Even when Brett was sober, which was now on rare occasions, my brother was not capable of looking after his own home. What most of us would manage as the normal day-to-day tasks of life—laundry, mowing the lawn, paying bills, and getting groceries—he was unable to handle. As a result, the once adorable little bi-level with huge potential was an absolute disgrace.

Brett's rotating shift schedule with too much time off and way too much money compounded the problem. On his days off, he spent his entire time drinking; nothing else. Added to that, he was repeatedly calling in sick for work. Always with the same guarantee: "I'll be there tomorrow." But of course that was just another broken promise that my brother was making.

As I snooped into his affairs like a crazed animal, I found he was once again heavily in debt, although I didn't understand why at the time. He still got paid, whether he made it to work or not, so he was making plenty of money. I was worried sick. I couldn't concentrate on anything else, certainly not on my own family. Brett was slipping into a deep, dark pit, and I wasn't sure what frightened me more: the fact it had taken over his life or that it had taken over mine.

Of course, his life—and his house—didn't fallen apart overnight. The downward trend had gone on for a long time; I would love to say that the time went by fast, but the truth is that those two and a half years felt more like twenty! They took a huge toll on me and my family. I was obsessed, trying to stop Brett from carrying on such a dangerous pattern of behavior.

Our mom blew in and out of town three or maybe four times a year; my sister came by even less. Even though they knew very well what was going on, they continued to ignore the now-frightening signs. As a result, my husband and I were left taking the brunt of it. We were the ones on the front line dealing with Brett's issues. They didn't live with this on a daily basis. But they certainly had witnessed it firsthand when he was drunk out of his mind, such as during Christmas dinner with all of us and the kids. Also, I told them exactly what I had seen. Deep down, I was simultaneously angry and frustrated with my mother and sister because no matter how hard I tried to explain what was going on with Brett, they believed his problems existed only in *my* mind.

My cousin Kelly was a constant presence during this stressful time. I wouldn't have survived without him. With a bouncy optimism, a huge heart, and a bright smile, he was a pillar of strength when I needed one. He was also doing everything possible to get Brett to stop drinking, to get him to understand his life was going downhill fast. I had taken Brett to a doctor; we had tried dumping out the booze; and we continually tried to talk rationally to an irrational man. We repeatedly warned him of the consequences, such as he would lose his job or kill someone by drinking and driving.

None of it did any good. Brett had become our full-time job. And both Kelly and I were failing miserably, despite our best efforts.

Kelly had a savior at home, just like I did in Jim. Kelly's wife Carolynn loved Brett, too, and that was obvious. Even from the time Kelly and Carolynn had started dating, she'd had to accept that Kelly and Brett came as a package: where there was one, there would be the other. They were cousins, best friends, "closer than brothers" as Brett would say. And there was nothing either one of them wouldn't do for the other. When the time came, Brett was completely honored to be the best man at their wedding. They had a young son, Tyson, and Carolynn selflessly put her own needs aside to make sure Tyson was well looked after when Kelly was preoccupied with Brett.

However, nothing Kelly and I did seemed to work. We were losing Brett to addiction. The downhill progression was startling and we both knew it. He would no longer go out and have fun; there was no going out at all. I would frantically call my mother begging for help. But each time I called to tell her what was happening with Brett, his behavior, and the conditions in which he was living, her response was the same. In some form or another, she would say, "By whose standards, Jodee? Yours or everyone else's?"

Our mother has always talked to me that way, always. Her snide, snippy comments stopped bothering me long ago. Her insinuation that I was saying those things about my brother because I am judgmental and condemning was so unfair and hurtful. So, although I kept trying, there would be no cavalry on the way.

Brett was losing his grip on life and sinking deeper into a hole of black despair. The truth is that as he was sinking, I was also losing a grip on myself. As my brother's personality started to change even more and his anxiety flew off the charts, he just wanted to be alone. Meanwhile, I was desperately trying to reach out to him. As his life shifted into nothing except drinking and being a recluse, I also became someone I didn't recognize.

At home, I was calm and logical. I did not yell to make my point. Jim and I talked openly about things with the boys and each other; we had a peaceful approach to conflict. Even as Rick and Ryan got older and into their teenage years, I was never the kind of mom who yells and screams to make her sons do what she wants. After all, that is what my own mother had done with me and I knew that wouldn't work.

But, that calm Jodee, the one who was level-headed and even-tempered, somehow became a different person when dealing with Brett. And I hated her.

Every time I caught him drinking after he'd promised he wouldn't, or driving drunk downtown in our small town, or missing work, or even just when he was stopping by to say "Hi" while he stumbled around my living room, my worry, disappointment, and frustration overcame me. Was I mad? Being mad was an understatement. On so many occasions, I showed up at his house yelling and screaming at the top of my lungs, "What the fuck is wrong with you? Enough!"

"Guns blazin'," as Brett would say.

I became the total opposite of who I was at home.

It didn't matter anyway; the yelling did no good, and I knew that. It didn't make me feel better and Brett just looked back at me with a dazed, glazed look on his face.

His mind was sodden from all the drink, living in a hazy world where

43

screams are muffled and pain is dulled with every slug of booze. I didn't even know exactly how much he was drinking, but it was a lot. If the tell-tale signs of missing work were not enough, the empty bottles scattered everywhere in his house told the true story. What used to be beer and the occasional cocktail now had turned into hard-core alcohol. No coke with a twist of lime, but pure vodka. Straight out of the bottle, sweet delicious vodka.

He would lock himself away, not just drinking enough alcohol to take the edge off, but devouring enough to knock himself out. He just wanted to stay asleep all day, waking only to drink some more, and pass out again.

The way he treated himself, often behind closed doors, was evident to me, but ignored by many, as no one except me and Kelly dared to say anything. Yet, Brett's disregard for his house was blatantly obvious and undeniable, or so I thought. One day in early 2004, almost four years into Brett's heavy drinking, I arrived at his house in the morning to find he had slipped further into the hole. Things were worse than usual, even though I didn't know that could be possible. I had my own key so he hadn't heard me come in the front door.

What once was a beautiful new home was now completely disgusting. Days' worth of dirty dishes were piled up, as were garbage and laundry. Also, it looked as though he had foolheartedly decided to paint a feature wall in the front entrance a sage-green color. I was not sure if he was drunk or sober when he painted it. His intentions were in the right place, but he failed at even this small task.

I was not sure what had happened in the living room, except that it was something violent and I instantly felt sick to my stomach. Scattered remnants of what was once a glass lamp with a lamp shade were in pieces all over the place. Blood was on the wall and the carpet, although not enough to panic me. After all, in the last couple of years I had witnessed this with him before. It could have been a nose bleed. Maybe, he had vomited it up. There are so many options when it comes to dealing with a loved one who is drinking as much as Brett was. As many times as I saw him in such an awful state, although I tried to be brave, I wasn't prepared and it simply broke my heart.

Cautiously, I entered the darkness of Brett's bedroom and I noticed that the windows were still covered so he could sleep without any reminder that it was actually day. My walking in spooked him so he flinched as he tried to pry his eyes open, and I could tell instantly he had been in a fight. My brother was unshaven, and the large cut on the top of his right eye was still fresh with blood. He wasn't wearing anything except a pair of plaid pajama bottoms, so I could see that his upper body was covered, not with bruise marks like you would expect from a fist fight, but with scratches up and down his arms and part of his chest. There was blood all over the sheets, clearly from his unattended injuries.

"My God, Brett," I said. But that was all I had to offer him. I was so exhausted and I knew that I was in over my head.

It didn't take long in this small town to learn of a bar fight that Saturday night where a guy got his ass kicked and left with a bunch of scratches.

I picked up the phone in the kitchen and tried to form the words in my mind. Instead of a peaceful conversation, my instincts and frustration kicked in and for once I said to our mother exactly what I was thinking. "Mom, you need to get here. NOW!" I was done trying to pussyfoot around her, scared of her reaction; she couldn't pretend this wasn't happening anymore. She was in the USA for work, so it was not until the next day that I saw her as she drove through the open gate at my business and into the parking lot in the back.

I cared about Mom's feelings. This was her son and I didn't want to scare her. After all, this reality I was forcing her to face would be very upsetting. I wanted to prepare her for the shocking state of what she was about to see when she went to Brett's house. I figured that it would be best if we talked a little first, in private. I let my staff go early and watched as Mom made her way through the warehouse to my office. I couldn't believe what I saw. Our mother is a woman who takes great pride in looking beautiful and staying thin, almost as much care and attention to this as to her actual job. She would run miles each day, always in full makeup with perfectly curled and styled hair. Her hard work paid off as she looked at least ten years younger than her fifty-five years.

But that was not the case this day.

Honestly, I had never, not once, seen her out in public looking that way—as though she had just crawled out of bed. I was stunned by the fact she had just stepped off an airplane looking so disheveled. She was actually limping towards me across the concrete floor. Quite frankly, she looked like shit. I could be sympathetic and understanding that she was worried, yet that was not my instinct; she was going to make this about *her*.

Mom sat down on a chair in my office without saying a word. I couldn't even understand it. I didn't even get a simple "Hi." A hug might have been nice. Somehow, for some reason, she was annoyed at me even before I whispered my first word.

"What do you want to know?" I asked softly.

"What do you mean, 'What do I want to know?'!" she fired back in her snarky tone.

I knew this wasn't going well. I have heard this tone before and I know how it ends, so I spoke as cautiously as possible.

"About Brett, Mom. I wanted to tell you what has been going on."

"I know what has been going on with Brett, Jodee! You don't have to tell me. I am his mother!"

She stood up and began to flail her arms, hitting a pair of sunglasses that she had rested on the corner of my desk. I have seen this stroppy act on many occasions, too. The sunglasses propelled high into the air and hit me right in the eye.

With a stinging shot to my face, I stood up quickly and hollered, "What the hell is wrong with you? I am just trying to explain what has been happening here!"

"What is wrong with me, Jodee? There is nothing wrong with me. There's something wrong with *you*. You and Jim are black and white people ... BLACK AND WHITE!"

I had heard enough. I stood up before she could say any more and I yelled, as loudly as I could, "You need to get out of here. There is enough going on without you making it worse. And let's make one thing perfectly clear, Mother: what is going on with Brett is in no way a shade of grey!"

I know what Mom meant about me being black and white; she didn't need to tell me. From the time I was a little girl, I had a distaste for the fighting, screaming, violence, feelings of embarrassment, infidelity, and divorce. My perception was that all of that came from alcohol. I developed a more defined sense of right and wrong, because I was always so damn scared of my life turning out the wrong way. Our mother was in a horrible marriage and I never condemned her for it. In fact, I am so proud and blessed that she was able to break free and give us a better life. It wasn't easy for her-financially or otherwise.

But instead of her being proud of the life I have created for myself—the choices I have made—our mother seems to resent me for it. She treats me like I think I am better. That could not be further from the truth. But she was right in some small sense: I didn't see it any other way than black and white, drunk or sober. There was no in-between for me when it came to my brother. No middle ground. It was one way or the other. And not because I am judgmental. Love was the only motivating factor for everything I had said. Something was seriously fucking wrong.

I held my eye as it continued to sting, while Mom spun around on her high-heeled boots, her limp magically gone. She slammed the back door behind her. I watched out of the side window as her little sports car got stuck in a snowbank in our parking lot, so I left through the front entrance to avoid her. I was in no position myself to take on any more stress; I didn't care how she was going to get out of there. I was so completely angry that I thought she could be stuck until spring for all I cared.

When Mom finally got to Brett's, Kelly and I were already there with him. He immediately denied to Mom that he had been in a fight downtown. He told her that he never even left the house all weekend. And, as usual, she believed every word he said. I didn't understand my brother's denial, but our mother's? You could see with your own eyes the destruction, the evidence. What was to deny? Did she think the lamp grew some arms and legs and beat the crap out of him?

My sister Nicole arrived a short time later. She still didn't come around that much, but she too has seen Brett drinking too much over the last few years. Her face told the story of her shock and horror, as she bent down to whisper in my ear, "I am so sorry, Jodee. I had no idea it was this bad."

The writing was on the wall, and if you missed it, the blood was there too.

Brett agreed for the first time to go to a thirty-day rehabilitation program in Calgary. I put aside my fight with Mom as she was finally being helpful. Together, we tried our best to maneuver our way through something we had no experience with. We weren't familiar at all with this type of thing. We didn't know where he should go, what type of program was best for his needs, what place was better than the other, etc.

Mom started asking opinions of some doctors that she knew and they gave some valuable suggestions. I didn't know exactly how much it would cost, and we are very blessed in this country that a substantial part of the fee for public programs are covered by our health care system, unlike the private rehabilitation centers that I learned later cost tens of thousands of dollars. The downside is that, depending on where you live, there can be a waiting list to get in, and some addicts are at a risk of dying while they wait, as they are so hard-core addicted that they just can't stop even when they want to. Luckily, we weren't in that position as this wasn't a life or death situation, so the wait was short, the fee minimal, and Brett got admitted immediately in Calgary.

However, there was one major requirement. My brother had to be sober for three days before he could enter treatment. Not all facilities are equipped with in-house detoxification programs—units that can bring addicts through the withdrawal process safely. This is why the addict needs to be alcohol- and drug-free before entering the facility. I wouldn't learn what all of this meant until much later, but I wouldn't have cared anyway. All I was concerned about was that he was going and I would have done anything to guarantee that happened.

As Brett was unable to give up the bottle—or unwilling, I still wasn't sure which—his being alcohol-free would mean we needed to watch him in shifts for the next three days.

To begin the process of purging Brett and the house of alcohol, Nicole, Mom, and I looked inside every cupboard, closet, toilet cistern, and even under the barbecue lid, any and all places where someone craftier than us might sneak a bottle of vodka.

Once we found Brett's secret stashes, we poured each bottle down the drain, then continued sweeping for hidden booze until our mission was complete. He looked at us with sad eyes, like he'd lost his best friend. Our mother takes sleeping pills to help her settle at night, so she gave a couple to Brett, which did make things a little easier. With him as peaceful as a baby, we could now take turns watching him every minute for the next seventy-two hours.

Brett still seemed at ease when he left to go to the rehabilitation center. It not only felt like a step in the right direction, but I was positive things were going to be quite different when he came home. Rehab, that is the answer; it is what we are programmed to believe. He was going to come back, go to work, be his old self, and stay sober. Everything was going to get back to normal.

Maybe that is the problem, our normal. And the unfortunate fact that we are never told what to do if it doesn't work.

It felt like I was going to rehab, like a weight had been lifted from my shoulders. There was an absolute sense of relief for thirty days, and it began instantly. I was no longer afraid of a ringing telephone that might tell me my brother was dead. I was filled with an overpowering feeling of calm. My husband, children, and even my employees had my full attention. A little part of myself returned to me.

And it did the world of good for Brett, too. In only a month, he was looking healthy and happy, with a new lease on life. Now equipped with the tools he needed to combat his alcoholism, he came back to his home with everything looking fresh and new. I had cleaned his house, done his laundry, and he was due back at work.

I have always known how my brother feels, even though he had trouble saying it out loud. After giving me a hug he simply handed me a tiny crocheted bag, with bright vibrant colors. As I opened the little ties slowly, I found a flat rock, engraved simply—Thanks.

"THE OTHER KIND"

By spring 2004, Brett was doing really well and I had been going with him to some doctors' appointments to show my support. He wasn't married, didn't have a girlfriend, and I wanted to know more about recovery, more about what I needed to do to support him in that.

We were greeted with a friendly smile at Brett's family physician's office downtown. He was not surprised I was there, as I had been there before. I listened intently to what he recommended. By this stage, Brett was on Paxil, which is prescribed for depression and also used to treat panic attacks and anxiety. The doctor had more of a religious approach when discussing Alcoholics Anonymous, which wasn't an issue for my brother. Even though we never frequented church, as our parents were not religious at all, Brett definitely believed in God, but in a spiritual, not preachy, over-the-top way. Brett's doctor encouraged him to find out what days the local AA meetings were and to make sure he went consistently. He also reminded Brett that he should not drink alcohol while on Paxil as that would be counterproductive since one is a depressant and the other an antidepressant. Also, drinking could actually make things worse since Paxil has been known to increase the effects of alcohol.

My brother only went to AA two or three times at best until he started complaining about it. His quiet nature and uneasiness about public speaking made him even more uncomfortable to share his feelings with a group of strangers. I never could put my finger on it, the why or how to explain, but he was never quite comfortable in his own skin. How could someone so incredibly popular and gorgeous have such low self-esteem? He has always had a deep desire to be liked and accepted, and this life challenged that on every level. AA meetings are filled with good people who have also made mistakes, deserve forgiveness, and are turning their life around. I hoped he wouldn't feel judged at AA meetings, as the people there were just like him. I was confident the meetings would get easier for him with time.

Since Jim and I continued not to drink, not a drop, not ever, I constantly reminded Brett that it is possible to live a beautiful life without alcohol. I didn't mind at all helping my brother where I could in his recovery. After all, if I needed something he would be there for me; that was just the way it had always been.

As I tried to lead Brett in the right direction, I got a sudden overwhelming feeling of failure, remembering when I desperately tried to make a positive impact on my sister's life when she lived with me and Jim.

After five weeks, it was time for Brett to go for a follow-up week in the rehabilitation center. Since that was in Calgary, he left his home to stay at Mom's for a few nights beforehand. Then I didn't hear from him, which left an unsettled feeling in the pit of my stomach. After three days into his follow-up week at Rehab, I was worried, so I called the center's main switchboard to talk to him. I was floored by their response: "Sorry, ma'am, there is no Brett Tisdale here."

"What? That's not possible. Check again."

"Sorry, due to patient confidentiality, we can't discuss any more details."

My heart began to race.

"Listen, he stayed there before—please do me a favor and go look at his file. You will see that he signed a piece of paper giving permission for you to talk to me about his progress. I will call you back in ten minutes."

I have learned from my previous visits with him to doctors' appointments that they won't say a word to anyone else unless he gives his consent. It continues to be one of the major parts of this whole process that I am dead against—a lack of information to the family. Our loved ones are dying right before our eyes and unless they happen to be under the age of eighteen, we are told nothing.

Since rehab is not mandatory, addicts can walk out the door at any time. I was worried that he would leave as he wasn't making rational decisions. I wanted to try to be one step ahead, so I had thought of this already.

After about nine minutes, I dialed the rehab again. They must have found the little note signed by Brett, because when I called back they talked openly with me. I quickly learned that they were very sorry, but since he walked in the front door under the influence, he had been refused treatment.

My first reaction was, *Oh, my God, where is he? That was three days ago*!

When I hung up the phone and called my mother, I put together at least half of the puzzle. She was oblivious. "What, he's not there? Where is he?" she said, acting completely surprised.

"They refused him. He was drinking. Mom, didn't you drop him off?" I asked.

"Yes, I did, Jodee!" She said in a tone that I recognized. "But he was really anxious and agitated here. And I was trying, but he was drinking all the alcohol he could find in my house! When I dumped everything out, I caught him in my bathroom drinking hairspray. When I took that away, it was my cologne."

She spoke so calmly, like this was a normal everyday occurrence and not alarming at all. Instantly, I could picture Brett frantically opening the bathroom drawer, removing the spray nozzle from the blue bottle of Finesse, and pouring it straight down his throat. When that was all gone, I could imagine him grabbing everything in her medicine cabinet, picking up her bottle of Anais Anais, spraying it on his tongue, and not stopping until the bottle was empty.

Oh, my God, that was utterly insane. I wanted to scream at the top of my lungs, but I sat silently on the other end of the line.

"I dropped him off. I didn't think they wouldn't let him in," she finished.

In other words, she didn't stay to find out. She knew the rules—three days sobriety. But I had no time to comprehend what this meant. I didn't even say goodbye. I just swiftly hung up as I needed to find him.

I began to look for the brother whom I loved so much. The one who was in a fog, rudderless, now so desperate he was pounding back any imaginable liquid that he could find. My mind was now my greatest enemy; it fed me images of hospitals, police stations, underpasses, dark corners of the city, any one of them hiding the lifeless body of my brother.

After an excruciating couple of sleepless nights and long days of wondering and fearing the worst, I learned that Brett was still in Calgary. He was also close to another of our cousins, Trevor. Trevor had been away on vacation and Brett knew where the spare key was hidden.

Trevor didn't have a clue that Brett had decided to stop by, uninvited. It was a rude welcome home for our cousin as he wasn't prepared for what he saw. After all, this was not the fun-loving, sweet Brett he knew, enjoying a few beers and eating turkey at a Tisdale Christmas gathering. Brett was highly intoxicated, barely conscious, drooling, and not making any rational sense. I know from experience, this is more than the average person can handle and Trevor wanted him gone.

Mom was unsuccessful in her pleading to get Brett to leave Trevor's. Although I was almost two hours away, I knew exactly what to do. We could spin this anyway we wanted—in my opinion this constituted a break and enter and that was a crime. My mother could continue to take her passive approach, but I thought my brother needed a dose of reality to come to grips with the severity of his situation. The things he was doing while under the influence now included breaking the law. I knew she wouldn't do what I was about to do and I called my brother. I hoped in his inebriated state he could comprehend what I was saying as I proceeded to tell him that I was going to call the police and have him arrested.

Looking back now, this might have been the best thing for him, but at the time it just seemed mean.

So, I delivered the ultimatum: "So, what's it going to be, Brett? Treatment or jail?"

Rehab. Round two.

"DEAR OL' DAD "

Cousin Kelly, Nicole, our mom, and I had been supporting Brett as best we could, although none of us had a clue about what we were doing. We were committed to helping Brett. That, we agreed on. But how to do that? That part wasn't so clear. Since we needed help and advice, we all went together to see a counselor. He was not a doctor, but a social worker and supposedly one of the best therapists in the Calgary area. His name was Terry.

With only slight apprehension, the four of us went with Brett. We all knew we couldn't go on as we'd been doing. We were lost. Well, at least I was.

Terry greeted us with a warm smile. He was an average looking man. Silky greyish sandy blond hair complemented with pale and slightly blotchy skin. His office was bright, with his master's degree certificate in clinical social work proudly displayed on the wall. He struggled slightly to find enough chairs, as clearly he was not used to a session with five.

Once seated, we told our story, our hopes and, yes, our fears. Well, really it was mostly Kelly and I doing the talking.

I looked over at our mother, sitting quietly next to Brett, waiting for her to chime in, to speak up. But, it was as though she couldn't bring herself to say anything that she perceived as "bad" about her son; she was visibly uncomfortable when we discussed some of the more personal details. And every time the word "alcoholic" was used, you would think someone pricked her with a pin.

I, on the other hand, was *never* uncomfortable with that. I do not look at "alcoholic" as though it is a derogatory word but rather, with my glass-half-full mentality, I always considered it a positive. My brother *is* an alcoholic; I think he needs to remember that every day when he wakes up. To look in the mirror, be grateful for the help that is offered, and never to forget this fact. I believe to this day that being able to admit to having alcoholism is what will keep a person sober. Being ashamed, hiding, pretending that it is not true will wear down self-esteem, creating self-loathing. Any of those things will just keep a person drunk.

We went to see Terry hoping for some valuable insight. Of course, Brett had been to rehab, but there had been no family interaction, so the process left us feeling isolated and alone.

We talked at length about what had been happening, although I doubt anyone could understand the gravity of the situation in sixty short minutes. How could he understand? We had every opportunity to tell the whole truth, but we didn't. None of us breathed a whisper about the cologne or hairspray, which likely would have aroused suspicion that this was a more complex and severe case of addiction. Brett didn't do much talking—he never did—but he never disagreed with anything we said. What had remained a constant, regardless of whom he and I had seen together, was that the only answer was absolutely abstaining from alcohol. And for Brett to use the valuable tools that he had learned in recovery to accomplish that. Terry's assessment was no different. Terry displayed a calm and understanding tone. I really liked him.

Everything we were told was what Brett should do, how he could stay sober. Everything was about him. What we were never told is what *we* needed to do. Our hearts were in the right place, but I believe we were all sick in how we were dealing with Brett, each in our own way. But at the time we didn't know any better.

Brett was fortunate to still be employed as he had great benefits that looked after the almost hundred-dollars-per-hour fee to see Terry. Even I was shocked that the gas plant hadn't fired him by now, but I understood. It was a small town with a family-type environment and they loved him. Everyone knew he was a great, kind-hearted person who did a hell of a good job when he was working. Their feelings for him swayed their management decision to make sure he still had a job no matter how many times he called in drunk out of his mind, or "sick" as he always told them. They knew what was going on, maybe not to the same level that we did, but they knew. I think alcoholics are the only ones who think these are secrets; it's part of their denial process. They may choose to ignore it, but people know, as it is impossible to hide. I did hope, even then, that his employer would fire him. Everywhere he turned someone was helping him along his path of destruction and it was just making things worse.

After seeing Terry, we were all pleased, and more importantly, hopeful. For the first time, Brett was willing to seek therapy on a weekly basis. But suddenly, just when we thought things were heading in the right direction, the therapy stopped. As sweet as he was, Brett had become a little stubborn over the last couple of years. A symptom of addiction, I suspected. Not sure if it was that or the fact that Terry was finally getting to the heart of the matter, to the depths of my brother's emotions and pain. Either way, when Terry challenged Brett, my brother simply quit going.

Instantly, the house was back in the same shambles as before. No money, no going to work, and when I made the mistake of bringing up rehab again, Brett was gone.

I spent days trying to figure out where he was this time, juggling my work and family responsibilities as best I could. I was not doing anything well. Not being a good wife, a good mother, or a good boss. The truth is if I hadn't been self-employed, I would have lost my job long ago.

Our mom's job at her "organization," as she called it, had always been deemed more important than the rest of ours. She had no problem reminding us all of that fact. What no one had ever considered, except my husband, was that when *I* didn't go to work, I didn't make any money, I didn't get paid. So, the time I spent running in circles had already cost us close to ten thousand dollars or more, although it was not as obvious as when someone had a check being deposited into their account every second Friday. And, despite my best efforts, I was still not feeling like a good sister; I felt somehow I was letting him down; I didn't know what to do to help him.

We did know he was alive, and that's about all we knew. He called Mom every couple of days on his cell to say he was okay. He did say he was in Edmonton, although he didn't say specifically where. And that was the only hint I needed to propel me to start calling each and every hotel in the area. After all, there was no point calling the police to make a missing person's report, because what he was doing was not illegal.

After nine sleepless nights and probably over a hundred phone calls to various hotels in the city, I tried calling the next one in the book. With a weary crackle in my throat I called the Pine Park Inn, I said, "Hello, can you please tell me, is there a Brett Tisdale staying there?"

"Hold, please," the hotel receptionist replied and I felt a leap of hope in my stomach—normally it was a quick no and a dial tone. I hesitantly waited for a response.

"Hi, yes, we do have a Brett Tisdale here."

Oh, thank God, I had found him. There was a short pause and I wasn't sure what to say next, but that didn't matter as she spoke first.

"I am sorry, this is awkward for me to say, and it is none of my business but I think you should know. He was in the lobby this afternoon … crying," the receptionist explained with embarrassment and concern creeping into her voice.

"Crying?" Tears welled up in my own eyes. "I am so sorry, thank you *so, so* much for telling me. I will be there shortly to get him."

I was overwhelmed with emotion. I have seen my brother in this state and it is not pretty, and many just simply look away in disgust. In a world with so much judgment, he was a drunk, a junkie, the lowest of the low. Yet this stranger had empathy and compassion for my brother and it warmed my heart that someone could see past the drunken man in the lobby. Maybe she knew someone else who was struggling, or maybe she didn't. Maybe her heart was open enough to understand that he was just a person, that he was someone's brother, maybe someone's father, someone's son, and that he was loved. Whatever her motivation, I was thankful.

I was on my way.

I was so relieved that he was alive, but my heart was also full of sadness at the thought of my grown, adult brother, sitting in a public place with tears rolling down his cheeks. My brother didn't cry when he was sober, not ever.

Dad picked me up to go and get him. He wasn't actively involved during this time with Brett's struggle, so I appreciated that he agreed to come when I needed him.

We sat in almost complete silence for the hour-and-a-half drive. I think we were both scared and just didn't know what to say. Our dad hadn't had anything to drink that day. Well, I didn't think so anyway and he was looking a bit vulnerable. Vulnerable. Not something I ever thought of when I looked at him. I stared at this very average, fair skinned, lightly freckled, red-haired man looking straight ahead, driving down Highway 2. I still couldn't believe that he was my father and that Brett had grown up to be so much like him even though we didn't grow up in the same home. There were so many times, before the "Golden Years," that I could never forget.

I would have no reason to think back, to reflect on some of the things that had happened if this hadn't been going so wrong with my brother. But I had no choice, trying to figure out; trying to decipher what potentially created what. I would never think about, or care that our dad thought it okay to bring some chick home to get laid, or that my uncle was drunk his whole life, wasting away alone, and dying long before he should have. I was haunted by these memories on my quest to unravel our lives, and to understand how some or all of these things perhaps played a part.

Regardless, none of that mattered; I love my father and I was glad he was there with me. We pulled up to the big cedar hotel and I made my way to the front desk explaining our situation as best I could. I was sure it would be against their hotel policy, but I could tell she felt badly for us as we shared our story. She politely but reluctantly gave us Brett's room number on the third floor. Our dad followed close behind me, not saying a word.

I felt anxious as we counted the numbers along the hallway. Even numbers were on the right side, odd numbers on the left. The hall kept getting longer and longer and I was not ready for this. As terrified as I was about what I might see when Brett opened the door, I was more afraid that he wouldn't. After all, it had been a few hours by now since anyone had heard from him and death was always one of my mind's options. We approached the door and I took a deep breath.

Two knocks and Brett cracked open the door. He was not expecting anyone and he had a befuddled, surprised look on his face. Or perhaps he was just in a daze; it was still so hard to tell. He hadn't shaved for days and was barely recognizable. His face was rounder than usual; his eyes swollen from crying.

"Brett, are you okay? Can we come in?"

He nodded briefly and I could see he was severely intoxicated as he stumbled back into the room, allowing us inside. The odor hit my nostrils; stale, acrid, and skunky, instantly reverting me back to childhood. Brett had been holed up in there, hiding from the world, obviously not even getting the bed sheets changed. The complimentary set of towels had ended up on the floor a while before.

I looked around. Everything was cockeyed, strange, and disheveled: the lamp shade was tipped askew, the pillows were at the foot of the bed, and the TV was on, but muted. There were empty mickeys and bottles of vodka on every visible countertop, probably close to fifteen or twenty by my quick count. It was an outrageous mess, much like Brett's own appearance.

It was dark so I made my way across the room, stepping over Brett's shoes in the middle of the floor, and I opened the large blind, exposing the bright sunlight, which made everything more vivid.

I felt just slightly better knowing he had been eating because on the desk, beside the coffee pot, there were various white and yellow wrappers from what looked to be McDonald's. When I glanced down, I couldn't help but notice the large wet patch on his beige cargo pants—urine, which perhaps explained *some* of the odor. My eyes continued to travel down to the floor where there were about fifty tiny white pills scattered by his bedside table. Our father remained completely silent, his eyes wide. This was worse than we thought.

"What are these?" I asked.

"Tic Tacs," Brett said as his head jolted back, a little in surprise, as if telling me that he was shocked I could think they were anything but a spilt box of little mints.

We explained to him how worried we were and that we were taking him home. He awkwardly went to the bathroom to "take a piss," while we began grabbing his things. I have never seen Meth. Or Coke. Or Ecstasy. I had no idea what they looked like; although, in my imagination, this was exactly what a crack house would be like. Minus the crack pipe, needles, and ashy debris on rolled-up pieces of tinfoil, like you see in movies.

I sat on the end of the unkempt bed and I slowly bent over and picked up one of the tiny white pills. With a brief pause, I gently placed it on the end of my tongue. No care for my own health or the consequence of my action. I knew that some people have become addicted to things like Crystal Meth after trying them only once. That's a game of Russian roulette since you do not know in advance if you are one of those people; one bad choice could change everything forever. But I didn't care; that is how far I had fallen; the reward seemed greater than the risk. I sat and I waited for some sort of sign; our dad's eyes were fixated on my every move.

"What is it?" I could tell he didn't really want the answer.

A slight tingle of peppermint now etched itself on the end of my tongue. I replied, "It's a Tic Tac." We both let out a sigh and our smiles turned into a chuckle.

Sometimes laughter comes at the most inappropriate times and, in this case, I think it was because we were both so relieved. I never thought Brett did drugs, although at the time this would have made so much more sense to me if he had. In my mind these were the behaviors of a severe drug addict. I had been around booze my entire life; yet what I was witnessing, even I could never have believed that all of this could be just from alcohol. This was off the charts, beyond what anyone could possibly imagine.

Brett walked out of the bathroom, his face damp from splashing water on his cheeks. He actually looked a little better, albeit bleary-eyed and in need of a few cups of coffee. We made arrangements and he went to spend the next five days in a detox center. He had been drinking so much for so long, we were worried about his health if he went off cold turkey, so we felt he needed medical attention as he came off the booze.

Early the next morning, while Brett was safely away at detox, my phone rang. It was the bank. They informed me that there was a check written in the amount of $7,000 that was going to be returned NSF, because there was only $150 in the account. Since it wasn't my usual bank, I knew what that meant. I had gone a few times with Brett to see his therapist, Terry, who had suggested for me to add my name to Brett's bank account in order to help

Brett get back on track—his finances were also in complete disarray.

I groaned and asked the bank representative who the check was made out to, but she couldn't read his handwriting. They soon faxed me a copy and it looked like it had been scribbled by a four-year-old. But, it didn't take long for the mystery to be solved. By early afternoon, I received another phone call; this time from an angry female "massage therapist" demanding her $7,000. Apparently, while in Edmonton, Brett had visited her office on several occasions. Just a couple of days earlier, he had been there, highly intoxicated. He became enraged, yelling and breaking things, scaring the staff. She claimed he did a lot of damage to her office and they could not see clients for the rest of the day. When she told him she was going to call the police, he became profusely apologetic and had promised her money.

Mom wrote a check for $2,000 to make this problem go away. We had no idea about those people and she was concerned that they now had *my* phone number and address.

Out of detox and sober for five days, my brother was now on his way back for another stint at rehab. When we tried to remind Brett that he couldn't keep doing these things as he had just cost Mom two grand, his lack of insight was completely evident. "She got ripped off," he said.

Mom looked to me with a hushed word in my ear, "It's okay, Jodee, he's just lonely." That reiterated to me, and sadly to him, that somehow this was still alright.

Once again, my brother entered a thirty-day rehab program in Calgary. It was so comforting to know he was alive and safe and that he wouldn't be using a checkbook for a while.

And, the big mystery I had been trying to solve of where all the money was going had now started to make sense. After all, rub-n-tugs are very expensive.

"COME AS YOU ARE "

Our mom went back to her life in Calgary and I to mine in Sylvan Lake.

The thirty days passed.

Surely I might have got used to seeing Brett looking so happy and full of life when he got home, but I hadn't. The best way to describe the change is a transformation akin to walking by a homeless addict, lying in the street, not bathing for days, intoxicated or high, begging for money. And then imagine, thirty days later, a "Brad Pitt" type, breathtakingly gorgeous and sweet, standing in front of you with a bouquet of flowers. It is unbelievable. His loving gift filled my heart so full of happiness that it almost burst. I knew once again he was sorry; after all that was what the flowers he bought me represented. If they didn't die after a week or so, I would have been able to open my own floral shop by now.

Nicole got married to a wonderful man Adam on August 28, 2004, her face beaming as our father and Jim both had the honor of walking her down the aisle. As much as we have had continued conflicts with my sister, I believe that showed deep down that she loved Jim and he was a stable force; a father figure in her life. We were surrounded by what I guess was one hundred family and friends.

And Brett had only been out of rehab for a couple of weeks. The only visible sign was that his face was still quite puffy, although no one would even notice nor would they know what it meant.

As the immediate family members posed for wedding photos, I couldn't help but notice how perfect everyone looked, like models in a magazine. I knew I should stand there and just be happy and grateful, but all my mind told me was no one could possibly believe what went on behind closed doors in the lives of these people. Our other family members knew, so did some friends. Although no one said anything directly to us, I could tell that some were uncomfortable and didn't know what to say. I mean, he had gone to rehab—he hadn't murdered someone—so why the awkwardness? What a positive it would have been if someone had simply come up to Brett, given him a hug and said, "Good for you, Brett, for changing your life." Instead, there were whispers, gossip, innuendo. I knew that bothered my brother.

Sobriety makes people very nervous and awkward, even those who just drink occasionally. Why? That is not for me to answer, I think that is a question each individual should ask themselves.

The photographer lined us all up perfectly. "Count'a three, everyone smile," he said.

Brett faced his fears and gave a beautiful speech for Nicole in front of everyone. And this whole night was truly a magical moment for all of our "beautiful" family; we hadn't had that in a very long time.

I was ecstatic when Brett hit the one-month-sobriety mark, attending Alcoholics Anonymous meetings and generally doing well. I could tell he hated going to AA, just like before, but that was hardly the point. I reminded him that some people go every day for twenty years; that this was about doing what keeps you sober, not what makes you comfortable. And even he could not deny, when he went, he stayed sober.

My brother was beginning to embrace his recovery, reading books on alcoholism, mostly autobiographies from addicted rock stars, plus the odd how-to book about the twelve-step program thrown into the pile. He continued writing in journals, which he had done for a long time, documenting his dreams and occasional night terrors that he had been experiencing lately when drunk and sometimes even when sober, and whatever else he was scribbling down. The night terrors scared the shit out of him, waking him up sweating, confused, his heart beating through his chest, and not being able to distinguish reality from the dream he was just awakening from. It seemed rational at the time to me, and the professionals, that these were either side effects from severe substance abuse or drunken hallucinations, given the level of alcohol he had been consuming. I certainly didn't give them a second thought.

Brett loves music, preferring it to television, although I wished he would play something more upbeat than all those damn Nirvana and Blind Melon songs, which to me seemed quite dark and depressing. I didn't understand his fascination with singers Shannon Hoon and Kurt Cobain, both of whom had struggled with addiction and were now dead. But I couldn't deny everything seemed to be working for him, so I was not going to complain.

I had missed the old Brett and looked forward to our daily coffees, even if it was just for fifteen or twenty minutes because he had to be back at work. Yet, one particular day's coffee together was different. His face lit up and he couldn't control the beaming smile on his face as he walked through the front door to visit me at work. He had been keeping a secret and he was sorry he hadn't told me before.

"Remember that girl I told you about? The one I used to see when I was living in Rimbey," he said.

"Ya," I replied. I remembered it clearly actually. Dawn-Marie —the only girl since Bobbie that I could tell he really liked. And she had broken up with him to get back together with an ex-boyfriend.

"Well, I called her. We have been seeing each other again," he said with a smile. "We are in love, Jode. You are the first person I want her to meet."

Instantly, my logical mind kicked in, since I had now been reading many books, too. I know it is a cardinal rule of recovery not to get into a relationship until after a year of sobriety. From what I understood, the recovering addict is supposed to abstain from new romantic relationships so he can remain focused. Brett was supposed to be concentrating on recovery alone until he was stable and settled in a new sober routine, without embarking on the highs and lows of a new relationship.

I always think that relationships, at the beginning, can be a little euphoric themselves—an unrealistic "high"—just like drugs and alcohol. But maybe that was not one of the reasons for waiting a year, I rationalized to myself. After all, I was just interpreting everything I was learning as best I could. I had hoped he would follow the program and advice from professionals. But I only let those doubts weigh on me for a split second, since my heart took over what my reasonable mind knows.

Dawn-Marie had a two-year-old son. Even as Brett told me, I knew that wasn't a problem. I had witnessed firsthand that Brett would love him like his own. When I met Dawn-Marie for the first time, I found her very pretty with dark hair, brown eyes, and a small frame. She was loud, funny, opinionated, and a loving mom, and I could tell she wouldn't take shit from anyone. I knew right away that we were going to get along just fine.

I watched such a complete metamorphosis in my brother. This sober Brett showed no signs of depression, went to work, and looked after his house. His love and dedication to Dawn and her son Matthew were obvious. He did get a little restless and jittery on occasions when he got anxious, but nothing he couldn't handle. We—Jim and I and the boys—spent the next couple of months growing close to Dawn-Marie and little Matt, often doing fun family things just like old times.

I was over the moon for Rick and Ryan too, as it had been so long since their real Uncle Brett had been around. They never said anything bad about him, but I know the drunken antics affected how they felt about him. My heart breaks for the families that are going through similar struggles. My brother is no different from the ones they love. Addicts do not mean to hurt the people they love most in the whole world, but that is *exactly* what happens. While we all have different limits, what we are willing to take, and for how long, it is almost unbearable to watch other people get hurt when we know our loved one is the cause of it. But, like everything else, we don't know what to do about it.

During that time, Dawn and I became fast and furious friends, but we didn't ever talk about Brett's alcoholism. I just felt they would have to sort through that on their own. She was a very good influence on my brother, loving, supportive, and understanding. He was so lucky to have found her.

Brett had managed to get an impaired driving charge during some of his escapades so he lost his license. He was relying on some of the friends on the same shift at work to pick him up or drive him home. The guys at his plant were tight. Kelly worked there too, and Brett constantly mentioned a guy named Mark. I had never met him—there were not many friends coming around those days—but I could tell by the stories that Brett thought the world of Mark and considered him a true friend. When the guys at work couldn't give Brett a ride, Dad agreed to play taxi, since he was now retired. Brett rarely got mad, but he was pissed right off when he told me that Dad had a drink between his legs when he drove him to work or picked him up.

That is why I love our talks; he could tell me what he thought and I could tell him right back what I thought. Our father has no concept whatsoever of what is appropriate. He never has had, and those are his choices. Brett either had to learn to accept Dad as he was, or not accept him, because he is never going to change.

It was always very confusing in my mind when Brett saw so clearly our dad's unhealthy behaviors, but he didn't see his own, or that what was happening to him was so much worse. Our dad does drink every day, which is a fact he's never hidden. He has lost much because of drinking: wives, the ability to live in the same home with his own children (twice), and other things that I do not concern myself with. He is also extremely high functioning, has many friends, has held the same job in the same position his whole life, and I wouldn't doubt he did all of that never once calling in sick to work. It is not anyone's fear that Peter is going to drop dead tomorrow of an overdose. Nor that he could be so desperate as to drink a bottle of perfume. So, no, he didn't have to change.

Regarding my brother, however, if Brett didn't stay on this sober path, I was sure he was never going to grow old.

My Auntie Sharon, my mom's only sibling, was planning a trip with our two adult cousins, to Australia. She invited Brett to come along. She was also deeply concerned about Brett and wanted to include him in this family trip. I don't think Brett had seen our cousins since late childhood, although I don't know exactly when, but it was natural that they would love him and miss him, so it was a really thoughtful offer.

My aunt and her family are the only relatives in the entire world on Mom's side that I have ever seen or heard about, besides Nana and Papa. I didn't know about Mom's grandparents. I didn't know if Nana and Papa had any siblings. There was no mention or meeting of any aunts, uncles, or cousins from that side of the family. Not one. It was like no one else existed.

I mean, our mother and aunt had to have grandparents at some point, didn't they? And it came later as a huge surprise at Papa's funeral that there were relatives and they were alive. I have never asked our mother why she has no association with any one of her relatives on this planet except my Aunt Sharon, so I don't know how or why. I learned at a very early age not to ask our mom those kinds of questions. All I know is it is just another thing that is really bizarre. It is totally against everything I want out of life, which is to be surrounded by my family.

Even though my Auntie Sharon had lived far away in Vancouver my entire life, she and I were always very close. I doubt she realizes, but I have mirrored my life after her and Uncle Jamie. Jim and I both have. Aunt Sharon and Uncle Jamie are the two people we trust more than anyone else in the world. They have always been fair, stable, loving, and completely rational, so I always looked up to her. From the time I was a little girl, she has been my role model, and she exemplified how I wanted my life to be.

I had called her months earlier to share more of what had been going on. She knew of course about Brett's drinking problem from Mom, but I filled in the gaps, all the unpleasant details.

Brett had been sober and thriving for a while, but I was bothered by this proposed trip to the other side of the globe. It just seemed unrealistic. Immediately, I called Mom to get her take on it. I know we rarely saw eye to eye, but since she was the one who had paid so much money to help Brett onto a new path, I thought she might see it my way this time. I didn't know exactly how much money she had given him in total—the cost of the treatment programs, eight grand in outstanding bills a few months ago (although admittedly, I had asked her to do that), the two grand for hookers—they all factored into my thought process. Paying for things to encourage sobriety in my mind was a matter of life and death; going to Australia was not.

I knew that Brett had not attempted to pay our mom back for anything yet. Truthfully, I don't think she'd even asked. He was making great money, but going on a trip like this did not seem like a reality to me. Jim and I work hard, every day, and we couldn't afford a trip like that. And if you can't afford it, you can't go. Everyone would have extra money for trips if someone else paid their other expenses.

I shared these concerns with our mother.

"Jodee, Brett needs something to look forward to," she said. And I knew the conversation was over.

They were set to leave in just a few days and I could tell instantly when I saw Brett that something was wrong. He shared with me that he didn't think he should go and wanted to cancel. He was feeling uneasy, a little panicked, although he was not sure why. I explained that the whole point of this process of recovery in general was to understand why you behave in a certain way; to acknowledge his triggers. That was something I couldn't do for him. I had already learned a lot about triggers from Brett, plus from the books I had been reading. Triggers are stimuli that initiate the desire to engage in addictive behavior. These can be things that affect a person's mood: a place, a stressor, people, and even a smell can give an addict an overwhelming sense to use and engage in a behavior that they are trying to avoid.

"Your anxiety is not going to go away a hundred percent with Paxil. There is no such thing as a magic pill; you need to work through those thoughts. I would listen to yourself, Brett. If you don't think you should go, then *don't*," I told him.

I didn't really understand the seriousness of his panic attacks back then. Unfortunately, neither did he.

A few days later when I came home from work—December 4—Brett had been at my house. Placed carefully on the mat at the back door so that I wouldn't miss it was a photo album with a huge logo, "Togetherness." It was over a foot square, with five cartoon cats excitedly playing on the front cover.

As I opened the first page, I read in big letters: HAPPY BIRTHDAY! ♥ BRETT.

The album was filled with over twenty pages of pictures from the "Golden Years" and beyond, which he had clearly scanned and copied on his computer. The Golden Years. That is what Brett called our childhood with Ron. Years of true happiness. I began to cry, feeling the love in this thoughtful gift. And

I knew why he couldn't be there that day; he had chosen to ignore what his instincts were telling him; he went to Australia anyway.

He had been back for a couple weeks when we knew something was wrong. Dawn-Marie thought so too. Instantly, his personality had started to change; he was grumpy, anxious, and not himself. We suspected he was drinking; although we came up with every other reason in our mind as we couldn't bear to believe it was true.

When we got together at Mom's for Christmas, Brett turned up, but he didn't invite Dawn. I found it strange that he didn't want to introduce her to Mom and Nicole, but that was his business. Our mother found him a little odd and had a hunch he was drinking, too.

Soon it was obvious—what he was hiding was a secret no more. Brett had begun drinking almost instantly he landed in Australia, although he used his manipulating techniques on my aunt, making her promise not to tell. That is what addicts do. They play on their loved ones' hearts, lie, make them believe a different truth, and loved ones fall right into the addict's trap when really all they are trying to do is help. It was not Auntie Sharon's fault at all; after all this time, I still fell for his charms. But she now told us the truth, feeling guilty to hold it in any longer. Although I didn't ask for all the nitty, gritty details, I believe he ruined the trip. After all, I didn't have to ask, I knew how it went once Brett hit the bottle.

From everything we are taught, it is very normal for an addict to relapse. Some of them relapse many times before they finally stay sober. For that reason, there were no alarm bells going off; after all it seemed like just an unfortunate, but normal, part of the process. If there hadn't been this little "bump" in the road, he would have been sober for four whole months.

While I was not sure how he managed it, Brett was able to stop the drinking on his own, so everything was quickly back on track. For the first time in such a long time he had so much motivation to change. He was in love and truly happy for the start of 2005. He had everything in the world to look forward to.

He called out of the blue just weeks later:

"Hello," I said.

"Hey," Brett said, cool as ever.

"Hey. What's going on?" I said right back.

"Okay, don't freak out," he said.

Yet, my heart was instantly racing, feeling like it would explode from my chest.

"What, what is it?!" I said in panic mode, with bad thoughts swirling and running through my mind.

"Okay, calm down." There was a short pause until Brett continued. "Dawn-Marie thinks she is pregnant. We have been planning it for a while. She doesn't know until we go to the doctor's next week, but she's pretty sure."

My heart was still racing, but those horrendous thoughts were quickly replaced. This was his happy ending. Every hope and dream I had ever had for my little brother was finally coming true.

"I AIN'T EVER SATISFIED "

That week seemed like it took forever as I just had to know; and I was about to burst with excitement. I was out of town in meetings for work the day of Dawn-Marie's appointment, but I made Brett promise to call me the second they found out. I did realize it was completely unprofessional yet I answered my cell phone when it rang and excused myself from the room.

"Hello," I said.

"Hey," Brett replied.

"Tell me, tell me," not even giving him time to say anything except one word. "Is she pregnant?"

"Ya, she just called," he said, but not in his regular voice.

"She just called. Didn't you go there with her?" I asked, raising my voice slightly, now suspicious and scared.

"No, she went on her own," he said, now not able to hide it in his voice.

"Brett, you're drinking, aren't you?" Although I wasn't asking him, I knew this to be true and I was freaking out.

"Jeez, Jodee. No, I am not," he replied.

Now, he had one hundred percent confirmed. He never said "Jeez"; never, unless he was drinking.

"Brett, now listen! DO NOT do this. I will be home in a couple of hours, you need to make plans to go to detox and nip this in the bud now. I mean it, Brett. This can all go away."

The same story persisted for the next couple of weeks; the constant lying, pretending he wasn't drinking, the arguing, the denial, the broken promises, just like I had witnessed so many times before. But now, this included a pregnant and confused Dawn-Marie. I don't think he had stopped drinking after Australia after all. The pain that I and other family members who love an addict endure is almost unbearable. Hope gives you the ability to get out bed in the morning, it gives you happiness, it gives you strength. Then, in an instant, there's a tightening of your heart, a sense of almost not being able to breathe. The realization that this will undoubtedly once again progress to those astronomical levels, that they may disappear for days or die tomorrow, none of which is in our control. But some of us hold on to the belief longer than others that we can control the situation as the alternative is too painful to bear.

My brother hid away from the world in a constant blur in his dark bedroom, locking all his doors, and pinning a note to his front door, "I'm so sorry."

I would not use my key; I could not take it anymore.

My fears were once again reinforced. For seven excruciating days, he locked himself away in his home. We knew he was alive because during his brief moments of consciousness, he called Dawn.

As usual, I tried to act normally for the sake of my own family. They didn't hear me come in the back door and walk upstairs where Ryan was talking to his dad.

"I hate Uncle Brett," he said. "All he ever does is make Mom cry."

I honestly had thought nothing could make my heart hurt anymore. But I was wrong. I cowered, tiptoeing back down the stairs. We were all struggling and my heart was being pulled in competing directions. I did not have any idea what to say to my young son.

It was later after dinner on day eight when someone knocked at the door. As I walked down the short hallway from the kitchen, I could see Dawn-Marie through the small window at the front entrance. As I opened the door, I saw little Matthew standing there with her and I could tell by Dawn's large eyes that something was wrong.

Frantically, she said, "I went to check on Brett. Jodee, he's passed out in his bed with a shotgun."

Rick, Ryan, and Jim were in the living room and overheard everything. I jumped three steps until I reached the cordless phone; Jim grabbed his keys, knowing exactly what to do.

"I am on my way," he said.

I dialed 911 while simultaneously yelling to my husband before he reached the back door, "DO NOT go into the bedroom." I shouted at him again with no reply. "Did you hear me? Wait for the police. DO NOT go in there!" I screamed out, fearing for his life.

The operator answered and patched me through to the police. After I gave her the quick details and address, I then begged of them to be careful. "Please, please have them be quiet. Please don't wake him, pleeeaaase." A combination of movies, newspaper stories, and television shows played out in my mind. I could envision the horror of the scene playing out. Jim or the police officers coming in and startling him—he jumps awake and accidentally pulls the trigger.

"Don't worry, ma'am. They will be careful. Help is on the way."

I hung up the phone and sat on the couch, holding Dawn-Marie, both of us breathing heavily and not saying a word. We were not crying, nor hysterical. We were trying to behave as though nothing was wrong for the sake of the children, all of them watching us with their young eyes. Matt was too young to understand, but Rick and Ryan, at thirteen and eleven, knew exactly what was going on. I waited about ten painstaking minutes, then I called Jim on his cell phone, having the same feeling of apprehension that I had each time with my brother.

I was so relieved he answered the phone.

"What is going on? Are you okay?"

"I am okay. The police have just got here. They are going in," he reported.

I could hear only the sound of silence on the other end of the line, although I dreaded a loud bang. My heart was beating wildly as I imagined hearing my husband tell me that my brother was dead. I was overwhelmed and my thoughts weren't making any sense. I had never in my life been this terrified. These types of scenes always end tragically, just like an episode of *Law & Order* with gunshot blasts, blood, and bodies. After what felt like an hour, in reality maybe two minutes, Jim finally spoke.

"They have him, Jodee. He's okay." I repeated Jim's words to Dawn. "He's okay." I dropped the phone and I crumpled to the floor and cried.

Pulling ourselves together, Dawn and I left Matthew with the boys and immediately headed over to Brett's. Brett sat quietly on the mismatched chair at the kitchen table, with a knitted hat nestled tightly on his head. He wasn't drunk out of his mind; drunk, yes, but not nearly to the barely conscious levels that I had seen. He was passive and reserved, and was trying his best to explain to the two officers, but he just didn't know why the shotgun was there. Taking no chances, as he was now a risk to himself, he was admitted to the psychiatric ward at the nearby hospital.

Dawn and I met Mom and Nicole at the hospital a few days later. It was slightly awkward as that was the first time they had met Dawn, but we made the best of it. Brett seemed better and mentioned he needed a few toiletries, so we all took a walk through the hospital to the gift shop. Walking down the hall seemed a little ironic to me. After all, this was the same hospital where Mom and Nana had been emergency room nurses. I had been there so many times, but those visits were for such different reasons.

I stood behind and chitchatted with Dawn-Marie while Brett walked through the tiny store. I wasn't paying close attention as he sauntered around picking up the things he needed. I began to take notice as he got to the front register laying each item, one by one, on the counter. Toothbrush, toothpaste, mouthwash, dental floss, a magazine, deodorant, and a pack of gum. I looked in our mother's direction. She was also watching his every move. I didn't get a response. I took two steps forward, leaned in, and whispered in her ear, "If you don't make a move, I will," coming across I am sure as a promise and a threat.

Mom acknowledged my request, said something to Brett that we didn't hear, he put back the mouthwash, and she paid the bill. Dawn looked at me with the same confused look that she had a few weeks earlier at our house. Brett had been out snowmobiling and we were sitting around the living room. Ricky came out of his bathroom holding a large, full-sized bottle of Scope that was empty. I had just bought it for the kids the day before. He didn't need to explain; my kids are old enough to put together their own puzzle pieces, just like I used to when I was a kid. Ricky had just waved the empty bottle in the air in disgust and disbelief, "Mom!!"

This time, I responded to Dawn's look of bewilderment.

"He'll drink it, honey," is all I said, without any further elaboration.

Once sober, Brett was released from the hospital. After all, society doesn't keep alcoholics locked up in hospitals because the families want them there. Soon the lies that he tells himself, as well as the rest of the world, started up again. First, a drink or two, doing a great job at hiding it for a while, then progressing to the lethal levels. Dawn tried hard to break things off with him, but it was an impossible task. She loved him very much.

History repeated itself and he locked himself in the house, but it was hard to destroy what was already damaged. The inside of his home was the epitome of decay and ruin. He had no concept of breaking things; the basic parameters of what a person does to keep a house clean.

After we all pleaded with Brett for days, he finally agreed to once again enter a thirty-day treatment program. It was up north in Grande Prairie and it cost $5,000, but they could get him in right away and he did not have to be sober beforehand because they have a medical detox there.

I called our dad and after once again explaining what had been happening, asked that he help pay for treatment for his son. "I can't pay, Jodee. I am retired and on a budget," he replied.

Our father was never equipped with the skills to know what to do. During this time, he hadn't been there emotionally either, so our mom once again carried the financial burden on her own, paying the rehab cost.

While Dawn unquestionably loved my brother, she was struggling to understand. They were in love, pregnant with their first child, and talking marriage. Then all of that bliss was ripped away and, in an instant, she had become the lead character in a scary horror movie. It turns out, the drinking had bothered her four years earlier and now it was back again. She hadn't actually broken up with Brett when they first dated because she got back together with an ex-boyfriend; she had ended it because all he ever wanted to do was get drunk. Brett had given me an addict's version of the truth. He continued to make every excuse he could come up with, except the reality—it had been the bottle.

What was happening now was in no way the same scenario as when they had dated, this wasn't just someone getting drunk. My brother was no longer a functioning alcoholic, not on any level. Dawn was a single mom, barely making ends meet, and she was now faced with the realization she might be alone with two little mouths to feed. Despite this, she stood behind Brett wholeheartedly and promised she would be right there by his side when he got home from rehab. But she was considering what—I would imagine—was the most painful and hardest decision of her life: whether to go through with the pregnancy.

Grande Prairie was a six- or seven-hour drive up north and there was just absolutely no way I could go. My husband, however wonderful, supportive, and understanding, was not impressed, and I didn't blame him. It had been years by now of these trials and tribulations that could push anyone past their limits. Nicole had just found out she was pregnant and already her marriage was showing signs of cracking. She and Adam had their own issues. Those were not my brother's fault but the added stress didn't help the relationship. Even so, Nicole and Mom agreed to drive Brett up north. He had agreed to go, although he wasn't happy about it.

I know we are told that an addict can't change unless they want to. No one can force them; they have to do it for themselves. And I do still believe that, although I think it is a little more complex. Can anyone dispute that addicts in the moment aren't thinking rationally? People have all sorts of motivations for change: "My wife will divorce me." "My boss will fire me." "I can't see my children." "It is a requirement of the courts." My brother wasn't the only one encouraged to go to rehab. I was always confident that with extra help from the professionals and thirty days of sobriety, he would come around, see clearly what was really happening to his life, and make the changes needed to live a sober life. My feelings are the same today, although standing back from a magnified version of the story, I think family has a huge impact. When our support includes buying into our loved one's altered reality, we will probably never see change, because the addict will continue to believe that nothing is wrong.

This time, he was clearly intoxicated as he struggled to get into the small backseat of Mom's Mercury Cougar, although it didn't matter; they would help him through his withdrawal when he arrived.

Mom turned to me, "I will call you when we get there."

"Okay," I said, as she got in the front seat, closed the door, and then rolled down the electric window.

"And, Mom," I said, taking a short breath. "Take away his shoes." After all, I wasn't about to take any chances.

"PROMISES BROKEN "

This time was going to be different, I was sure of it.

What I loved about Grande Prairie is that they have a "Family Week," which means the closest member to the loved one can attend in order to learn about recovery. If the previous centers had any family interaction or programs for us at all, Brett hadn't told us. So I was overjoyed at the prospect that someone at an actual rehab facility would be willing to talk about what goes on behind those walls. I was determined to finally find out why our previous attempts were such an epic failure and what we needed to do to help Brett fully recover.

My brother wanted Dawn-Marie to come for that valuable week, but she had her own responsibilities. She had little Matt to look after, plus she had a job; she wasn't in a position to be able to take five days off work. Brett told her he understood, but I knew him so well; he didn't. This was an example of one of his biggest personality changes early on, selfishness. I too had been reading up on symptoms of addiction, and they fitted my brother to a tee:

The adjective "selfish" is one of the most commonly used responses when individuals are asked to describe the addicted person they love. By definition it means lacking consideration for others, concern for primarily one's own pleasure.

My brother no longer saw the world from others' points of view; selfishness and self-centeredness reared their ugly heads with his constant, insatiable desire to fill his own needs. What Brett told Dawn and what he felt inside were completely opposite sentiments. He was hurt deeply and really believed Dawn should just be able to leave her son and her commitments because he, Brett, needed something from her.

Since that thought process wasn't a symptom unique to my brother, it was no coincidence that one of the things addicts were there to embrace was "humility." Humility. It is one of my favorite words, "Not thinking less of yourself, but thinking of yourself less." I used to use it to describe my brother, but not anymore. I thought it would do him good to be reminded that he was not the center of the universe.

I was confident that when he talked about this with his therapist or in group with the others in recovery, they would help him see things differently. Just because Dawn couldn't come didn't mean she was not a hundred percent supportive. Besides, I was willing to leave my life, my job, Jim, and the boys for a week to help him. But of course, Brett had other plans. If Dawn-Marie wouldn't come, he didn't want anyone else there. It was a quiet family week for my brother as he continued to make poor choices and, in my opinion, didn't engage in what was recommended.

Dawn-Marie talked to Brett on the phone every day, and he was so lucky to have her in his life. Together, she and I spent that time organizing his house and getting it ready for her to move in. While cleaning up, I discovered that his finances were still a mess. He had accumulated a huge mound of debt in just a few short months; my brother was another $15,000 in arrears.

As I dug my way through his pile of bills, I could see everything was way past due. Utilities, cable, cell phone, and credit cards. As well as a couple of bills from those high-interest loan companies that air commercials on television, promising "quick money" just until payday. With an annual percentage rate at a whopping 521%, that is fucked up in itself. The only thing that was current and not in the pile was his mortgage payment, thank God.

Dawn was shocked and confused while looking through these stacks of crinkly papers as Brett had told her that she could quit her job and be a stay-at-home mom. A stay-at-home mom? That was far from reality—he was in no position to be making that promise.

When I got the chance, I talked to Brett on the phone about my concern over his debt. I thought he should really consider selling his house, as his bills and commitments were now exceeding what he made. He absolutely did not understand and quite frankly it was as though I was speaking a foreign language. This was a man who had to pass advanced calculus for his Power Engineering Certificate, so I was perplexed that this simple math did not make sense to him. To prove my calculations were right, I faxed him a thorough list, with the column of monthly expenses on the left and wages on the right, for him to see in black and white the enormous shortfall. But he wouldn't listen to reason, barking "For fuck sakes, Jodee, I make over eighty grand a year."

That statement was true as he continued to keep the same job with pay when off "sick." He was adamant that I was wrong. But eighty grand doesn't matter if he spends a hundred.

Over the next few weeks when Brett was in rehab, we corresponded via telephone and the occasional letter. Brett talked to me more at length about the things he was learning and seemed to be opening up. I took that as such a positive sign. He had learned that the addicted person stops maturing at the age when the addiction begins. "Basically, I am sixteen," Brett said.

Sixteen? Swirls of happy memories raced through my mind.

I remember his sixteenth birthday like it was yesterday. I had left home long before, but I made sure to come home since he was getting the gift from Mom, Dad, and Ron that I had lovingly picked out for him. Although I didn't get such an extravagant gift for my sixteenth, that didn't matter to me. I had a great idea for my brother and talked both my parents into splitting the cost of a used car. I then went vehicle shopping, putting my big surprise in place.

Brett was beyond excited when he opened the neatly wrapped package. When he undid the tiny bow and opened the small silver box, he was surprised to find a single key inside, attached to a key chain marked with the iconic emblem, "MUSTANG."

I can still see him beaming with pride and happiness with his childhood best friends, KC, Tyson, and Jazzy, zooming off to their newfound independence. I honestly didn't care that my parents never bought me a car; my brother was happy and, in turn, so was I.

This was valuable insight for him, but it was for me as well. This was the first acknowledgement I had ever heard that drinking in his mind had become a problem so long ago, during our youth. I had never thought of it that way before, at least when it came to him. We had so much love during the Golden Years, but what we also had was complete and utter freedom. We were teenagers, after all, and teenagers don't usually make the best choices. I have no idea what exactly he was doing during those years as I had already moved away, but it obviously involved excessive drinking.

And no matter how hard I try, I can't remember my own sixteenth birthday. Weird.

Once again, Brett was receiving group therapy in rehab, as well as one-on-one with a counselor. I hoped they would really get to the bottom of his emotional pain, and ultimately concentrate on and help him understand the triggers that make him reach for the bottle. He seemed so excited, relishing in the newfound knowledge regarding certain things that were not good for him and could set off a relapse, such as isolation, boredom, loneliness, self-pity, a sense of failure, criticism, or people and places that remind him of using.

"Dad's at the top of the list," he said.

I was careful to just listen and offer support as best I could, as it was not up to me to diagnose or to figure it out for him. My brother loves his dad very, very much; he needed him during this time in his life. And unfortunately that was not the card he was dealt. It was a struggle for Brett, but I was so relieved that he was being honest up there and having insight when it came to those negative influences. I was relieved and thankful for the education and help he was getting, but I was always so grateful that he continued to call and that he didn't hate me. After all, I did feel that once again we had forced him to do this.

"Don't ever say or think I hate you. I wasn't even mad, just very scared the first couple of days. Thought I had lost everything. I talked about what I did, and it's more common than I thought, still pretty lame, but I'm over it. I have to be," Brett said with such confidence.

"We've got things narrowed down to self-sabotage. I just have to take the time to grow into happiness."

Dawn was unwavering in her love and support. After thirty days, my brother returned home to a beautifully manicured lawn, clean house, new bedding for his bedroom, all compliments of Dawn and me. And, just like in a five-star hotel, we even placed a little mint on his pillow. Welcome home.

Mom came to visit about a week later and she always chose to stay with us. Brett had a spare room so she certainly could have stayed there, but that was just not her routine. She arrived while we were eating dinner and the boys had to witness their obviously intoxicated Gramma stumble into our home. It scares me to think that she had been driving in that condition. She was another one not considering the consequences of her actions. She was glassy-eyed and carrying a white, plastic bag that you would get from a grocery store, glass bottles clinking together inside. She neatly placed the bag on the island for all to see and pulled out six mini bottles of wine, setting them on the counter one by one. Jim and I and Rick and Ryan just sat quietly, heads down, chewing on roast chicken with mashed potatoes and gravy, occasionally making eye contact with each other in disbelief.

I love our mom very much. I somehow feel the need to clarify that in advance, because when I say things about her, I feel guilty. In society and especially in families, you are not supposed to say anything perceived as negative about your own mother. You just aren't. And when you do speak up, you are made to feel like you have done something wrong and it does cause me great anguish. But as I know when you don't say anything it just continues. In my opinion, our mom has a drinking problem. Well, I suppose that is arguable. When does something become a problem? When it starts to negatively impact that person's life? Or when it negatively impacts someone else's? That is the burning question, isn't it? Our mom changed around the time she and Ron divorced.

The mother I remember from childhood no longer existed. Her drinking now was having a direct impact on my life, and sadly I believe it was doing the same for my brother, even if I and everyone else continued to deny it. She had no problem having lunch downtown with Brett, never minding to enjoy a few glasses of wine or two "double" Caesars (*aka* Bloody Marys) in front of him during those infrequent visits. I didn't understand why she couldn't just order a diet coke or a lemonade when her son had just got out of rehab. Nonetheless, I knew my brother was going to tell our mom something important, life changing; that Dawn was still painstakingly considering whether or not to terminate the pregnancy.

Later that evening when everyone was getting prepared for bed, Ryan walked downstairs dressed in his pajamas and I could tell that something was wrong. "I just watched Gramma take a bunch of pills. Mom, this is not right," he said in disgust.

"Ry, I am sorry, just ignore her," I said, which had become my automatic reply. I kissed him on the head. "Good night, love you."

"I love you, too," he replied and he turned around and went back up to his room.

I knew he couldn't ignore her. The spare bedroom was right across the hall. It was impossible to ignore anything that you witness with your own two eyes.

They were her much-needed sleeping pills. But the truth was I didn't even know what she was taking. The only mention of them was a while back when she said that everyone, when they get older, needs to take something to help them sleep. I thought that was a completely ludicrous statement. But I was not going to get involved; I didn't have the energy for that fight. Our mother is a nurse. Although she no longer works in a hospital environment, her job is leading health and wellness. If she didn't know better, she most certainly should have.

Jim was already in bed when I came upstairs and reached the top of the landing. I could see Mom tucking herself in for the night.

"Jodee," she called.

"Ya," I said as I poked my head in.

"Come in here," she asked.

"Can you tell Dawn that if she has the baby, I will raise it," she said matter-of-factly.

Now I have heard and seen crazy. Our mother, who was approaching her fifty-seventh birthday, who had briefly met Dawn-Marie only once, at the hospital no less, was going to raise *her* baby? Holy shit. I did not even respond, but turned back around to go to bed.

As I took the first step into my bedroom, I heard her yell at me. "Don't you dare tell her what to do, Jodee! Don't you dare!"

"What was that all about?" Jim asked turning over, bleary-eyed and half-asleep.

"Don't ask," I said as I crawled into bed and pulled the covers over my head. I just wanted all of this to go away. I just wanted to hide.

It was a constant conflict; the lessons my children were potentially absorbing versus the morals I was trying to teach them. I wanted to tell our mother to leave, that this was not appropriate, this wasn't fair to me, least of all to Ricky and Ryan. I wanted to tell her that she needed help, we all did, as this wasn't working. But as usual, for the sake of at least some peace and calm, I said nothing. I was trapped between both families—the one I was born into and my own. I just didn't have the skills to know what to do.

And I would never say anything to Dawn-Marie. You can't decide for someone else what they should or shouldn't take and what choices they should make.

Hers was not my life to live.

"ALL APOLOGIES "

But life and its problems don't just go away. Not with alcohol, not with sleeping pills, and certainly not with a burgundy-colored four-hundred-thread-count bedsheet.

Our imagination can be our best friend, or our worst enemy. I did my best to shake off the images of what could be: a beautiful, brown-eyed, exuberant little girl, watching her at dance class, taking her to Build-a-Bear, and having sleepovers at my house. Or a round-faced little boy, with infectious laughter, always happy, and my proud brother teaching him how to skate and play hockey at the neighborhood rink. The squeals of "Auntie Jodee, Auntie Jodee" echoing through our halls.

I wouldn't get to make a big family dinner, or give a toast with non-alcoholic wine to celebrate the baby-on-the-way, or buy pink and blue balloons for the shower to welcome the new addition to our family. Dawn-Marie had made the agonizing and painful decision to get an abortion.

She was still right there by my brother's side, promising him they could try for another baby at a better time. But her mind was made up, allowing her logic to lead her, not her heart. Brett wanted to go with her, but she told him that she really needed her Mom to hold her hand on that day.

Brett went to work and I was home alone waiting for what seemed like an eternity, knowing what was happening in a clinic not too far away. I knew it was selfish to think of my own desires while Dawn-Marie and my brother's insurmountable heartbreak was far greater than my own. Everyone from both sides of the family was struggling with hurt on so many levels. I couldn't help yearning for the memories that would never be. Dawn wanted that baby. We all did.

As always, life went on. Dawn-Marie called me and asked if I would do her a favor and watch little Matthew for the day. Brett was at work as he had been sober for about two weeks. I was surprised to see him when he knocked on the door. He had just got off the midnight shift, so I knew he had to sleep. I was taken aback that he was there.

We bantered back and forth as I really didn't mind watching Matt, but Brett was adamant that Matthew was his responsibility. "I'll take him, Jode," he said, and off they went. Never did it occur to me that things would go south.

When Dawn arrived at his place about six hours later, Brett was wasted, although he denied it. It's crazy—she, I, we, all know deep down these are lies, but you want so much to believe what he says to be the truth that, somehow, you actually convince yourself that it is. Well, for a few days.

Dawn had almost four months of joy and happiness in the beginning of their relationship, but she had now added four months of living in an unbelievable, drunken nightmare of constant arguing, disappointment, and tears. Once again, Brett was back on a permanent bender.

I see now that her shock and fear was magnified a hundredfold as no one had breathed a word to her about her boyfriend's addiction. Not a whisper. Not even I, who at the time had become a good friend. It is hard to formulate into words why I didn't say anything. When I look back now, I wonder that myself. I really felt that it was their private relationship and that was my boundary, I suppose.

I would not find out until years later that he never told her he was an alcoholic. He said he had gone to rehab as a requirement for his impaired driving charge, and that couldn't have been farther from reality. He was so ashamed about what he had become, to be unable to tell someone he loved, someone he wanted to marry, when he should have been able to tell her absolutely anything. But he couldn't find the courage; shame is very powerful. Never in my wildest imagination did I ever think he wasn't telling Dawn the complete truth.

I ask myself, if I could go back, would things have worked out differently if I had talked openly with her?

As families, I think we hide, we don't tell our friends, our neighbors; we don't even talk about it inside our own four walls. You learn silence from the time you are a little child, and you are programmed not to speak of things, like addiction in your family because that is considered as negative and insulting and these are people that you love. I think that is a breeding ground for shame. I was always different. I was never ashamed of my brother, not ever, that was not my motivation for staying silent. It was never up to me to tell others, Dawn included, what my brother was really going through; that was up to him. And I trusted he was doing that. I guess I hadn't learned the lesson yet, that it is not a good idea to trust an addict.

The reality that it was not only possible, but probable, that there was no end in sight caused Dawn-Marie to end the relationship with my brother. I knew that Brett putting Matt in danger gave her the extra bit of strength and courage she needed to say goodbye. I heard the shrill, desperate, heartbreaking cries of Dawn as she asked him: "Why? Why? Brett, I loved you. Why are you doing this?" in the last voice-mail message she left for him. And it was over.

In continued denial, my brother believed it was all Dawn's fault; she was to blame. After all, if she just would have stood beside him, he would have stopped drinking. He could say what he wanted. I knew he no longer needed a reason.

There was no longer a way out of the financial hole that he had dug for himself, and he was most certainly going to lose his home. His bills far exceeded what he made. Deep down I knew he still had no comprehension of this, but he had always trusted me. Although it hadn't been happening lately, he finally took my advice.

It took some serious persuasion, but he eventually agreed that the house had to go. In order to save money on realtor commissions, I placed a large BY OWNER sign in the front bay window. After all, I had been very successful at selling homes this way in the past, so I was quite capable. I asked Mom if she could front him the money for his overdue bills, giving him another $10,000. House prices had gone up the last couple of years, so he would make a healthy profit of close to $25,000. He would be able to pay her back as soon as it was sold. The remainder would go to the credit card balance and then he would have to start fresh all over again.

Even Ron came to help make Brett's home perfect for an open house.

Although Brett and Nicole hadn't kept in close contact with Ron since his divorce from Mom, I had. With no questions asked, he was there to do whatever he could to help. The house sold quickly to a lovely young couple, with a possession date at the end of May, only five weeks away.

I knew Brett had only been back from rehab less than a month, but he agreed to return. We didn't know what else to do. Where else do you send your loved one for help? And quite frankly, thirty days just didn't seem like enough, but that was our only known option at the time. I did recall one little detail about Grande Prairie's facility: if it didn't work they would take him back for an additional thirty days, no charge. So at least this wouldn't cost our mother another five grand. It did seem like he was failing and at times it felt like there was no hope at all. There are so many varying statistics on failure of treatment, but I prefer to focus on the positive ones, that there are over twenty-three million people in the USA in long-term recovery and close to five million in Canada. That is the statistic we should all concentrate on.

My brother had trepidations about returning to rehab on Monday morning, and I didn't blame him. It is a scary concept, the unknown. Or maybe his fear was that he could never drink again, I wasn't sure. So the Saturday before, in order to show my support, I decided to spend the weekend with him. I kissed my family goodbye and went to pick up a few groceries.

I arrived at Brett's at dinner time with a grocery bag in each hand. He was lying on the couch, the sound of "Smells Like Teen Spirit" that I have heard so many times before blaring in the background, as I heated up some oil on the stove. I began frying little chunks of beef for supper. While it crackled and spit, I cut up vegetables, every few minutes I went into the living room to talk to Brett, then back to the kitchen, back and forth. He picked up the large FOR SALE BY OWNER sign that was still in the window and, with a black felt marker, scribbled "SOLD by JP." It struck me as odd because he wasn't acting quite right. He was a little agitated, but I knew how stressed he was about going back to rehab, so the restlessness certainly made sense. He promised he wasn't drinking so as completely crazy as that sounds, it didn't cross my mind that he might be.

"Hey," I said. "Wanna watcha movie? Maybe I'll call Ryan and see if he wants to come over and you guys can pick something out."

"Ya, sure," Brett replied.

I called Ry and soon he would be on his way. Meanwhile, Brett continued to act jumpy and anxious, going downstairs into his unfinished basement to shoot a puck at the empty hockey net. Ryan arrived a short time later and, by then, I could no longer deny the bright bold signs all pointing in the same direction.

Ry followed my lead and together we hunted through drawers, cabinets, closets, anywhere that alcohol could be hidden. Without saying a word, Ryan and I poured the vodka down the drain as a fresh pot of stew cooked on the stove. Brett, now sitting silently on the edge of the couch in the living room, realized that the jig was up. For the first time ever, I witnessed a full-on anxiety attack; he was panicked, worried, nervous, and was breathing more heavily than usual. If I hadn't known better, I would have thought he was having a heart attack. I tried to calm him, reminding him everything was going to be okay, to just breathe. We were there for him and we were so proud that he had agreed to once again take this step. He left the room to go to the bathroom, but it didn't matter, the bottle wasn't there any longer. Ryan and I had found the half-full "forty-pounder" floating in the toilet tank.

My brother strolled out of the bathroom about five minutes later, his face damp with sweat. "I am sorry," he said in a whisper to the two of us sitting on the edge of the couch, not knowing what to do.

As Ryan and I both looked at him, he stood still, with nothing more to say. He raised his hand, which was holding three empty pill bottles.

"Oh, my God!" I screamed. "What have you done!"

"I'm sorry," he repeated himself.

I grabbed the bottles from his trembling hand, found the cordless in the kitchen, and dialed 911. Twelve-year-old Ryan stood there silently, with no reaction at all. Since we lived in a small town, our ambulance service isn't immediate as they are called in from their homes. I knew it was going to be a wait, plus another twenty-minute drive to the hospital. I just didn't know if that was too much time before he died from an overdose.

The 911 operator calmly asked what he swallowed. "Ummm; Paxil, although I have no idea how much or how many were in the bottle! The other bottle was Antabuse." I have the foresight to know these are the pills sometimes prescribed to treat chronic alcoholism. It is not a cure, but a deterrent for drinking as they become deathly sick if taken with even the slightest amount of alcohol. "I imagine that bottle was full," I continued. "And the last one, I can't tell what they were as the letters are faded on the label," I said in hysterics. "Brett, what was in this bottle!?" I asked, frantically waving the empty pill container in the air. He did not answer.

"Help is on the way, ma'am."

And I hung up.

I was trying to prepare myself, waiting for Brett to drop on the floor, unconscious, but that was not the case. He was far from still, in fact quite the opposite; instead frenetic and pulsing with fear. Within minutes, his face began to get flushed and he was pacing like a crazy person, realizing what he had just done.

My sense of hope is so deep that I had truly believed what Brett told me at the time; that he wasn't drinking.

It seems inconceivable, mindboggling, that I would have invited my son into this horror.

I finally grabbed enough sense to call Jim to come and get Ryan, giving him the quick rundown of the current disaster. The ambulance arrived first, so I placed Ry safely in the front seat, as he waited for his dad, while the two paramedics worked to stabilize Brett on the stretcher in the back.

Ryan had been absolutely silent during this whole thirty-minute ordeal. He didn't speak. He didn't flinch. He didn't cry, just being a little boy assessing what was going on around him.

And finally Ryan shared his thoughts. "Uncle Brett is fucked," he said calmly.

I do not condone the language, but it was hard to disagree.

"NOWHERE ROAD"

Brett was released from the hospital after a few days.

Our mom arrived to show her support, this time with a box of granola, yogurt, and an armful of health magazines encouraging Brett to "get healthy." I barely blinked my eyes and he began drinking again, and the house instantly reverted into a disaster zone.

It was the middle of the day and he was asleep in his room when I got there. Oh, who was I kidding? He had passed out. I was used to the broken furniture, the garbage, the piles of laundry, and the dozens of empties. But on that day, sitting perfectly in among the empty vodka bottles was an empty cereal box. Scattered everywhere across the beige linoleum kitchen floor was granola.

I was standing there all alone, and no one could hear me, but that didn't stop me from speaking out loud: "I understand Brett—that is how we all feel."

I couldn't explain at the time why none of us dared say anything to our mother; we all needed deep therapy to answer that. The thousands of spilt pieces of rolled oats and almonds each represented our frustration. Granola was not the answer for my brother. As confused as he was, he knew that, and so did I.

I turned and left the déjà vu, knowing there was nothing more I could do. Not because I had given up. I just couldn't take the pressure anymore. I tried my best not to think about what was going on in the house in Fox Run, but that was an impossible task.

For me, Brett's alcoholism was something I was unable to escape from. For more than ten days, I hid my tears from my family because I knew with each drop, they hated him even more. He was causing me severe anxiety and pain; my brother was hurting the one they loved.

I couldn't sleep at night with every imaginable scenario playing over and over in my mind. He was going to overdose, he got killed in a bar fight, a family was dead as he killed them drunk driving. I was not some drama queen; each and every one of these scenarios was a very real possibility. I went to work in the morning, trying as best I could to coordinate the staff with their duties. They were clearly struggling with no form of leadership as I was rarely there those days.

I would sneak home in the middle of the day, walk through the front door, and unplug each and every telephone, because I was afraid that if it rang, it would be because my brother was dead. I felt like I was going to go crazy, perhaps I was already there. I would go into the spare bedroom and crawl under the covers to find darkness. Quiet. Peace. If only for a couple of hours. When I woke, I plugged back in all the phones, greeted the kids after school, and made dinner for my family, pretending I'd had a great day at work. I too had become a master liar and deep down I knew they were worried about me. I was worried about me, too.

Days later, my cell phone rang and it was Brett in his talkative but slurry, blubbery, drunken tone. The booze always made him so sad, lonely, shameful, and despondent. The feelings he hid so deeply when sober overflowed through the phone and the hysterical crying was too much to take. I was not up for it; I had to have my shit together that day as I had a busy trade show with my candle products in Rocky. I told him that I didn't want to hear from him until he wanted help, real help—do-all-the-work-and-decide-to-change kinda help. And I hung up. I arrived at the loading dock and spent the next three hours, with meticulous detail, setting up my booth. As they opened the front doors, streams of eager customers instantly filled the aisles, then lined up at my lime green and hot pink counter.

I was saying "Have a great day" to one of my customers when my cell phone rang. "Mom, it's Uncle Brett," a panicked Rick was saying, barely giving me time to even say hello. "He drove here and has cut his wrists!"

"Oh, my God, Rick, what?!" I screeched, unable to catch my breath. "How bad is it?"

"There's lots of blood, Mom," Rick said.

"Ricky, go grab some cloths and wrap his wrists. I'll call 911. And I will call you back," I said, the bustling blur of the trade show closing in around me.

I hung up on my son, dialed 911, and once again whipped through the details, begging them to get to my house. As soon as they assured me they were on the way, I hung up and called cousin Kelly to go help since he lives only two minutes away. I then called Jim, filled him in; but he couldn't get home for at least an hour as he was out of town.

I paced back and forth in my booth, frantically trying to get back through to Rick. When he finally picked up, and I asked what was happening, he told me that Brett and Kelly got into a fight on the front lawn. Well, it was more that Kelly was in a fight. He was yelling and pushing my brother around on the grass so badly that Rick had to run across the street to get a neighbor to help intervene! I was not impressed. I didn't know what the hell Kelly was thinking; this was hardly the time for this kind of behavior.

For his young age of fourteen, Rick was remarkably calm. "The ambulance is just pulling up, Mom," he said, taking complete control of the situation.

"Okay, honey. I'll be on my way as soon as I can," I replied. And we hung up.

By now, everyone at the trade show had realized something was seriously wrong. I called one of my staff; told her we had a family emergency, and asked if she could please come and take over. She told me she would be there as soon as she could, although it would take her an hour to arrive since she was about fifty miles away.

I dialed Nicole's number and told her what had happened and asked her to meet me at the hospital. I would be there as fast as I could. I then dialed Mom and tried as best I could to explain. She too would be on her way.

I paced for about half an hour, but I was so distraught, I couldn't wait any longer. My sense of despair was overwhelming so I left over $10,000 of merchandise unattended at the show and drove fast and furiously to the hospital. I was absolutely frantic, paying no attention at all to the speed limit shown on the highway signs.

My mind was elsewhere. I could imagine the blood shooting from my brother's arms, spilling onto the plastic floor mats of his truck, stumbling to the door as red streams flowed down his pant leg, then holding out his arms to Rick in a desperate attempt to get help.

I pulled up to Emergency in Red Deer and quickly found a parking spot, barely shoving the truck into park, jumping out, and racing through the automatic doors. When I found Brett's room, Nickie and Kelly were already there with him. But this normally quiet, kind, soft-spoken guy is not who I saw. Brett was being loud and belligerent to the doctor in the white lab coat, with a few fuck-yous thrown in for good measure. He wanted to go home. NOW! Of course, that was not an option as two police officers were standing guard outside his hospital room. I was used to this. Until he got an assessment from a psychiatrist and was deemed okay and not a risk to himself or to others, the cops would once again stand at the door, watching him 24/7.

I took a few steps, walking up to him lying on the steel metal hospital bed. "Brett, look at me. Brett, look at me," I repeated softly as we made eye contact. "You need to relax. The doctors, they are here to help. Okay?" And although he didn't say a word, it took less than thirty seconds for him to calm down.

As I sat quietly in the corner, trying to process everything that had happened, I looked over at our wonderful cousin Kelly and realized I had judged him unfairly for having a fight on my front lawn. I was pissed off at him for yelling at Brett before the ambulance arrived. Now, as I watched him closely, I saw the love in his eyes. He was so hurt and concerned, being there for Brett for about the hundredth time, never asking for one thing in return. I could see he was trying desperately to stop his best friend from doing these things. With so much pain filling his own heart, all these crazy things that kept happening, his anger and frustration finally overcame him. I got it. I did it, too.

Our mother arrived about an hour later. I expected a nurturing, caring, scared mother in sheer panic arriving at the ward. Instead, we got a cold, emergency room nurse. She walked in, didn't say a word or make eye contact with any of us. When she reached my brother's bed, she nonchalantly picked up his wrists, took a quick look, then set them back down. Both his wrists were stitched up with little black pieces of string, sharp and pointy with still some visible signs of blood.

"Brett, why are you doing this?" she asked calmly. He did not answer.

I knew they were going to let him go. After all he had already been there twice before. The gun. The pills. I suppose the average person would think, "Oh, my God. He is going to kill himself," and would think that he would be locked up. I wish that was the case but that is not how this works. Step 1: Call 911. Step 2: Get admitted to hospital. Step 3: Have a quick, few-minutes interview with a psychiatrist without any family member present ("Sober up; you don't want to die."). Step 4: Go home.

We would not accept that answer this time. The four of us, begged and begged and begged some more. "Please. Something bad is going to happen. Keep him here for observation," we all said in our own way. They finally relented, they listened to our pleas. Instead of being admitted to the psychiatric ward, Brett was placed in the back of an ambulance and taken to another hospital forty-five minutes away. That gave us so much peace as we knew my brother was safe for now.

I was not sure what time it was when I got home. It was late and I was too exhausted to even look at the clock. The kids were in bed and I could tell that Jim was not pleased. He didn't ask how Brett was, nor say "Hi" when I entered the house. He was sitting on the living room couch; the expression on his face told the story. "It is funny how you rushed to the hospital to make sure that Brett was okay. You didn't even call to ask how your son was."

And what was so much worse than what he said was that it hadn't even occurred to me.

I never did talk to Ricky about this. I certainly fell short in getting him help to talk to someone about it, which I should have done for both sons, immediately. How could these boys not grow up to feel deep down that I was putting someone else above them? And what would all of this look like as they maneuvered their way through their adult life?

My mindset at the time was that my sons had an amazing father; loving, attentive, fair, stable and a completely hands-on dad. And that I was an attentive, understanding, loving mother, making up for all of this in different ways when I had time to focus on them. That confidence I had in Jim gave me the freedom during times of distress to shift my priorities to those of my brother. I knew, even while it was happening, that I was putting my children in harm's way by allowing them to be exposed to Brett's perilous behavior. And how unfair that was of me to put that responsibility on my husband. But every minute of the day was consumed with the thought that someone I loved was going to die. That clouded my judgment on every level. That was my justification for my own behavior.

I have always known, for as long as I can remember, why I am who I am. I knew that those childhood Friday nights developed my personality more than anything that has happened in my life; they were where my strength and determination came from. I always knew that was why my brother had such an attachment to me (although he didn't know it) and I to him. My husband and I worked so hard to give our sons a different life, a sober life, so that their childhoods wouldn't be filled with constant chaos and alcohol that would affect who they would become. And yet, that was exactly what I was doing. I should have protected my own children; and I feel nothing but heartache that I didn't. I should have talked calmly and compassionately to my brother, explaining that the children could not be exposed to this any longer. I should have done that a long time ago. But my heart was in charge, so I didn't do that, not by a long shot.

"NO RAIN"

After a few days, my brother could have visitors and I was instantly on my way. I really needed to work, but I drove right by my shop and headed forty-five minutes down the highway. The hospital to which Brett had been transferred was tucked away. Once I turned off the main highway, all I could see in all directions were beautiful trees and spring flowers. I had never been there and as I drove through the windy road, my own feelings of anxiety began to set in, since I was not sure what to expect when I got there. I had been having panic attacks more and more since this journey began, my heart rate rising and feeling like it could explode in my chest, my voice filling my head with illogical thoughts and a constant feeling of dread and disaster.

"Whoo, whoo, whoo. Whoo, whoo, whoo." I let air escape through my pursed lips as I tried to calm down.

A few minutes later, I saw the sign: ALBERTA HOSPITAL

When I arrived, the front doors were locked and I had to buzz to gain entry. As I walked through the glass doors, my head was filled with images from movies I had seen. And it was exactly the same. Quiet. White walls. Security. Sterile. There were no pillows on the simple beds as I turned to look in some of the rooms. And the dozen or so people I saw were not laughing, visiting, or talking. It was one of the most serene and atmosphereless environments I had ever been in.

I sat and chatted with Brett at a small table in the corner. He still didn't look particularly well and we didn't talk of anything of real importance.

"I need to go home, get out of this fuckin' puzzle factory. This is ridiculous; I am here for a couple of scratches on my wrist," he said harshly, quite unlike his usual soft-spoken tone when he was sober. But he couldn't go home. This was a psychiatric hospital. For the first time he was being held against his will.

I had the immediate urge to grab him, shake him, hug him, yell at him, kiss him, anything to make him see what was really happening, but I didn't. Instead I just stared at him blindly from across the table. After all, in my own way, I had tried all those things and they weren't working. After our twenty-or-so-minute visit, I walked back down the cold white hallways to leave. I could feel myself no longer being able to control my emotions and I was unable to breathe. I hurried out the front door, gasping to catch my breath as I inhaled the warm air and the bright sunshine touched my face. I propped my back up against the brick wall, and then slid slowly to the ground and sobbed, the tears streaming down my cheeks, wiping them with the sleeve of my grey hoodie. *This is not happening. This is not happening* was all my mind was telling me. But it *was* happening.

I went back the next day, and the day after that. As we sat and talked, I slid a card that I'd brought across the plastic table and asked Brett to sign it. He made no acknowledgment of what it was for, just wrote his usual "love Brett." I took it with me and promised I would see him again in a couple of days.

Mom and I went together and he was looking much better as we sat and talked in his private room. We stayed for about an hour or so and just as we were walking out the door he said, "Can you please tell Dad I am here?"

That moment was one of the weirdest experiences I have ever had. My brother sat there calmly, his legs hanging over the side of the bed, and I didn't envision my adult brother. What I saw was his short brown hair, chubby cheeks, and round face. A five-year-old boy, so weak and scared, just wanting the love of his father. I gave him a quick hug and a kiss goodbye, "Of course," I replied.

As Mom reached her car to head back home, I handed her a blue envelope and she slowly read the card from Brett. It was one of the rare moments that she seemed thankful for something I had done. She looked up and smiled, "Thank you, Jodee." It was Mother's Day, 2005.

"Oh," she said before taking her last step to climb into the front seat. "Are you going to call Peter and tell him Brett is here?"

"He knows he is here, Mom," I replied.

I had called him, many times, looking for any support at all, financial or otherwise. And my requests had been denied repeatedly. Yet, I had tried again days earlier. I was mad and resentful at the time that Dad didn't come to visit his son in the hospital after he had cut his wrists. What Brett was looking for from his father I feared he was never going to get—emotional support and understanding. That completely broke my heart for my brother. I don't believe our father is capable of putting someone else ahead of himself. I worked very hard in therapy coming to terms with that truth for myself a long time ago. I thank God that I am not one of those adults with any Daddy issues at all. And I would *not* call our father again.

My feeling of relief while Brett was locked up was short-lived. Knowing he was safe and out of danger is what kept me going day after day. I had no preconceived notions about the future, but I was completely blindsided when I went to the mailbox and opened a letter from the hospital.

Since Brett had listed me, not Mom, as the next-of-kin, they were letting me know that they felt he was no longer a danger to himself. His involuntary status would be removed in two days, and he would be discharged.

My head instantly began to spin, by now I did unfortunately know how it went. If you are a danger to yourself or others they will keep you locked up. But, just like before, these suicidal gestures only happened when he was drinking severely, and once he was sober, those thoughts subsided. And so, it was time to go home.

At the time we were all so consumed with keeping Brett alive and I was desperately trying to hold my own life together that I didn't fully understand what everything meant. My brother so much wanted to live that I wondered why he kept making these constant suicide attempts. The truth is startling. Some statistics show the risk of suicide for alcoholics is 120 times more prevalent than in the general population. It is worrisome because long-term alcohol abuse deepens and creates social isolation, which is exactly the deterioration I had watched with my brother. This leads to depression. It increases impulsivity and a negative self-image. Certainly, consuming those high levels of alcohol that Brett was consuming interfered with his rational thought process. In fact, many alcoholics don't really wish to die, but their emotional pain becomes unbearable; overwhelming emotions take control when they are in that condition. To them suicide seems like a reasonable option once their sober inhibitions disappear.

I suppose this time we were fortunate; the hospital kept Brett for about ten days. The other times, they had only kept him a couple of days or a few hours before sending him on his way. I hoped then that he could be locked up indefinitely, for his own sake. But that of course is not how the system works at the hospital; there are human rights, laws, privacy acts; no doctor was going to call me, to hear my version of events, even if I am a relative.

I wish they had made an exception for my brother, but locking him up so he couldn't drink wasn't the answer either. Every professional therapist, doctor, and psychiatrist can offer tools and advice on what he needed to do. What they *can't* do is stop him from using alcohol. He had to do that on his own.

During my final visit to the hospital, I took a glimpse at Brett's medical chart hanging on the edge of the bed. I had talked to a few professionals with my brother by now, but on that day, it was written a little more bluntly than it had been communicated in the past. I could decipher the typical physician scribble and I got it loud and clear. I had known this for a while.

Brett is missing valuable insight. It is a concern that unless he accepts and understands the gravity of the situation, he is going to die.

"WITHOUT A TRACE "

Only forty-eight hours after leaving the hospital, Brett was once again AWOL.

He had gone off to a sleazy hotel for days with a "crack addict" (his words, not mine) he met on the street. She was a "nice girl," he said. After partying it up and doing God knows what, he gave this stranger his truck and his debit card, although it didn't really matter: the account was dry. He ended up waiting for two days for her to return and when she didn't, he finally called the police. She showed up a couple of days later, but by then the hotel had asked him to leave; they had seen the police car and didn't want any trouble. That seemed ironic to me, since this was the type of hotel you could rent by the hour.

My brother had run out of money and despite my telling her not to, Nicole delivered him a crisp one hundred dollar bill.

During this current fiasco, I was thirty minutes away on my hands and knees sweeping up granola and scrubbing vomit and blood off a shag carpet. I was having a complete meltdown, trying to erase the stains that seemed to run far deeper than the beige carpet; fighting back tears of despair, sadness, and loneliness. The crushing pressure of the ever-present state of stress got the best of me that day.

Brett's landline rang and when I answered it, it was our mother. I sobbed uncontrollably.

"Just go home, Jodee. You don't have to do all that," was her advice.

"Yes, Mom, I do. After all, *I* have sold the house to those people."

I hung up the phone and eventually calmed myself down, pulling it together. I made my way through the house, room by room, throwing everything into boxes. Going into my brother's bedroom and opening the white closet doors, I removed a large bag of porn movies and threw them on the deck. I shook my head. I had previously found he was watching these types of shows on his computer so I'd had his internet service disconnected while he was at rehab. I guess that hadn't worked. It didn't faze me and I don't think any less of him; it's a symptom after all. I have never read any extreme addiction story that hasn't led the addict down the same path, whether it be porn, affairs, risky, casual sex, and, yes, even prostitutes. I had been doing my best to guide him, to encourage a real loving and nurturing relationship.

I already knew about "Charmaine." I had asked Brett who she was when I saw her name and number on a pink post-it-note on his fridge. We talked about her a lot.

"I met her on one of my rendezvous to Edmonton, the one when I sold my quad there and stayed for a week in the Pine Park Inn, like a drunken prince. She told me one of her clients comes in on the way to the airport to pick up his wife. Terrible. At least I'm single," Brett shared.

That is how the conversation started about healthy relationships, I was taken aback that he was trying to find her when he was sober. "She's real, Jode," was his answer, although I thought that couldn't be farther from the truth. Paying someone to give you a handjob is not part of a real relationship.

My mind was trapped in a whirlwind of thoughts. I was unable to really know for sure. Was it just his desire to fill his own addictive needs? Was it because hookers won't ask him to change? They just accept him as he is. Or was it something more?

I couldn't help but wonder if it were just the effects of alcohol that drove his behavior? He didn't know anymore how to have a good relationship with women because alcohol got in the way. But he never lost his ability to love. Or was it something else that had happened that confused him? Haunted him? Was there another demon that clouded his vision and distracted his thoughts?

My mind turned once again to childhood and another painful secret. Our parents were divorced; that wasn't out of the ordinary. But things happened back then on the visits with our Dad that would not go on in every home. Brett and I would stay up late playing cards at the kitchen table. Dad would go to bed with his lady friend and they would begin to have loud, powerful, all-consuming sex even though they knew we were awake and less than ten feet away. My brother and I didn't say a word to each other, but continued counting our cribbage hands, "fifteen two, fifteen four, fifteen six," while her screams of desire echoed through the house.

When they finished, after about fifteen minutes that seemed like hours, we could hear the bedroom door creak open and she walked out. Casually strolling into the kitchen, slowly opening the refrigerator. She would open the cupboard door, pick out a glass, and pour herself a drink. She stood there with her long, popsicle-stick legs, skinny white thighs, fuzzy pubic hair, and large round breasts. We saw it all. She took a couple of sips, turned around, and then casually sauntered back to the bedroom. Both my brother and I tried to ignore her bare white bottom as she left the room.

It was just another thing that we tried to pretend wasn't happening, but it did happen, again and again. My brother was only nine years old.

Could her naked body in our kitchen have had an impact? We were just children after all, but children grow into men and women. I have never discussed that with Brett, everyone has things that they experience and interpret differently. I don't believe I ever would have even thought about it again had all of this not been happening. If Brett felt this made an impact on his life, he needed to bring these kinds of deep private issues up in individual therapy. I come from a place now where I think this was so completely and utterly fucked up. And could be characterized as abuse. Seeing the busty women on the covers of his porn collection made me wonder what he thinks is acceptable, normal.

In the living room, scattered across the wooden flip-top coffee table that Jim made for Brett one Christmas were about a dozen of my brother's personal journals. I opened the lid to find more than a dozen more, most in a variety of coiled notebooks with lined paper, some more fancier in various shapes and sizes.

I stopped and for the first time I began reading the pages. This journey down to the depths of hell had made me capable of doing things that I would normally never do. A part of me wondered if he left them out for me to read. After all, he had left a few at my house years before. Was this a quiet cry for help? My brother knew me, inside and out. I had his keys and full access to his home, and most of his journals were sitting there in plain sight. For me, I didn't really care why they were there as I sat down on the wet carpet propping myself up against the couch. I began reading.

It wasn't what I was expecting, necessarily; certainly not what I would have thought to find in a personal journal. It was not long stories or deep feelings, but rather glimpses of thoughts. Paragraphs, quotes, simple sentences, and documented dreams. I sat on the floor flipping page after page, book after book, occasionally wiping tears from my eyes for nearly three hours. But I didn't find what I was looking for, some magical clue, a deep dark secret that maybe he was hiding. The one "demon" that would be the puzzle piece to put this all together.

Our mom was none too pleased that I had resorted to this, not that we needed a reason to argue those days.

"Those are his private thoughts, Jodee. You have no business reading them," she said sternly.

But I didn't care what my mother said. Reading his journals was not beneath me at this point. I didn't care if he was a teenager or this thirty-two-year-old man. I wasn't going to let someone I love die little by little without doing everything in my power to try to help him.

Soon my brother was once again out of money and on the run. Mom would get a play-by-play version of his life each and every time he called her on his cell. He was driving to Calgary while hammered, dazed, confused, and hallucinating. He believed the "nice girl" had put a bug in his radio, but he couldn't find where the voices were coming from.

Days passed. I had no idea what had happened or how Brett got sober, but he arrived at my door two days after the possession of his house. I had already put his belongings into storage.

"LITHIUM"

Finally, Brett's employer had also had enough. By law, since alcoholism is no different from any other disease, they had continued to support him by placing my brother on short-term disability. I hoped they would follow through with requirements for sobriety and not just let him continue being off work with pay. But the fact was, I didn't know exactly what they asked of him, or if they asked him anything at all.

My brother should have received close to $28,000 from the sale of his house, when all was said and done, from the nice increase in real estate values and the fact that I had saved him having to pay someone commission. Instead, I would soon come to realize that he had put a second mortgage on the house for twenty grand about eight months earlier. Addicts burn through money; there never seems to be enough. So, with lawyer fees, penalties, and the remaining loan he came out of it with just over three thousand dollars. I was left shaking my head from this startling news, in total disbelief. Another harsh, financial reality. But sadly, maybe not.

Without skipping a beat, Brett rented a cottage in town. Something was just not adding up, at least not to me. But that wasn't anything new in those days. There was absolutely no way he could afford this new place and I begged my mother to try to talk some sense into him.

"Mom, he isn't even working right now. This is NOT an option."

She adamantly refused and snapped back, "It is up to him."

Brett found a way to secure the rental home and began moving in immediately. It was not new or fancy and it had rough hardwood floors with a wood-burning stove in the living room. Surrounded by thirty-foot-tall pine trees, the house looked as though it could be nestled in the woods, rather than sitting on the busy street corner it was actually on. Brett was eager and happy while setting up his new digs, bringing load by load in the back of his pickup, leaving the things he didn't need in storage.

I walked through the brown picket gate, down the path, and in the side door to find Mom there helping with the unpacking, as he had finished moving everything earlier in the day.

"Hey," I said.

"Hey," Brett answered right back.

Before I could ask how they were making out, I could hear the muffled sounds of nails scratching on the wooden floors. Scampering around in sheer delight was a small golden lab puppy, obviously just weeks old. Brett bent down to pick him up. "I have someone to introduce you to. Look at his eyes. Aren't they the deepest indigo blue?" he asked, so proud. "This is Indie."

I knew this breed of dog was expensive, so when my brother was out of earshot I asked our mother how much the dog cost. She was instantly uncomfortable when she explained that she lent Brett a thousand dollars and he was going to pay her back as soon as the house check was ready at the lawyers.

I didn't understand this train of thought, especially since she knew she wasn't getting the ten grand back that he'd promised. But also, when he had to start back at work—twelve-hour shifts—who would look after a dog? I didn't know if I was the one going crazy or if they both were, but I said nothing more. I was getting beaten down, exhausted. I didn't have the strength to continue to fight them both.

It never mattered what I said or thought anyway. My brother and Mom always seemed to come up with a different plan. They had spent the day together shopping, looking for another housewarming gift from her. They had settled on a brand new sofa and love seat that was soon to be delivered from The Brick.

Our mother was ecstatically happy when she told me the news a couple of days later that Brett was going to spend five or six days in the psych ward at the hospital for a complete assessment. I had no idea how this had been arranged or why this was happening. I was dumbfounded. All I knew was that my brother's family doctor requisitioned it and made the arrangements.

I was so confused, particularly because he had just stayed at a psychiatric hospital. I couldn't help but wonder what he and Mom were looking for. An answer that wasn't "Quit drinking"? But I supported him. Maybe I was totally off base, I am not a doctor. When he asked for a ride, I dropped everything and drove him to the hospital.

It didn't take long for our mother to ask me for a favor; after all, favors seemed to be all I was doing in those days. She wanted me to somehow tell the psychiatrist in charge everything that had been going on. She just couldn't bring herself to say those things about her own son. I knew exactly what she meant; she didn't need to elaborate as I continued to be the bearer of bad news, the sharp reality in the family. These responsibilities that I have had since as long as I can remember created my outspoken nature with the ability to say exactly what is on my mind. With me, be warned, what you get when you ask for my advice will be the truth as I see it. Painful or not. Don't ask if you don't really want to know. I will never choose sides, but if you insist that you need to know, I will choose who is right, and that will not necessarily be who I am related to.

It was made clear that I needed to somehow get word to the psychiatrist and, as always, I complied. All the doctors would know about the gun, the wrists, the pills. That was documented as he had been admitted to the same hospital three times. But I wasn't confident Brett was telling them the truth about everything else. The scarier part was that he seemed now to be in such deep denial that he legitimately believed his version was the truth. So how could anyone help him if the things he was relaying were not reality?

It was no guarantee we would be given even five minutes in person, so just in case I wrote a letter with all the details and symptoms of what my little brother's life had become.

To whom it may concern,

As you may or may not know my brother has been to treatment centers and hospitals repeatedly for his severe alcoholism. We all know my brother has a serious drinking problem and are worried that something else may be going on; we just don't know what else to do. I am not sure if this plays any part, but alcoholism is on many branches of our family tree and we have a close relative that is bi-polar. I thought it would help if you knew some of his symptoms as this is not who he used to be.

Besides severe addiction, here is what we know about:

- *drinks lethal amounts of alcohol, once he starts he can't stop on his own*
- *light sensitive*
- *anxious*

- *avoids family & friends (wants to be left alone)*
- *hates people*
- *excessive watching of porn*
- *visits prostitutes, thinks this is totally okay (he would never have done or thought that before)*
- *no concept of debt or the money he is spending*
- *unrealistic, grandiose thinking (he believes every female he meets or is in contact with wants him)*

And this is the scariest part of all. Once he sobers up, he says that he thinks everything is "fine" and not so bad; I don't think he is lying. I think he believes it.

Please help us,

Jodee Prouse

I hated the letter that I wrote; it felt like a knife piercing through my heart. I hated writing it but, more so, I abhorred the things on that page. Even so, they were all true; every word, every letter was written with nothing but love. Someone had to share these painful realities as we all continued to run on a hamster wheel. Someone had to really know what was going on. I gave the letter to Mom to deliver to the doctor. I felt if it came from his own mother, it would make more of an impact. They would take it more seriously. I was just the sister after all.

Almost a week later, when Brett got out of the hospital, he and Mom both came to pick me up. I could see that he was reading something in the backseat and I knew what it was. I felt sick at the thought of him reading that horrible letter. That was not ever meant for my brother's eyes. It was private, meant for the doctor only. Brett was holding it, absorbing every hurtful word.

"You said these things about me?" he said and I turned around in shame.

I saw it in his eyes—I knew that I had broken my brother's heart.

To this day I am unsure whether the psychiatrist ever received this letter from my mother. With everything that continued to go on, I don't think it really would have mattered one way or the other.

"CHANGE"

No different diagnosis was going to make any or all of this go away. Brett was to continue to see the hospital psychiatrist, once a week. The wonderful thing about this was that since he was seeing a physician, the cost was covered by provincially funded health care (unlike private therapists). So there was no excuse not to go.

My brother asked me to go with him to his first appointment; and he handed me the report to read beforehand so I knew what to expect. As I read each word, I realized how at times he did try to be honest with me and tell me everything. He just had such trouble communicating his deep feelings. I always took what I could get and I read his hospital report from June 15, 2005 very thoroughly.

Brett's report explained more or less that my brother was a thirty-two-year-old single man who was living in Sylvan Lake and working as a power engineer. He had been off work for some time on a recommendation from his occupational health nurse. He admitted to the doctor that he had a major problem with drinking and that for a short period he had stopped before beginning to drink quite heavily. He was admitted to Alberta Hospital in the last few months after getting drunk and slashing his wrists. At the time, Brett was treated with Lithium (a drug that studies show can significantly reduce suicide risk and prevent future manic and depressive episodes) and Paxil, which he was currently on at 20 mg per day.

Brett reported he was sober for almost two weeks prior to being admitted and said that when he is drinking he thinks and acts differently; he becomes another person. He characterized himself as a binge drinker who goes on for a week consuming about 26 ounces a day of hard liquor. He shared that he has been in treatment centers three times, one in Landers, one in Grande Prairie about three months ago, and another center he could not recall.

He managed to stay sober for about a month when he was attending AA meetings and Counseling with AADAC (Alberta Alcohol and Drug Abuse Commission), but he relapsed and was admitted to the psychiatric hospital. He denied feeling depressed or having any mood swings but said he sometimes cannot sleep because he feels anxious and worried. My brother shared with the doctor his fears and his feeling of panic, that he did not like big crowds, and did not feel comfortable in the mall, in restaurants, or standing in line at the cashier or bank. When he goes to the bar he has to drink a couple of shots before he is comfortable. And when he is not drinking he feels really good.

Brett had said he was really worried, however, about his job and his family. He is one of a six-member crew at work and he describes himself as well-liked and getting along quite well with other people. At home, however, he feels enormous pressure from his family, particularly from Nicole and me. He admitted we are both trying to back off, to give him time to think and settle. He has learned his lesson and he is going to settle his problems with drinking—he isn't going to drink anymore.

He stated that the last three months had been very difficult for him as he got drunk three times and each time he had suicidal gestures. First, three months ago, he decided to use a gun. The second time, he overdosed on medications, also while drunk and after a fight with his girlfriend. Once he found he had overdosed, in fact harming himself, he phoned friends right away to get help.

At this point, I looked up at my brother, not knowing what to say, because I know this wasn't really what happened. I continued reading.

The third suicide attempt had been a month ago. He had slashed his wrists when he was drunk and when he realized what he had done, he called someone right away. Again, I knew this wasn't how the events had taken place.

He denied using street drugs or having any psychosis. My brother admitted to enjoying good health and having no history of any serious medical conditions.

I tried to absorb each word, insight, and explanation from his point of view. I thought about everything long and hard as we entered the doctor's office together. Brett had got some of the details wrong. Believing that he had a fight with his girlfriend, and then calling some friends when he had overdosed on meds spoke volumes to his incapacity for knowing reality while under the influence of the insane amounts of booze. After all, Ryan and I had been right there. And he was in complete denial about how much alcohol he was now consuming each day. It was not 26 oz. a day, but rather almost double that. All it took was just one, which turned to two, to three before his body became so immune to those levels that 26 oz. just wouldn't cut it. At this stage my brother was drinking up to at least 40 oz. of vodka a day. That's forty straight-up drinks to you and me. I had seen the bottles, counted them closely, and physical evidence doesn't lie.

Together, Brett and I sat and listened to his psychiatrist. He reiterated that he understood my brother did have anxiety and some symptoms of depression most certainly made worse by alcohol consumption.

"You need to commit to sobriety, abstain one hundred percent from alcohol. You have been consuming so much for so long it will take up to a year for your head to be totally clear. Do you understand?"

My brother nodded.

"If something else is going on, and that is a big 'if,' we won't be able to figure that out until you remain sober for a period of time."

This was an entangled weave of complicated symptoms and diagnoses. Where did one thing end and the other begin? Had his anxiety advanced due to years of severe alcohol consumption? Of course, alcohol will do that. But is anxiety why it all started?

What was suggested by the health care professionals we saw and the stints at rehab was to concentrate on the drinking. That is the opposite of what many—but not all—believe today, which is that there are concurrent disorders (also called "dual diagnosis"). This means there is a mental health illness such as depression, bipolar, borderline personality disorder, schizophrenia, or mood/anxiety disorders, as well as a substance or drug abuse problem. Both require treatment at the same time. Social and medical sciences have advanced our understanding of why these mental illnesses begin and where they originate. Nowadays, we try to get to the bottom of that, rather than zooming in simply on sobriety. Without looking at the deep down root cause of the problem, our addicted loved one's chances of success are greatly impeded.

Brett's symptoms were jumbled and mixed as they fell within the parameters of mental illness, but they were also *all* symptoms of long-term alcoholism. The lines were blurred, so the doctors—and in turn we—focused on the drinking.

"And Brett," his psychiatrist said with a short pause, "If you don't stop drinking, you will die, either by your own hand or as an accident."

Brett didn't say much during the twenty-minute drive home. I pulled up to his place and put my SUV in park.

"Thanks for coming with me again, Jode," he said as he gave me a hug.

"Of course," I replied squeezing him tightly.

"And please, I don't want you to worry. I'm not that selfish. I don't want to die."

"Brett," I paused just slightly. "I think you are missing the point. No one has ever said that you *want* to die."

He still wasn't getting it. When he was heavily intoxicated, he was *not* in control. I know my brother didn't want to die, those feelings surfaced only when he was drunk. And of course there lies the problem.

For the next two weeks, there was peace and harmony for all of us as Brett settled into his new home and was back at work. Jim and I were taking the boys on summer vacation and I asked Brett to please check on the house for us, and pick up the mail. I gave him the spare key.

Within a couple of days, I called to check in and he was drinking again. Judging by the tears and the slurring of his voice, he was within a few days of consuming lethal amounts. Mom soon arrived to look after him and the puppy, with Nicole occasionally stopping by.

My quiet, relaxing holiday at the beach with my own family was disrupted every morning as I called Mom to be assured that Brett was still alive. My kids waited patiently as I spent fifteen to twenty minutes on the phone before heading to the lake. Mom was staying there to watch over him and make sure he didn't pass out and choke to death on his own vomit.

Upon my return with my family just over a week later, I found a full bottle of vodka, which I kept in my freezer for when we had guests, frozen solid. I know vodka doesn't freeze so my brother had done a little bit more than check the mail. When I called Nickie to get an update, she informed me that Mom had said they should, "Wait for Jodee and then make a plan."

I didn't even know what to say. Why was all this on me? I was trying so hard to follow the lead of the ones who knew more than I did; the professionals who knew what works for sobriety. I never, not once, faltered in my belief that embracing recovery will and *does* work. I didn't believe my brother was listening. I was getting more and more frustrated with our mother. I didn't think she was listening either. I always felt, whether she admitted it or not, that she was indulging Brett on his every whim, always giving him a Plan B.

By now, my brother couldn't stop drinking. And I mean *COULDN'T*. Many people not experienced in this lifestyle, this nightmare, have the simple belief that addicts can just stop using if they want to, that this is just simply a choice. Quit. Of course some can, even if for a short amount of time, if they are high functioning and not taking drugs and alcohol at this level. But this was not one of those cases. This had progressed from "innocently" partying as a teenager, to having a drinking problem and it having a negative impact on his life. But now my brother was a *severely* addicted young man. Once he took that first swig of alcohol, his body would take over.

Brett was downing lethal doses of alcohol. It was not only impossible for him to go cold turkey; it had reached a level where there was a risk to his life if he tried on his own. Not that it mattered, he *couldn't* quit on his own. Brett detested having to go to a detox center for the withdrawal phase as by now he had been there a few times before.

"Detox is the longest five days I've ever known. Some sleep on the floor, some are scared, but I am pissed off. I want to tell every fucker with a smile on their face to wake the fuck up. I want to tell the holier-than-thou nurses to get fucked. 'Give me my pills and bed, and let me suffer like I should.' Days of pure agony pass and I want out. People play pool, smoke in groups, and enjoy that shit, not me," he told me some time ago when he called from there.

My brother is blunt and edgy when he has booze in his system. I don't know why he believes he should suffer. I know he doesn't believe alcoholism is a disease;

that could play a part in his self-hatred. If it's not a disease maybe he buys into some of society's preconceived notions that this is all simply a choice, that this just means he has a character flaw. That he is weak and that if he just had more willpower he could just stop. For us, I think at first, we used a detox center as a convenience. A facility to help us get respite for a few days, to sober him up. But now we all knew how serious it really was.

He needed medical supervision and help as he came off the booze. It would take four to six days in which he would be given things like Valium to ease his way through the excruciating pain and suffering of the withdrawal process. Delirium tremens (DTs) is a state of confusion of rapid onset that is usually caused by withdrawal from alcohol. Alcohol is actually one of the most dangerous substances to come off. Alcoholics can experience symptoms like nightmares, vomiting, diarrhea, shivering, sweating, racing heart, fever, shaking, tightness in the chest, and difficulty breathing.

That is if things go well.

If things go badly, our loved ones can have a stroke, a heart attack, or a grand mal seizure. During withdrawal, long-term alcoholic abusers can suffer psychosis that manifests as hallucinations and delusions (like hearing voices from a truck radio), which is why they need to be monitored by a health care professional. DTs can sometimes be associated with severe, uncontrollable tremors of the extremities and secondary symptoms such as anxiety, panic attacks, and paranoia. My brother was very aware of what could happen; the good and the bad. Although, admittedly, none of this has steered him clear of not taking that first sip.

Instead, he lay in the permanent fetal position on the bare mattress in the corner of his bedroom, waking only to guzzle some more booze to continue living in a half-alive, half-zombie state. He refused to go to detox and he came up with a better plan for getting through this. Mom agreed to help him go through the withdrawal at home. She got him a prescription for Ativan to which she added Gravol and her sleeping pills for four days (although she had to give him three times the required dosage to keep him compliant). And when he sobered up he assured me "I'm fine."

Plan B was in full effect.

"HOLYMAN"

Brett and I had an appointment together, this time with a local psychologist, Dr. Mark Dimirsky. It had been such a long time since Brett had seen therapist Terry; the two-hour drive from Sylvan Lake to see Terry wasn't ideal so the fact this psychologist was so close eliminated that excuse not to go.

We sat in the meticulously perfect waiting room, talking freely as we were the only ones there.

The secretary told us that it was our turn and within a split second something changed. Brett turned to me with an instant sense of panic and fear.

"Please, Jodee, can you tell him everything that has been going on?"

I know now that on so many occasions I was my brother's voice; at the time I didn't even know I was doing it. It wasn't fair to him or me that I was doing much of the work. That certainly isn't esteem and confidence building. And it didn't give him the opportunity to challenge these attacks, but rather to succumb to them. Which of course is a valuable lesson; confronting your fears. I wish I had turned to him and said, "Listen Brett, I am here to support you, but *you* need to tell him the story."

But instead, I introduced ourselves to this straight-faced man with glasses and cropped salt-and-pepper hair, and for the next thirty minutes or so, I told him the whole story. As fast as I could, this whole, twisted, complicated story. He asked Brett the occasional question, and Brett answered "Yes," corroborating my version of events every single time.

Dr. Dimirsky shared with us a little bit more about himself and told us what he did differently than some psychologists as he specialized in Cognitive Behavioral Therapy. Neither of us had ever heard of that therapy before. From what I understand now, Cognitive Behavioral Therapy teaches people ways to control their anxiety levels, working on irrational thoughts.

"Cognitive Behavioral Therapy, or CBT as it is often referred to, is pretty straightforward to understand. But it gets tricky to do sometimes, so it is best to have someone who knows it to help you with it. The idea is that by changing what and how you think, you will change your feelings. And by the combination of changing thoughts and feelings, then problems get dealt with differently. So what happens is that you change patterns of responding to behaviors from the unhelpful kind to the more helpful kind.

"For example, using alcohol unwisely is actually a lot of different patterns. One pattern is impulsiveness; another pattern is negative self-talk that you want to go away or you want to quieten, so you drink to forget or not hear. Another pattern is setting yourself up for failure through unrealistic expectations; another pattern is how you interact with family or friends or your employer, where the result may not be healthy."

Brett and I sat silently listening.

"CBT really deals with the internal talk more than the other patterns. So, CBT by itself won't be enough to quit drinking. But it can be really good for changing negative self-talk patterns and also for helping to point out some places in other patterns where things can be changed so that you aren't as likely to relapse. And if you do relapse, it isn't so disastrous.

"My points are that drinking too much and too unwisely is a complicated issue and won't be solved only by CBT. But it can be one powerful tool to stop or slow down. For CBT to actually work, you have to see me or another expert in it and be prepared to do homework in between sessions. The idea of the homework is to help you practice healthier ways of thinking and to see what if any barriers stop you from thinking this way. Then you bring your homework in and we go over it and find ways you can think about things differently that fit for you. It doesn't work to just tell you how to think because it won't last … they have to be ways that make sense and come to feel right, over time, for you."

I didn't understand the relevance, difference, or importance of this meeting at the time. Dr. Dimirsky was the first person I am aware of who really was interested in getting to the bottom of Brett's anxiety. Even on the first meeting, Dr. Dimirsky wasn't focused on the drinking part, but rather on the patterns and what went on in Brett's mind. He made it abundantly clear, though, that Brett had to do the work. This new approach had the potential to be life changing.

Dr. Dimirsky paused and stared at us with great concern in his eyes.

"Do you understand? Does this make sense?"

Brett and I both nodded our agreement.

"I apologize for going on with so much to say, but I want to clarify roles and boundaries. If you decide to be my patient, Brett, then our relationship is a private and confidential one. It does not matter who pays. It doesn't matter how sincerely concerned the other parties are. It is a private and confidential relationship … except if you are a danger to yourself or others or there is a court order that tells me to reveal information. So, if any family member calls, I cannot and will not reveal your information. That puts a lot of pressure on you, Brett, to communicate what you need to say to your family and not leave it to me to be a message provider. If you give me permission, Brett, then I can talk to your family about you but I may not want to. I might want you to be the person who talks to them. Is that fair, Brett?" the doctor asked.

"Yes, definitely," Brett answered. After all, it was the same agreement he and I had with regards to Terry.

"Finally, I don't want to be discouraging, but I also want to be honest and direct. It will be an uphill battle for you to quit drinking. It sounds to me from what I've heard of your history that it would be fair to conclude that once you start, you can't stop. If you agree, then, you have to really look at a target of total abstinence. Some programs will offer what they call 'some form of controlled or social drinking.' That won't work for you, I believe. You need complete abstinence."

Brett and I looked at each other and locked eyes. We had heard this plenty of times before. We thanked Dr. Dimirsky and Brett made his next appointment.

Stop drinking.

That was something that Brett couldn't do, and after only one other individual session with Dr. Dimirsky, he was back on the run.

We knew he was alive and in Edmonton as his infamous calls to our mother and sister told us as much. I was now refusing to take his calls. If the long, never-ending days and sleepless nights of ominous tension didn't kill me, then the wailing cries, begging, and sobbing on the other end of the phone would.

It was day seventeen of Brett's current disappearance. Jim was working up in Edmonton for the day and, by sheer coincidence, directly from the main highway, he saw Brett's truck parked outside a sketchy motel.

Jim gave me the news and in an instant my heart told me to run and save him, but there was no way I could go. Regardless of what catastrophe was going on in Brett's life, I could not disappoint my sons again and miss their lacrosse tournament the next day.

Not only was I caring for my brother, but I had two active boys who needed my attention. Trying to balance our schedules was another added level of stress. Ricky and Ryan were always involved in different activities: swimming, baseball, soccer, skiing, snowmobiling, guitar, drums. Lacrosse was their new passion that year. It was violent and dangerous; and I hated it. On one occasion a couple of weeks earlier, I actually had to leave and wait in the car. I got so completely overcome with anxiety and pain at the thought of them getting hurt, watching as the boys knocked each other into the boards, that I just could not sit there any longer.

Since all this had begun with Brett, my constant fear and dread that something bad was going to happen to my sons was unshakable. My sons paid the price for the constant panic I carried around with me—I had become very overprotective of them. They would not have been able to understand that then. How could they? I didn't understand it either. I too was struggling with what I believe now was a more active, progressed form of my anxiety disorder due to everything that was going on. I, however, wasn't on any medication and I didn't consume alcohol to temper the sting. Every moment of every day I was overwhelmed with the thought of death or disaster for my brother, Rick, or Ryan. My sons were just teenagers, so I am sure I came across as some kind of "crazy mother," not even letting them do things as simple as jumping on a friend's trampoline, eating a hard candy because they might choke, or being worried sick when Ryan was forty-five minutes late home after a movie night with buddies. I would already have Jim and Rick up out of bed and dressed, heading out the door to search for him, as I instantly envisioned the smashed car and his limp body on the side of the highway.

These are not logical thoughts on any level, but you can't shake the feeling; there is nothing logical about anxiety.

And, I could and would disappoint my sons again.

This is when I ditched them at their lacrosse tournament after less than an hour, heading up north to Edmonton with my mother to go rescue Brett, eventually arriving at an emergency room to be greeted by a judgmental nurse.

And my brother entered detox once more.

"FEARLESS HEART "

I had become accustomed to making the most of those few days when Brett was away on alcohol withdrawal. I revelled in being able to catch up on some sleep, dote on my family, and get some of my old life back. I began to feel "normal" and myself again.

When I came home from work a few days later, after a full uninterrupted nine-hour day, I found a beautiful bouquet of flowers with a card sitting on my kitchen table. It was a small bouquet filled with short-stemmed roses in a shiny, patterned ceramic vase. I picked up the envelope, ripped the seal, and pulled out a poem card.

It was Brett's way of telling me how much I meant to him, that I never failed to come through when I am needed the most, with no strings attached. He said how generous and selfless I am and how grateful he was to have me for a sister.

It ended with "how much you mean to me," although Brett neatly inserted the word "guys" after "you."

Finally, in Brett's handwriting, in red felt marker:

Jim, Jodee, Rick, Ryan, Cole
Thanx for saving me. X10
♥ *Brett*

And that was exactly what I was doing—saving him, over and over again.

I always knew how appreciative he was (he even thanked our dog) and how much I meant to him. What hurt my heart was that he didn't understand, although I had tried to explain it to him, that by this stage the flowers had the opposite effect of what he was trying to achieve. Typically, when you get the "I'm sorry" flowers, it means that you won't make that same mistake again. And for me at least, those sweet-smelling petals represented that he just didn't get the gravity of what was going on, but that he actually believed they could make up for the damage that was being done. So, while they were pretty and are just as beautiful today, dried, sitting next to my wooden memento box on the dresser in my bedroom, the flowers became just another reminder that made me sad.

But, my closest friend was back. He had been sober for close to a month and going to work. He really seemed to be happy. I looked forward to our daily visits, although I admit I would have preferred that he didn't permanently have a paper cup of coffee in his hand, whether it was 6 a.m. or 6 p.m. My brother still had trouble sleeping; my not-so-subtle hint to him was to perhaps cut back from guzzling cups of coffee late into the night. But as usual he brushed off my suggestion.

It became my routine to stop by to walk Indie while he was at work. Brett was keeping his rental house looking meticulously perfect, except for the scattered CDs spread out near his cherished stereo: Nirvana, Steve Earle, Corb Lund, and Blind Melon are what I saw at a glance. I had no reason to suspect anything was wrong, yet I still couldn't help but be a private eye— nosing around, analyzing, making sure everything was still on track.

I giggled out loud as I noticed, sitting on the kitchen table, the calendar I'd bought him a couple of weeks before. We had talked at length about his recovery plan, including meetings, and that scheduling everything in your life, including work, should revolve around this sober plan.

"I don't have a calendar" was his smart-ass reply. So I changed that.

Penciled in the little numbered boxes were his hours of work, hairdresser, and CBT appointments with Dr. Dimirsky whom he had resumed seeing on occasion, but no AA meetings. I took about eight steps to the refrigerator, stood there for a split second, and I am not sure why my first reaction was to open the freezer door. It was completely empty, except, standing in the middle, was a frozen bottle of beer.

I turned quickly, darted down the hall, and opened his bedroom door. Instantly, I dropped to the ground like I had been hit with a baseball bat to my gut. The mattress was bare except for a pillow, with visible signs of vomit stains. The unventilated musty odor brought back a stream of visions that I couldn't ignore. As my eyes turned to the left, there was a garbage bag FULL of hard liquor bottles in the corner of his open closet. Not a kitchen catcher type bag, but a yard bag to hold leaves, big, bright, and so orange it burned my eyes. As always, he could control and hide it for a while.

Once again, free will and strength did not work to keep him sober, so days and days turned into long, excruciating weeks. No more work. No more daily coffees. No more normal.

I continued to do my best to hide my feelings at work while he locked himself away to the world. I snuck away to my office almost each and every hour like an obsessed animal dialing into Brett's voice mail with his password. "You have two new messages." And I would hang up never listening to who had called.

I called his voice mail the rest of the day, even after I got home and again, late into the night. "You have four new messages."

I woke at the crack of dawn, rolled over, and before my eyes could focus, I dialed my brother's voice mail once again, "You have *no new messages*." He had cleared his messages. Whew, he was alive, and I could survive my day.

Within days, I got a call that my sister Nickie was in labor, so I spent a couple of hours with her and others at the hospital. But, reluctantly, I couldn't stay because I had a weekend craft show out of town. I promised to check in as much as I could, but I was barely down the highway when she called me between her contractions. Brett had shown up stumbling drunk at the hospital carrying a bouquet of flowers.

My sister was crying and she didn't need to elaborate. After all, I knew how she felt. No matter how many times I saw him in this condition it brought me to my knees with pain. All this, on one of the most important and happiest days of my sister's life was so far past being good judgment.

"It's okay," I assured her. "I will call Mom."

Ricky was driving as he had his learner's permit. I asked him to pull over into a Walmart parking lot. I dialed our mother's number, wanting her to put a stop to this. Take control for once; tell Brett that his behavior was wrong and unacceptable, do something, anything.

When I explained to her what happened, that Nicole had called me, her analysis was simple: "They are just flowers, Jodee."

The next day, September 15, 2005, my sister gave birth to a beautiful baby girl, Kadince ("Kaddi" for short). It was Brett's thirty-third birthday. Such a complete and utter coincidence. What are the odds of that?

When I got home from the weekend away, my first priority was rushing to see my new niece. When I got there, Mom and Nicole's husband (and even Nicole) were noticeably annoyed at me, apparently, for stirring up trouble during the delivery. I was away minding my own business and now everyone was mad at me. I was so damn frustrated that no matter what I did, how much I tried to help, I always ended up being the bad guy. And, I was also mad at myself. Why didn't I stop getting involved when they asked me? I began to shut down, avoiding Mom and Nicole, as the unnecessary drama was far past what I was capable of handling. Or should I say I tried to avoid them? But that is not an easy task with family.

Two never-ending days later, I received a message from Brett at work. I wouldn't have answered if I had known it was him, but I was on the other line with a customer so he had left a voice mail that I couldn't avoid:

"Pleeeeeeeaaaase, Jodee, I am really hurt this time," Brett begged. His voice was panicked and scared, as though he was in real trouble. And instantly my heart began to pound through my chest.

In a flash, I ditched my employees and was on my way to his place. I didn't know what to expect, I was dreading every second, fear rising up my throat. Scared, I quickly called Kelly and was relieved when he picked up the phone.

"I am on my way," he assured me.

It was only a short drive from my office so, in less than five minutes, I was outside Brett's door.

I gently turned the doorknob, and slowly opened the door. I thought I was prepared for the worst, but no one could prepare for this as the disarray inside his house was indescribable. From dirt to dog shit, the damage that can be done by someone locked up in the confines of four walls for a few weeks is astounding.

"Brett, what's wrong?" I asked terrified, scanning him for any signs of injury.

Our eyes met and Brett turned around, calmly lifting his plaid shirt to reveal that his entire back had turned a deep purple. I instantly thought *internal bleeding*.

"Oh, my God, Brett," I shrieked.

I grabbed my cell and, just as I have done before, I dialed 911. When they were on the way, I sat him down on the edge of the couch.

"Are you okay? Are you in pain? What happened?" I laid him back carefully, to rest on a throw pillow.

My brother looked sick and ashamed as he slowly told me the whole story, in vivid color.

"Monday was creeping up, time to work. Since I am on probation, and random piss tests, I went to bed early, got up at 3 a.m. and looked in the mirror—no fucking way, they will know. I phoned in sick, and the cycle started. I needed and wanted booze. Called in all week and they knew, so the guilt and the need for relief was in full swing.

"I woke up at 6 or 7 a.m., NO BOOZE—I needed it bad—fuck it, paint thinner."

Paint thinner. He drank paint thinner. Holy fuck. I sat stone faced and continued to listen. He was lucid and calm and seemingly sober, but I knew he was intoxicated as this had gone on for weeks. Plus his story was far more elaborate than it would have been if he'd been sober. He continued like a Chatty Cathy doll.

"It worked until I puked and shit for two hours. Indie knew and looked at me with sad eyes—I had to get some vodka to flush that poison out. I drove to Red Deer to a hotel with a mini bar. No luck, so I ordered room service. I ordered three double Caesars, but I had to wait until 10 a.m. Fuck. I did it, but I went to stock up on juice, so I wouldn't have to turn to paint thinner ever again. A 60 oz. and 26 oz. mixed into a cranberry elixir.

"Phoned cousin Kelly to let the puppy out, then phoned Mom. She was coming to pick him up, phoned work, and made some doctors' appointments. Then my birthday came—and Nicole was in labor. I took a cab to see her—disrespectful or not, I went—and it felt good.

"Probably 26 oz. later, I had enough of doctors, piss tests, work, lying, pain. I called the plant and gave my two weeks' resignation. After seven and a half years—fuck, seven and a half years, Jode. Thought I'd take my pension, and move on. BC was the plan. Just me, puppy, sled, and the highway; Steve Earle style.

"The long and careful road home, bought a 60 pounder and walked into a fucking crack house. Piss, stuffed animals torn in disgust, broken taps, bottles, puke, piss, and demons. Didn't have enough energy to clean, I fell asleep and woke to my cell phone. My boss, Dan, told me to page him. He was pissed off—he talked me out of my resignation, told me to sober up; I had ten days to get it together. He was genuine, and I had some motivation to clean up."

You could hear a pin drop—I was like a fly on the wall. I sat in complete silence, my eyes wide open.

"At one point that night, I had one of my fits and fell down the stairs. Not sure where, or how long, one or two days and when I woke up my back was very bad. I sat up on the couch, too much pride to phone for help. Going to the jar store was a must—I found twenty bucks, forced myself up and out for a 26 ouncer of Alberta Vodka, since that is always the brand for the finale. One swig and I felt my insides burn, I wanted to get sick, a few more slugs, and *Of Mice & Men* was the background movie of the day.

"My body was giving out—no food for days. Water was my chaser so that helped. I choked down a bun and thought if I just got a half bottle in me I'd be good. I made the decision to check out my back—BLACK, like a shirt. I had to call someone, so fuck; I swallowed my pride and called you again."

Kelly arrived while he was telling the end of the story, so I quickly exited to the backyard to call our Mom about the current disaster.

"He called me already, Jodee. I hung up on him. There's nothing you can do if he doesn't want help, just leave him and go home," she said.

Our mother and I are complete opposites. I wanted her to be firm with him when he was sober, not tough and dismissive when he was drunk. After all, she knew I had tried that once and it ended with a pool of blood at my son's feet. But I didn't know who was right and who was wrong; that was the problem. None of us knew, so we all just kept rolling along in this vicious cycle. So, after less than a fifteen-second conversation, I closed my flip phone and waited for what seemed to be hours.

Once the ambulance arrived, the paramedics secured Brett with a back brace and lifted him into the back. I hugged Kelly goodbye since there really was no reason for him to come to the hospital. And I promised I would call him later with an update on his best friend's condition.

When we arrived at the hospital, all the rooms were once again taken so they put Brett, the two paramedics, and me in the hall. Brett was lying impatiently on the gurney, while I sat next to the two paramedics, waiting for someone to call his name. It was not a life or death, do or die situation at the moment and this was an emergency department so our turn would come based on the needs of others in more serious situations. Within the hour, Brett really had to go to the bathroom and couldn't wait any longer. The two men carefully helped him up by his arms. They were responsible for him and because they didn't know what type of injuries he had sustained, they wouldn't leave him unattended; they escorted him to the bathroom.

"That better?" I asked as my brother a short time later as he was being helped back onto the stretcher.

"I couldn't fucking go. How's a guy supposed to take a piss when a complete stranger is standing there staring at him?" he said.

Without saying a word, I walked away and came back a couple of minutes later with a stainless steel container used for urine. I held it at Brett's eye level, moving it to and fro, "C'mon, let's go."

"Fuck you, Jodee," he said. And together we laughed and laughed. Even in the worst of situations, we were always able to make each other happy and lighten the mood, if only for a short time.

There was an awkward silence for the next ten minutes until I said something to one of the paramedics.

"Is my sister here?" Brett said in a surprised tone when he heard my voice.

I looked up at the attendant, not knowing what to say, and I shrugged my shoulders. We had been there together for over two hours. Once again, it was a jolt of reality as my brother was seemingly sober to the outside world. But in that condition, that quantity of booze, he really did not have a clue what was going on.

After eventually getting Brett in for an x-ray, it was determined that there were no serious injuries, just a bad bruise, and we were sent on our way. Since we had no ride, I reluctantly called my husband and Jim came to get us.

There was nowhere for my brother to go and today, in 2016, I feel the desperation and despair of all family members whose loved ones, for one reason or another, don't seem to change. But change begins with changing. He can't stay at the hospital. The beds are full and they don't just admit you for being drunk. He can't come to my house, my God; my children couldn't keep seeing this. What do we do? And so, with no other alternative, we dropped him off at his house of demons.

Less than two hours later, my home phone rang and an hysterical, crying Brett was on the other end begging me to take him to detox in Calgary. My family was once again left alone as, without hesitation, I went out the door.

When I arrived at his house, he was just polishing off the last drop of a 26 oz. bottle of vodka. I sighed, took him by his left arm, and directed him out the door.

As I drove the hundred miles in the dark, he was in the passenger seat, drooling, with his head swaying in and out of consciousness. I tried to concentrate on the highway and the steady stream of traffic, while I kept screaming his name, "Brett! Brett!", looking over in his direction, trying to keep him awake. I believed he was going to overdose right in front of me.

I pulled up at the five-minute parking sign in front of our mother's building almost two hours later, and shook Brett awake. He was staggering, barely able to walk, but he was alive. She was as cold as ice when we walked through the door, and didn't say a word to Brett, except to hold out her hand with about three or four little white pills.

"Take these. Go sleep in there," she said as she pointed to her spare room.

And he would be compliant for the night after taking his dose of her sleeping pills. There were no other options for him. The beds would be full at detox this late at night, so Mom would take him in the morning. I stayed less than two minutes; I didn't even know what to say.

As I drove back home in the dead of night, I was so beyond exhausted, on so many levels, that I didn't have the energy to cry. During the long drive home, I finally had time to think about everything that had gone on that day. In his condition, his logical plan was to quit his job and "move on," believing again that was the answer (or even a viable option).

My mind then turned towards nostalgia and I saw his handsome face in such a frenzied state that it was beyond my comprehension. I envisioned him vibrating and stumbling out his back door across the yard and into the small garden shed, rummaging around tools, used tires, and weed eater until he found a bottle of turpentine. He pressed his lips against the plastic, tilted his head back and swallowed.

Would anyone—just a regular person, average, maybe like you, maybe like me—be able to truly wrap their mind around how this is possible? An addiction, a need, a desire so deep that when nothing else is available you would resort to drinking paint thinner to ease the pain of withdrawal?

Terrible visions ran through my mind, which left me in insurmountable pain. I wondered, *How could this possibly get any worse?* I wouldn't have to wonder for long.

"YOU KNOW YOU'RE RIGHT "

Rehab, round…? I was losing track.

Brett threw his canvas duffel bag into the back of his old Chevy, revved the engine, and off he went on the seven-hour drive up north back to Grande Prairie for another thirty-day program. I really felt this was the turning point as, for the first time *ever*, it was his idea and he really seemed to want to go. And he was willing to drive himself, another positive sign. Brett was taking advantage of his "free card," as they guaranteed the program, so he could return if he relapsed and it wouldn't cost Mom another five grand.

We talked almost daily on the phone and my brother shared what he was learning there. He really seemed to like his therapist, a girl named Sarah. He talked about her often. I have to admit that I, as well as my own family, once again got something out of rehab. I got peace, serenity, happiness, just knowing he was safe. My kids got their Mom and my husband got his wife. Everyone in my house got my complete attention and devotion—if only for thirty days.

I cherished the letters he sent, another thing we always shared.

He thanked me once again for everything I had done and promised me that things were "all good." He couldn't explain what was different but he was learning. He was hanging out with the nurses in the mornings since he got up at 5 a.m. He said that many there thought he should be a counselor or in the least he should share his story.

"Fuck yeah," he agreed, which made me smile.

He asked how his house was and said he wasn't sure he wanted to come home to a run-down TEE-PEE, but he would let me decide on that. He wondered perhaps if I could just get the empty forty pounders out of his room, but he would leave that up to me. And he thanked me again for all the "fucking around" with the doctors.

And he would call just a couple of days later.

"Hey," Brett said.

"Hey," I replied.

"Thanks for the letter. It made me think and feel strong. I'm actually learning new things, and really AA is one of 'em. The rest is hard to explain, but don't be scared. I have some new insight, huge.

"I am being totally open and honest here. Sarah got punched out by a chick who threatened to kill another chick. Meth Head, bad shit. There's also a Meth Head we think, from detox, robbing everyone.

"I admit getting those doctor reports pissed me off. Dr. Benoit never even remembers my name and is so burnt out when I see him I'm sure he's not even listening. I'm gonna stick to Dr. Dimirsky, AA, and occasionally Dr. Sullivan. Not twenty doctors making a prognosis when they hardly know me. That Alberta Hospital doctor saw me twice for ten minutes."

I was stunned and concerned but I didn't offer a response. I continued to listen.

"I get my keys back tomorrow, I'm taking Ray to see his mom and then we're going to the Keg. We're starting to get a little bit of 'Get-me-the-fuck-out-for-a-couple-hours syndrome.'

"Oh, yeah, Sarah wants me to concentrate while here on the ABORTION. I am starting to really resent Dawn and her fucking Mom. I wrote her a letter and gave it to Sarah—that's on HOLD. Have ya seen DAWN? Just curious.

"Miss All You Guys," he said as he hung up.

I didn't answer some of these questions, but I hadn't seen Dawn. Not that I hadn't wanted to. I adored her, but there was no way I could face her back then. Just the thought of her reminded me of what could have been a beautiful life for my brother. Love, happiness, stability, a child of his own. My eyes instantly filled with tears as I tried to shake those feelings. I forced those images out of my mind, and avoided Dawn-Marie like the plague in our small town, as I just couldn't handle any more pain.

I worried after we talked. Once in a while, there seemed to be a glimmer of insight, but then there were things that made me think "not at all." His thought that somehow Dawn was to blame and his bitterness toward her mom, who was just there to love, support, and protect her daughter, scared me. I was there; it was bad. Over the top, dangerous, insane, run-as-fast-as-you-can-and-don't-look-back bad. This was not Dawn-Marie's fault, not one ounce of it. She was just a casualty.

And there was something else that seemed to be changing in how he interpreted what was going on. I embraced all the hospital stays, the different doctors as people trying to help. After all, my brother was the one who had put himself there. If there were three reports floating around or three hundred for that matter, that was because of Brett's choices; that is not the fault of the professionals trying to help him. And now he resents them for it.

But what frightened me the most was when he wrote "making prognosis when they barely know me." I had known this for a very long time and it had been getting increasingly worse as time went on. He still did not buy in to the fact that he was no different from any other alcoholic. By this time I had read at least a dozen of the most hard-core, raw, real, and graphic books on addictions by both self-help authors and memoirs of people who have gone through it. Honestly, you could take every single copy and insert Brett's name and it would be about him. Every symptom, story, conclusion would be him, exactly him. Everything I had learned thus far was coming true. Yet, my brother believed somehow that he was special. That he was different. That he was an exception. And he was wrong.

I feared that he was now putting the blame on everyone else and none of the responsibility on himself. Resentment and blame are particularly dangerous emotions for people in recovery. Actually resentment and blame are quite dangerous emotions for anyone, not just for an addict. By focusing on someone else's behavior, we do not focus on our own. And it shifts the accountability to someone else. When we stay in a position of blaming others, we can never get better and move our life forward. After all, this unhealthy thought process would mean that you don't have to change as it is always someone else's fault. You become the victim. And everything continues to get worse—exactly what was happening.

I said nothing directly to Brett, but I was going to say it and no one could stop me. Family Week was fast approaching so I decided I would be patient and wait and share my feelings and concerns with the professionals there. I don't know why I was surprised, but yet again I was when he refused for me or anyone else to attend. But there was no way I was making the same mistake again. I looked up the number, dialed Grande Prairie, and asked to speak to Sarah.

She had to call me back when she got a spare moment and I was truly appreciative of her taking the time to talk to me, being careful to stay within the boundaries of confidentiality about my brother. I shared with her his refusal to have me come for Family Week both this time and the last time he was there. When I hung up, I immediately called our mother to share in our conversation.

"Mom, Sarah says that Family Week is a very important part of recovery. She said that, with or without his approval, someone should be there."

Our conversation was instantaneous and short. She always made it that way if she didn't agree. She told me to call her tomorrow after she'd talked with Brett.

The next day, Mom and I had one of the most heated conversations we have ever had. Without any flexibility at all, she barked, "I have talked to Brett, Jodee. He does not want anyone there. It is up to him."

"Are you fucking kidding me, mother? You have paid tens of thousands of dollars and I am investing all my time, and it is up to HIM?! He is sick and confused and not participating in the program!" I responded in a loud, harsh tone, unable to hide my feelings of anger and frustration any longer.

She started to speak and I interrupted. There was nothing she could say to me that would make me see it any other way.

"For the record, I do not agree!" and I hung up.

Family Week came and went, which made me wonder about the other families. I envied them; they were probably getting along, a close family working together, and not fighting continually like we were, which was making things so much worse. For us and for Brett. And they were learning something that I was aching to learn. I knew what we were doing wasn't working and I just wanted someone to tell me what to do. "If I am doing something wrong, tell me. I will do anything."

I did not go to Family Week. I guess someone (our mother) *was* able to stop me.

My last letter arrived, just two days before Brett came home.

He thanked me for cleaning out the bottles and said that he was looking forward to a fresh start again. He really missed his home and knew he had taken too much for granted, mostly all of us and Indie.

He had been in the hot seat for two days in group and, surprisingly, he liked it. His counselor Tim was really digging into my brother's emotions, although Brett got annoyed a couple of times. He said that everyone was impressed with the "family tree," how we've all remained close. He said that Tim thought Dad is a very sick man. My own feelings continued to jump back and forth between hopefulness and hopelessness.

I always knew what he meant about "family tree." He always talked about and shared in letters with me how close Mom, Nicole, he, and I were and how proud he was of that. I wouldn't characterize the four of us as close; not in our adult life anyway. I believe Brett was holding onto his childhood, at a time when this statement would have been very true. But life is about perception, we are individuals, we do not all see things the same way.

Mom and I had sent Brett some brochures to look over about a longer rehab program. He promised to think about it with an open mind, but said he was burnt out with institutions. "Trust me, 30 DAYS is exhausting & 12 days in DETOX."

I see now continued rehab wasn't the answer for Brett, at least not one that was strictly for alcohol abuse. Rather, a dual diagnosis facility was what he needed, keeping in mind I had no idea what that even meant at the time. There was no follow through or change on any level, not from any of us. When a loved one goes to rehab and comes home, going back into the same unhealthy patterns and dysfunctional family structure diminishes their ability for success in sobriety. But when these are the people that you love, your vision is blurred by your heart; you don't see it at the time; certainly you don't want to admit your family is troubled. And that in turn, although unintentionally, puts all the burden on the addict.

We were all doing the same things over and over again and my brother was getting tired.

I finished reading his letter and then carefully folded the piece of paper, just as I did each and every time, and tucked them away in a special box with all the cards and letters from him that meant so much.

I don't think he'd been home for five minutes when I excitedly went to meet him at his house. It didn't resemble what it had been a few weeks earlier. It is amazing what I, with simple soap, water, and ammonia can accomplish.

We sat in the living room. The hardwood floor was cold on my bare feet. His usual tunes lightly played in the background as he shared with me more about his time away.

"I met this guy Steve—he would actually drink with his kids in the car. FUCK—can you believe it, Jode? Not caring that your kids are in the backseat and he is hammered? That is messed up."

I said nothing and kept listening.

"I talked tons to Sarah; she's cool. She thinks I need to get back to work right away, that it's the best place for me; she doesn't think that long-term treatment is for me. She has a little crush on me—I can tell."

For a split second, I thought this was actually possible. Lots of things had changed by now, but when sober he was still so sweet, good-looking, kind, and quite frankly irresistible to females. I had watched the reaction my whole life. My little voice spoke to me, Jesus Christ, Jodee, snap out of it. They can see through all this in treatment." But could they?

"I also told her everything about Dawn. She says I need to give her the letter I wrote, that she owes it to me to explain some things."

What made-up stories was he telling them there? The crazy thing is I am not sure they were stories at all. Brett legitimately believed that someone driving drunk with their children was so much worse than what was happening in his own life. I would consider that bad judgment. A person doesn't even need to be an alcoholic to make poor decisions. After all, how many people are guilty of that? And Dawn-Marie, that poor girl. I love my brother dearly, but what could a person possibly say to a therapist to have the result that he was the one who deserved all the sympathy? What I do know, however, from experience during my separation from my own husband, is that therapy is directly relative to what you tell the therapist. You can bend, twist, and turn what you say to ensure you get the answer you want. Or you can be uncomfortable, deal with the pain, tell the truth, and get help. I was not convinced that Brett even knew what the truth was at this stage.

I knew within five minutes of seeing him that this hadn't worked. Nothing had changed.

"COPPERHEAD ROAD "

I had never in my life been so happy to be wrong.

It was such a blessing to see my brother so completely content and settled. He had been sober for about a month and a half and working really hard, still employed at the nearby gas plant. He was challenging his anxiety, which he told me caused severe discomfort when attending his meetings. I wouldn't ever want someone who is struggling with addiction to believe Alcoholics Anonymous is the only way to recover. I don't believe that. The key is for addicts to find out what works for *them*. I am so proud of those in recovery and there are many different ways to ensure sobriety.

Now, years later, I have a slightly different feeling about AA. I certainly do not want to offend, nor diminish the fact that it has and continues to bring millions throughout the world to sobriety. What I feel now though is that we have progressed. How we view addiction and alcoholism is changing. In fact, we aren't even calling it "alcoholism" anymore, but rather "substance abuse disorder" as those words seem more compassionate, caring, and understanding. I grasp why Alcoholics Anonymous helps its attendees with anonymity. There would be judgment and stigma from strangers, friends, co-workers even family members sometimes if they were to find out. And that without that security of anonymity, alcoholics might not find the courage to seek help. It's not the premise I am against, just the word "anonymous." Doesn't that in itself breed stigma, judgment, and shame for the individual and for the families? After all, it means secret, faceless, unknown, characterless, incognito, nameless. Who would ever want to be those things?

I respect those who for reasons of their own are not wanting to ever open up and share their personal journey; that should always stay intact. But the world is changing. We are no longer encouraged to be silent, quiet, and hidden, but rather to share our painful stories and experiences in order to help others. How freeing it is to your soul when you have the courage and confidence to speak openly and honestly; without shame. I have no interest in being anonymous.

For my brother at the time, at his non-functioning level, he needed the structure, the accountability, and the support of AA. It was available to him wherever he was, for free, which was a huge bonus. Once, a girl questioned him about the scars on his wrists in front of everyone, which he told me caused his face to go "cherry red" and he was embarrassed to have to explain. I don't think it ever occurred to Brett that someone could ask from a perspective of kindness, care, and concern. He hated what he called "people feeling sorry for themselves," telling their stories. But, as I reminded him, with any help that is offered, absorb what works for you and ignore the rest. And I believe, to be truly a part of a changing world where eventually people will be as comfortable talking about their addiction and experiences as is someone with ALS, Alzheimer's, cancer, or Parkinson's, we need to start the conversation in our own family and find a better word than "anonymous."

On his many days off, to make extra money, Brett was helping me around the shop. Although I had staff and didn't need the help, I found odd jobs that he could do, for a couple of hours a day. He didn't even notice that the files I had him put away this day were the same ones I had had him file a few days before. I just pulled them back out of the filing cabinet and shuffled them up a little, setting them on the corner of my desk. After all, I wasn't just going to give him money—there was no lesson in that. I paid him ten dollars an hour cash. It was much less than the usual wage of a power engineer, but his bills were mounting and so every little bit helped. I enjoyed his company. We had fun together at work, even when things were a disaster.

We had had a little bit of a fire (nothing too serious; no one got hurt) while I was pouring candles about three weeks earlier. Brett was annoyed at me when he went to grab the fire extinguisher and it didn't work. It had expired two years earlier. I knew I should have noticed, but I could tell he was proud when he took the canisters in for me, got them recharged, and made me promise never to neglect them again. I guess it was one of the many things that I let slip through the cracks back then.

I was teaching him how to make our blue colored crystals that are used in floral arrangements. When they are added to water, they puff up to a hundred times their size and turn a bright, bold color. They are tiny, white, rock-type pellets that are put into a drum and then sprinkled with powdered food colorants. While the drum is spinning, water is sprayed to disperse the color. Because these tiny particles of color get airborne and are invisible to the naked eye, it's essential to wear a full, white protective paper suit over your clothes and shoes. You even have to pull up the hood over your head, and then put on a face mask, latex gloves, and a pair of goggles. It's a bit of an ordeal and the outfit looks quite over the top once you're fully garbed.

Brett, of course, had other plans. He did put on the suit, with one of his beige baseball caps, no hood, no mask, no gloves. When I reminded him of the other accessories, he confidently replied, "It will be fine."

"I am sure it will," I said with a smile. "Unless you get wet."

Brett went outside for a smoke about an hour later and casually, like nothing was wrong, walked back into the shop and around the corner. He didn't even smirk and I was having a hard time controlling my bellowing laughter. His beige hat was now stained, his hands were completely covered, bright blue streaks streamed down his face and dripped off the end of his nose. It looked like he had been doused with a bottle of food coloring.

"Uh, ya," he said, off the cuff, "It's raining out." And nonchalantly, he turned and walked away.

I love this guy. After all that time, he still made me laugh and I had missed those simple, special moments with the person I know to be my brother.

To be honest, I needed the comic relief. Jim and I had had struggles of our own during the last few months, although no one would know the truth as we kept it to ourselves. Our business had been hurting financially and we were close to bankruptcy. We were not sure what to do, but that wasn't the only stressor. I had been diagnosed with pre-cancer and I was having surgery in a few days.

We told no one. Instead, Jim and I had spent what felt like weeks waiting and waiting for my appointment with the specialist. Crying together at night, we waited some more. I am one of those people who is usually totally healthy, so if I have nothing wrong, I don't go to the doctor. And that would include skipping my yearly physical. It had been almost ten years and then—boom. Apparently, I wasn't so healthy after all, as the results came back with "suspicious cells."

When we finally got an appointment with a specialist, we sat patiently in a busy waiting room while Jim held my hand in support. I remember quietly looking around and saw some women by themselves, some couples. Almost every chair was filled with people of various ages. It was a gynecologist's office, so I wasn't sure how many were there for cancer or for other reasons. Maybe all, maybe just me, but I couldn't help but think some may die.

We listened quietly as Dr. Helford made her recommendation of a hysterectomy—the removal of my uterus and perhaps ovaries—depending on what they found. It was a serious, major surgery. I would spend three to five days in the hospital. Then I should be off work to recover for about four to six weeks. She confirmed that it was only pre-cancer and she was confident that it had been caught early enough. She had no reason to believe I wouldn't be totally healthy afterwards. With this diagnosis, I was filled with an overpowering sense of gratefulness as I don't ever feel sorry for myself. I couldn't help but imagine what someone would feel hearing those same words if they had not yet had children. I was truly blessed.

When I received my diagnosis, I finally broke down and told our mom and siblings. It wasn't that it was a secret; it was more that Jim and I deal with issues ourselves in our household. Plus I didn't want to worry them unnecessarily as we already had so much going on with Brett. It was a relief to get it out of the way, and then I could focus on happier times ahead. Christmas was fast approaching and that is my favorite time of the year. Since Carolynn, cousin Kelly's wife, and I were hosts, we made sure all the plans were in place for the annual Tisdale Christmas Dinner that means so much to all of us.

Our family had become so big over the years that it was no longer possible for my aunts and uncles to host the annual event at their houses. We hadn't gathered for a couple of years and Christmas just didn't feel the same. It was always so important to my Grandma Tisdale, and I remember the fun times of enjoying the holidays as one big happy family. Maybe it was my way of holding on to the past, just like Brett was trying to do. We all seemed to be so happy and close back then. I hope the tradition of getting together always continues, otherwise my kids won't know my cousins' kids and eventually the next generation won't know each other at all. Families need to make an effort. Sadly, I think they get so wrapped up in their own lives that they forget that sometimes. Well, in my family anyway.

So, the invitations were sent, the room at the golf course was secured, and the only thing they didn't know is that I might not be there.

Jim and I and the boys, then fourteen and twelve, sat patiently with me in the hospital room. Eventually the nurse brought me a light blue gown. Jim and I didn't share all the surgical details with the boys. They knew I was having surgery but we played it down a little because we didn't want to worry them.

We laughed and joked together as I opened the robe my family had bought me, and my thoughts turned for a second to Brett. He told me once that he thought I hid my feelings of anxiety and discomfort through laughter and sarcasm. Right then, I thought he might be right.

After about an hour, the nurse came to get me. I kissed each of them and told them I loved them and that I would see them later. I could see the fear in my husband's eyes as I whispered in his ear, "It's okay, don't worry."

Worry. I didn't take more than three steps into the long, cold hall towards the operating room when it became safe to cry and my eyes fill with tears. I *was* worried. I was scared, terrified. I was afraid of the potential pain. I was scared to be put to sleep. But mostly, I was frightened that something would go terribly wrong and I wouldn't wake up and I would never see my family again.

I suppose everyone has those same fears before an operation under anesthetic. And, of course, I did wake up. I felt surprisingly okay, although nauseous and disoriented while my eyes tried to focus on a room I had never seen before. It didn't take me long to drift back to sleep.

I was more coherent a few hours later, sitting up in bed, trying to eat some tasteless hospital food when a bleary-eyed Jim walked through the door. I was still a little groggy. My first instinct was how sweet it was that he was so worried about me that he had tears in his eyes, that he was overwhelmed with relief that I was okay.

"Hi," I said, pushing aside my tray, having lost my appetite before I'd even tasted it.

"I am so sorry I'm late," he replied. It was almost 8 p.m.; visiting hours were almost over, and I had been out of surgery for quite a while.

"Oh, my God, it's alright. You're here now," I said, as he sat on the edge of my bed.

"What's wrong?" I asked. Knowing my husband so well, I knew something had happened. It was more than just relief over my surgery.

He leaned in to give me a hug. "I am sorry; I don't want to upset you. I just can't believe your mother."

"Now whaaaat?" I asked, hesitant for the answer.

He shared how worried he had been about me all day, trying to concentrate at work but feeling sick inside that I was there alone. He just wanted to get back to the hospital as fast as he could. But he knew that Mom and our older sister Jane, the one who had been given up for adoption, were coming later to see me. He picked up the kids from school, and rushed home to make dinner for the boys, Mom, and Jane. Mom had shown up at our house well past 7 p.m. "Sorry I'm late, I took Jane for dinner," she told him as she casually walked in the door.

I wish I had something better to say, to make this easier for him since my mother has no instinct to come and help him with the children, let alone to get to the hospital. I wanted to find a creative excuse for my mother's self-absorption. But I didn't have one, so I just went with the standard: "I'm sorry."

And I certainly didn't think Jane had any responsibility for this. After all, she had just been brought into our family. How could I expect her to say something when I myself continued to bite my tongue?

I thought it was so thoughtful that Jane would come all this way to visit me. What meant the most was that she came to make sure I was doing alright and expected nothing from me in return. I, of course, wasn't used to that.

I can't help but wonder how different things might have been had Jane not been given up for adoption. She would have been the oldest in our family—maybe there to take care of me as that no longer would have been my job. All of our roles and responsibilities would have changed when we were little children. Had she not been given away, who would I be today? Is it possible, would I have become an addict instead of my brother?

I stayed in the hospital for a few days, but I didn't hear from Brett, nor from Nicole, either. No visit, no call, no card. My feelings were hurt, even I admit that it would have been really nice in this instance to get some flowers.

Early Saturday morning, I tiptoed to the bathroom and began getting ready. When my roommate awoke, she yelled from across the room, "What are you doing?"

"I'm leaving today," I said.

Our conversation was overheard by a nurse who blasted, "You are NOT leaving. The doctor needs to discharge you."

As I poked my head out the door, I said kindly, "Then I suggest you get her, 'cause I AM leaving. I have a party to go to."

And so I did go to the Tisdale Christmas party. Although, I didn't stay long as I was still extremely weak and in a great deal of pain. But the happiness I felt was far better for me than any painkiller. I love my family very much.

By Christmas Day, once again, I was not speaking with my sister. I don't take it lightly. I love Nicole but it is a fight, a conflict, almost every time I hear from her. For what felt like the hundredth time over the years, I fell into the trap of giving her a job as she called begging for money and really needing a job. She promised it would be different this time. Within a couple of days, it was obvious that it was going to be the same old story, as she had some excuse for not being able to work and I once again was left scrambling to find a staff member at the busiest time of the year. She was absolutely furious at me for letting her go; no concept that I had a company to run and that you don't do this to your employer. Once again, she suckered me into helping her in her current disaster. And it seemed that to her, I became the bitch. And she has no problem letting me know it. My silence became my way of surviving. If I said something back, it would escalate into a war zone that was impossible for me to win. My sister would never see life my way. I had accepted that a long time ago.

Nicole was having her own Christmas celebration at her house and our mom had chosen to spend it with her, Adam, and the kids, Payton and Kaddi. I didn't mind at all. In fact, deep down I think I preferred it. But what I hadn't expected was that Brett wasn't coming to our house, but going there instead. I didn't make a big deal about it, but I was filled with an overwhelming sense of hurt as he barely had a relationship with our sister.

Mom swung by my house really quickly to show her face before heading off to Nicole's. Over and above my sadness, deep down I was concerned. My brother had been doing remarkably well; he should have been so proud of himself, sober for almost three whole months. But I was still worried, always on edge, and I knew the celebration at my sister's would be quite different from the one at my house.

"Mom, no one is going to drink tonight are they?" I asked, cautiously waiting, not necessarily for her response as much as her reaction.

It was obvious why I was asking, although I certainly didn't feel I needed to explain what I was worried about. I absolutely agree, alcoholics definitely need to take responsibility for themselves. Drinking is everywhere. It can't be avoided, and they need to do things to ensure their sobriety in those situations.

I think even the therapists would agree that it was too soon for him to be around people who were sharing a few glasses of alcohol. After all, Brett and I both knew (and our mother should) that the core premise behind his recovery is avoiding the triggers and finding "sober friends," good influences, people who support his recovery. That rule would include his family, wouldn't it? Surely our mother and my sister wouldn't expect Brett—someone who didn't just drink too much but was so profoundly, painfully, actually "addicted"—to be able to go his whole life without a drink, if they couldn't do it for just one evening?

"Yes, we are drinking!!!" Mom snapped, and I was blessed with not only her raised voice but the arm flailing as well. "What do you think, Jodee? That we aren't going to enjoy a glass of wine at Christmas?"

I knew this wasn't really a question, and I wanted to snap right back, "Yes mother, I do actually think that, exactly that." But in the hopes of avoiding more drama, more conflict, more disruption in my life, I just shook my head in silence. So, she blew out the front door as fast as she had blown in.

Jim, Rick, Ryan, and I had a beautiful Christmas together, like we always did. The stockings filled with special things just for them, the laughter, the love, and complete happiness filled the air. I knew in my heart my family was delighted it was just the four of us as it was a rare occurrence those days.

The kids were growing older and they had spent much of their lives witnessing all of these disasters firsthand. And not just the addiction of my brother, because that would not be fair to put all this on him, but all the added complications of their grandmother's and aunt's behavior as well. I was beginning to wonder what to say. After all, it didn't even make sense to me, so how could I explain it? You hear other families say, "Every family is dysfunctional." My God, I hope every family doesn't have all of this going on, shit flying in every direction, or I might just lose faith in the human race.

I kissed the kids goodnight and crawled into bed after our peaceful day of fun and festivities, turned out the light, wrapped my arms around my husband, and closed my eyes. Instantly, I could no longer contain my underlying sense of hurt that Brett chose to celebrate at Nicole's instead, and tears began to stream down my cheeks.

On December 25, 2005, I cried myself to sleep while my brother was a half-hour away enjoying a glass of wine.

"HOMESICK"

A bump in the road, a binge, a relapse: we learn they are normal parts of recovery after all. But my brother could not afford relapses. Whereas others can stop after a weekend bender and get quickly back on track, a relapse for my brother would always end the same way, with him hanging between life and death. Perhaps in his mind, it was "only a glass of wine." But what we all know by now is by this stage of his addiction: one burning glass and he *couldn't* stop. Within days, he chased that glass of wine down with bottles of vodka and the saga continued.

By the second week of January, when I snuck home early to get some much-needed rest, I awoke to receive an incoherent voice message left on my cell phone, echoing cries of my brother: "Please help me, I can't feel my hands."

As hard as I tried, I just couldn't stay away. I found the courage to go to Brett's house later in the day, although he was no longer in need of my assistance. He had taken a bunch of pills earlier to sleep, begun hallucinating, and believed Dawn-Marie was hiding in his basement. In his panicked state, he had dialed my number. When I didn't answer, he called 911 as by then he was having chest pains. Then he bolted from the hospital just an hour later. He wasn't going into cardiac arrest; it was in fact an anxiety attack. I let out a big sigh as only in my brother's world could consuming a half-full bottle of Tylenol chased with lethal doses of vodka not require medical intervention.

He got a moment of clarity, if even for a split second, a few days later, knowing he had to stop drinking. He refused to go to a medical detox center and instead was withdrawing at home with help from a girl named Barb. I had never seen her before and I didn't know her deal, and really I didn't wanna know. When I asked him who she was, all he said was, "She's my best friend."

I had never seen or heard of that chick in my entire life, and she was his best friend? OMG. I mean no disrespect at all to her; after all I realize that her own family would be worried sick if they knew she was with Brett. No girl without problems of her own would be having sex with my brother in that condition. Within a couple of days she was gone and I never heard her name or saw her again. He sobered up and had a new life's plan. He quit his job at the plant, made some calls, did a resume, and without skipping a beat had a new job.

He was excited about his new power engineering career with another oilfield company; great pay, a benefit package, and a brand new company truck to drive. His thought process scared me. It was as though the last few weeks and years hadn't happened. Barely sober for a week, in my brother's mind, he had a brand new future with endless possibilities. Yet, within a couple of days, he was phoning in sick, with his empty promises of "I will be there tomorrow." Then tomorrow, then the tomorrow after that.

For me, every moment was more excruciating than the last. It is torture watching a loved one caught in a downward spiral, over and over again, worrying that this time they wouldn't be able to pull out of it. Time stood still, moving in slow motion, the days never ending, and the nights filled with tears, tossing and turning, and trying desperately to sleep so that the images of my brother's dead body could leave my mind.

Our mother had been practically raising Indie and once again had picked him up long ago as Brett couldn't manage to look after a dog. Long gone were the days of doing things with friends or playing hockey games or having any sense of a life at all. His financial situation was dire because of his mounting bills, including being in debt to those high-interest cash-advance companies. And let's not forget all the ambulance bills that he had not yet paid. We were fortunate, hospital visits are free in Canada, but each time he dialed 911, another three hundred dollars for the ride was added to the pile. Collections agencies were calling him on a daily basis, although that was nothing new. The only thing current was his rent, as he did have the foresight to pay that first (well, I believe he was the one paying it).

Mom, Nicole, and I once again begged for him to get help. He refused. And then, finally, with no more money for booze, and nothing left to pawn, Brett was out of options. He was backed into another corner, so he once again agreed and this would be his sixth attempt at rehab.

I had been frantically communicating with an admittance counselor named Diane in a place that I had found in Montreal. It was supposed to be one of the best, although really how would I know? What I did know for sure were two things: it was a longer program—ninety days—not this three or four-week stint so it had to be an in-depth treatment. And it was expensive. As in twenty-five THOUSAND DOLLARS expensive. We were so grateful and full of hope. Ninety days. This was what he needed; we were sure of it.

Our mother, without hesitation, once again wrote a check to help save her son. I must emphasize our Mom is not wealthy, but she found the means, even if that meant debt of her own. Brett was set to experience the "best" treatment money could buy.

As usual, I was supportive in helping my brother tie up some loose ends. Someone needed to explain to Brett's employer what was going on and since he was not available to do it himself, I volunteered. As a complete coincidence, his boss lived just around the corner from me in a quiet neighborhood in town. I explained to him as gently as I could that my brother was sick, in the hospital, and wouldn't be back to work for an undetermined amount of time. I didn't give more specific details than that, although I was sure he knew. Brett misguidedly thought he was fooling everyone when he called them with his excuses in his condition, but he was not.

Brett's new employer called me within two days to pick up a letter for Brett. My brother was already in Montreal, so I opened the bright white envelope from his employer and instantly I was beyond furious. Not because they had written him a termination letter, but the reason that they gave is what made my blood boil. They had the audacity to put my name in the letter and claim that his termination was because of what *I* had told them.

I may be calm most of the time, but when someone pushes me, they had better watch out. I picked up the phone and called their office, asking to speak to someone in charge to tell them exactly what was on my mind. "How dare you blame me or make me responsible at all for your decision to let my brother go."

As this person from the human resources department was making excuses and trying to interject, I kept on talking, getting louder and louder to muffle the sounds of his voice.

"Listen. I didn't tell your company a damn thing. My brother is sick and in treatment. You hired him; you are required by law to support him with that." I was still choosing my words carefully not to tell them exactly what was wrong. I suppose my instinct was still to protect him. "What I certainly won't let you do is put in writing that whatever your decisions are surrounding my brother have anything to do with me. I suggest when you hang up the phone you call your legal department; they are going to tell you exactly the same thing!" And I hung up.

You can debate it all day long: alcoholism is considered a disease in this country, no different from cancer, and legally they couldn't fire him. I knew I was right. If I pressed the issue, Brett would have his job when he got back. In fact, I think they would have probably had to pay some or maybe all of his rehab costs.

But my logical self won this fight and it didn't take me long to calm down. I believe Brett's previous job was a huge part of the problem. Employers are not equipped to handle addiction and, after all, it is not exactly the same as cancer. When a person is off with pay for cancer, the support is not perpetuating a problem; it is very clearly supporting someone through a tough time, often through chemotherapy. But what legal rights do employers have with someone addicted, especially one who will not stay sober? One, that is not following the treatment suggested. The world has a long way to go in education but I do not believe that keeping addicts employed, with pay, and no follow through or expectation of a recovery plan is the answer.

When I calmed down, the truth was I was glad he got fired. They did the right thing, maybe not what was legal, but the right thing in my mind. I felt my brother needed a dose of reality, to be broke, to struggle, to suffer the consequence of his choices. That hadn't been happening and it was about time. I backed down and decided not to contact his employer again.

Mom got Brett safely to rehab. She arrived a couple of days later to see me. "Oh, my God, Jodee, you should've seen how fearful he was. It was heartbreaking."

It was not what our mother said sometimes that was so shocking, but rather the way she said it. It was said with such pity, like you should feel so sorry for him, like this had never happened to anyone before and none of the other people that have ever gone to rehab are fearful. PITY. It is an emotion I am not capable of having. That does not mean I am not empathetic to others and what they are going through. But my help will never come from the word I hate most in this world—"pity." I believe pity wears you down. It will break your spirit. It makes you believe that the situation is hopeless and it is not hopeless. And *Mother*, I wanted to say but didn't, *Brett was having a major panic attack.*

Mom and I entered the front door of his rental home cautiously to see what state it was in. It was mind-boggling; weeks of destruction. My first instinct was perhaps it would be easier if we got a jerrycan of gasoline and lit a match. Instead we cleaned every inch from top to bottom, just as I had done many times before. We put all his things into boxes, as he would be away for three months. I gave his thirty days' notice to the landlord.

It all happened so fast that Brett hadn't taken much with him. I grabbed a big canvas bag of his clothes when I left and brought them home to wash. Urine-soaked, filthy, and bloody, many of his pants were as stiff as a board, and caked with vomit. I sat for a few minutes on the little wooden step in my garage before I entered the house.

I was so conflicted. Every bone in my body wanted to close the zipper, put his belongings in a box, and ship them to him that way. I loved him so much. I didn't care if he got mad at me, if he hated me. I wanted it to arrive across the country via Federal Express, my brother opening it up when it got there, his nostrils stinging from the stench. I wanted him to drop to his knees, in shock and disgust at the reality of what his life had become. I wanted his roommate to say: "Oh, my God, Brett, what the fuck?" And he would have to explain the truth, that he had made that disgusting mess himself. I wanted to do that so badly, but I just couldn't do it. Instead I opened the back door to our little laundry room and I began throwing his clothes in the machine, with an extra cup of Tide.

Jim came around the corner, while everything was still fresh and warm from the dryer, as I neatly folded a pair of Brett's jeans. My husband, although struggling himself with everything that was going on with my family, continued to let me do my thing where my brother was concerned. But I could tell by his body language that he did not approve. There was no point me saying anything to him, trying to excuse what I was doing as I understood. I didn't approve of what I was doing either.

The next day, I met the movers at the house, showed them around, and told them where to shuttle all Brett's things. When they were done loading, they would give me a call. I would drive with them the short distance to the storage unit that I still held from when Brett had sold his house.

When I got back about two hours later, the man was not impressed. "Listen, we've moved his stuff but we *are not* going to touch that couch. My guy almost puked when we went to move it."

As I walked across the room, I realized that with all of our cleaning and organizing, we hadn't even touched the couch, sitting perfectly in the middle of the living room. Oh, but the movers had. Lying underneath were days-old pools of vomit, the smell almost knocking you off your feet.

"I am so very sorry," I said, but he didn't really accept my apology.

Once out of harm's way and back to his reality, as usual, my brother was *not* happy he was back in rehab. He begged for our help, and we continued to jump like kangaroos. Once the booze was out of his system, he resented us for helping and for the fact that he was there.

Day 4, "I think it's a mistake that I came here."

Day 6, "I met this guy named Sandy. He has a son far away. It's sad. We both get up really early so we have been walking on the grounds—he's cool."

Day 12, "Twenty grand for shit pens. Getting frustrated with the Nazi fascist shit here—oh well, I'll use it. Dreams are pissing me off, I can't remember them."

Day 15, "I want to come home."

We weren't writing letters to each other this time, but rather talking on the phone at least every second day. I am not saying he was totally happy and cheerful, but he sounded in better spirits, like he was coming around. He really liked his roommate Sandy; he talked about him often and it seemed they spent a lot of time together, as he didn't mention anyone else.

"They got us working on tons of worksheets, tons of these fuckin' things. Never really done that before."

"Really, like what kind of sheets?" I asked.

"You know, like how I spend my day versus how I *should* spend my day. How much has my addiction cost me? How do I make up for lost time? Shit like that."

"Read me something."

There were a few seconds of silence until I heard the sound of crinkly paper coming through the phone, "They got us to write down reasons why we don't want to use—supposed to keep it in our pocket. Like a reminder."

"And?"

"Why I don't want to use: Indie. Why I don't want to use: Nicole. Why I don't want to use: Mom. Why I don't want to use: Rick, Ryan, Payton, Kaddi. Why I don't want to use: Jodee. Why I don't want to use: Integrity."

I did not notice that he never once said he wanted to quit using for himself.

"I'm supposed to set a boundary for Dad. Things will never be like they used to be. We created a very close relationship. Unfortunately, booze was the bonding force. He told me I am not the way I used to be. I'm not. We were drunk all the time, fishing, quad biking, hunting, camping. It is time for me to move on, with or without his support."

This made me painfully sad. I believe Brett's relationship with our dad was one of the things he struggled with most during this time. He loved his father very much, so he was deeply conflicted. At least these were honest feelings, and it showed me that he understood what the rehab centers were telling him regarding his relationship with his dad. Brett had been told many times before that in order to embrace a new life he had to change his lifestyle and his relationship with the people who were bad for his recovery. I wished things were different. I wished some of those people were not our family. But they are and neither of us could change that.

"I learned something else too, Jode."

"Oh, what's that?" I asked, trying to learn from everything he shared.

"I expect things to change too fast. I need to slow down, accept things will get better with time."

"Brett, that's awesome. I am so proud of you."

"Ya, thanks."

And once again my heart was full, not of happiness, but with hope. I had hope.

For only the second time, Nicole came with me to see a professional. She too was overwhelmed with the situation, and we could no longer avoid the fact that nothing seemed to be working. We entered the office and I introduced my sister to Dr. Dimirsky and once again shared what had been going on.

"I have Brett's permission to see you and talk about him," Dr. Dimirsky began. "I understand he is in Montreal as he has been in contact with me. He knows what I'm going to be talking about with you but not my exact words, of course. Everything I say to you about him will be told to him. I understand you both are here for help for yourselves as you deal with your brother's pattern of relapses. Is that right?"

We both nodded our heads. "Yes, we don't know what to do," I said.

"I've seen Brett a number of times now and believe I have a pretty good knowledge of him. I'd like to make some comments and some observations about him and the two of you and your family.

"I do think Brett is sincere in saying he is sorry for his continual relapses. I do believe he regrets his wasting of the opportunities to turn his life around and I think his self-concept suffers because he judges himself to be a failure and in lots of ways a burden.

"That sincerity is a trap for him and for those who want to help him. After all, it would be easier to turn your back on someone who appears to be manipulative and not sincere. It is a trap because both of you (because you are a close family) and people like me (who think of ourselves as helpers and healers) get drawn into being part of a pattern. A pattern that can be too comfortable too quickly and that just winds up not working to get Brett away from drinking permanently.

"So I'm saying that all of us need to understand that Brett's sincerity has to be put aside and we have to deal with behaviors. Not excuses, not reasons, not what will happen in the future. We have to be grounded because he isn't and his sincerity invites us to overestimate how grounded and realistic he is."

I sat there listening intently. I couldn't have agreed more with his assessment of the situation.

"A second point I hope to discuss is that Brett is totally responsible for his behavior. But there is a 'but.' People and events from his past and present play a role in either having formed some patterns of his behaviors that don't work and/or maintaining those patterns now.

"I'm not blaming; he isn't blaming; and certainly I don't want blame to come out of this discussion. But I do think that what I've heard from Brett and from the two of you suggests to me how the family typically deals with Brett needs to be explored. It may be that the way the family deals with Brett winds up supporting some bad patterns for him."

Okay ... this guy's good, was what I was thinking.

"For example, I've seen in lots of instances where women take the role of helping someone who doesn't take their fair share of the responsibility in maintaining a relationship. I've seen this a lot in marriages where the wife assumes most of the responsibility for making changes to herself and excuses the husband when he should be making some changes also. I think I'm seeing and hearing from you, and from Brett, that he might have two or three women who wind up carrying too much of the responsibility and, therefore, shielding him from that responsibility. This is called 'learned helplessness.'

"So, I'm asking both of you not to blame yourselves for creating Brett's problem of drinking. That would not be good to do and also would not be truthful, because your patterns only have limited influence on Brett. But I am asking you to examine whether something that happened in childhood that needs correction might be at play here. I am asking whether some patterns that started a long time ago by one or both of you might need attention. In short, if we are talking about what you can do to help Brett then I'm saying I think some issues from childhood or later that happen or happened in the family should be examined. I don't know what those are specifically now, but I think they need to be explored, because they are likely continuing in one form or another and are not effective. They may actually work against Brett gaining ground in his fight."

I was overwhelmed with emotion. My chest felt tight but in a positive way; full of so much hope. Dr. Dimirsky must have finally broken through the surface, got my brother to open up. This was the help we had been dreaming of.

For the first time, someone mentioned our childhood, and for someone who had just met my sister (and never our mother), he was remarkably spot on in everything he said.

Nicole and I have talked about our early years with our dad. I never would have told her about them unless for a good reason, as she wouldn't be able to remember the drunken fights because she was just a baby. But she struggled for a long time when Mom sent her away to live with me. I couldn't even say how many times throughout the years I heard, "She was done being a Mom. She washed her hands of me." I just thought we could share some of our pain. I understood it's important to work through things, make sense of them; otherwise they can ruin our life. And if we can work through things, we can forgive and move past them.

But our early years—our father, the violence, the yelling, the chaos—that wasn't what Dr. Dimirsky was talking about. I didn't think so anyway. After all, I don't believe my brother remembered those days either, as he was only three, four, and five, so he wouldn't have been able to tell the story. He was so young. He couldn't possibly remember the fear and running out the door in the middle of the night. We were never told, nor did I ever read anything at the time that had any correlation between childhood trauma and addiction. What many believe now is that adverse childhood experiences can lead to mental illness and even alcohol and drug addiction later in life, even if the child can't remember. If I had had any idea at the time, I would have screamed the truth from the rooftops.

Without this knowledge at the time, I thought what the doctor was referring to was the three women in his life, us. I knew our mother, sister, and I were all in a pattern of doting on Brett's every need, and it started so long ago. Probably right after our dad left. Brett was always the one who was perfect, the one who could do no wrong, and the one we each loved just a little bit more than we loved each other.

Never was anyone dismissing the fact that my brother—indeed any addict—must take on their own personal responsibility. What I believe Dr. Dimirsky was saying is that we must do the same and that we were doing things to perpetuate Brett's problem.

There were unhealthy patterns going on. You would have to be blind not to see that. I was prepared to do exactly what the professionals told me to do. We were not children anymore. I got that. I was just not convinced anyone else did.

We said goodbye, thank you, and left. As I pushed the elevator button, Nicole and I were talking about our new scenario. After all, if we weren't prepared to change, then why would we be there?

We chatted all the way to her house and remarkably, she and I agreed on something. We had so many differences of opinion on life, but there was nothing more important to us than helping our brother. We were in total agreement and aligned firmly in our plan to support Brett and encourage his choices for sobriety. We would no longer spoil him, nor do the work he needed to do for himself. We were going to change our reaction; we were going to hold *him* accountable.

"Okay, Nicole, you need to make sure. No more giving him money, no calling in sick for him, no sending cigarettes to Montreal as a sweet little gift," I reiterated. "It just keeps him in this pattern of denial."

"Oh, I know," she replied. But the truth is it was not my sister I was worried about but rather the reaction of our mother.

We had wanted Mom to come to see Dr. Dimirsky but she refused. I called and tried to talk rationally to her, letting her know not what Brett needed to do, but what *we* needed to do as a family, what changes we should make. Each of us should take responsibility to change. And she completely lost her shit! Once again, this professional was incorrect.

"I am not going to listen to this, Jodee," she snapped. "I have done nothing wrong!"

The real reason why I remain silent and rarely challenge our mother is to keep the peace. I have been doing it since I was a little girl. We were at a crossroads. My brother was not changing so I wanted the rest of us to change. I wanted so desperately for all of us to trust in the people who were also trying so hard to help. Maybe it would have an impact on the outcome. That was my hope anyway.

But Mom wasn't interested in listening to Dr. Dimirsky's advice, and I felt we were left with me on one side and her on the other. And although Nicole agreed, I knew my sister was teetering right in the middle.

Day 24, "Hey," Brett said. "Sorry I didn't call ya for a couple days. Sandy took off a few days ago. They found him yesterday in a downtown hotel room. OD'd."

"Oh, my God. What? He's dead?" I shot back in complete surprise. "Brett, his poor family. Are you okay?"

"Yup, I'm good."

And after about two minutes of me asking more questions that was the end of that conversation.

Sandy. I had heard his name so many times over the last few weeks that I was completely caught off-guard that he would take off from rehab and die from an overdose. You can leave rehab at any time as the doors are unlocked. That fear is always with me. I was even more shaken by my brother's matter-of-fact reaction to Sandy's death.

Brett lacked emotion about the situation—no tears, no shock, none of the normal reactions if a friend were just found dead. Perhaps this could be just another one of the things he buries inside? But deep down, I believe there is more to it than that. What I think is that Brett couldn't relate. In his mind, this could *never* happen to him. And so much had happened that even when he was sober he was losing feeling; he was numb.

He continued to call every couple of days, opening up and sharing what he was learning. Never again was there a word about his friend Sandy.

"I've learned the real problem for me is seclusion, living alone, and having too much time off. That and boredom," he said.

"Hey, that's great," I replied, although I did know he had been told that before. And the astronomical amount of money he made certainly didn't help either. But I am pretty sure he was not telling them about that. "That's huge progress, Brett."

Days of treatment turned to weeks. Then, Nicole called to tell me the news, "He's coming home, Jodee."

"What? He has another month!"

"No, Mom has agreed to let him come home early." Oh, my fucking god.

I instantly dialed her number and like a broken record I heard, "It's up to him, Jodee."

I agreed it was his choice. All of this was his choice and he would be free to hitchhike across Canada if he bailed on rehab, but we all knew that is not what was happening—she was making the arrangements and he was flying home. Once again I felt completely deflated.

Brett was going to live with Mom for a while when he got home, since he had no money and no job. I didn't believe it was the environment that my brother needed and I would have loved it if he committed to a sober living facility where he would gain the proper support. But he always said no to me on that suggestion.

I shared with Jim this big news and I got that he was feeling nervous. In all this time, we had only ever had one knock-down, drag-out fight about my brother. That certainly didn't mean my husband doesn't have his own strong opinions. He is hardly passive. It just means that yelling and screaming isn't our way. We prefer talking calmly through conflict.

The fear in Jim's eyes was valid, especially since Brett was coming home thirty days early. I could have understood if my husband had snapped, if he'd finally had enough. "I just need to ask you one question," he said to me calmly, before taking a short pause. "If it were me, would you have divorced me by now?"

I am ashamed at the pain I was causing my husband. The silence was deafening. I said nothing. After all, he knew the answer.

The answer was yes.

"SOAK THE SIN"

Brett was staying at Mom's, frequently driving the hour and a half to spend the night with Nicole, and occasionally coming to help me at the shop.

Things were going well for me. The last sixty days helped. I had been given a clean bill of health—the hysterectomy had done the trick. There was no need for chemotherapy or any further treatment and with me having regular check-ups every six months, my doctor was confident I would be just fine. Our business was doing much better: I had transitioned from making candles into making beauty products as I had the foresight to see there was a shift in what was becoming popular in the market. We had come so close to losing it all (finally having no choice but to add fifty thousand onto our mortgage to keep the business afloat) that that was just the motivation and focus I needed.

Brett had had barely a couple of weeks of sobriety and stability when he decided to move up north to Edson for another oilfield job. It was about four hours away. He knew absolutely no one there, so there was no support at all. It was the same schedule as usual and, of course, the ridiculous sums of money that he just couldn't refuse. These were all the triggers he had just learned about.

Even though I knew this, when he asked me to help him move, my heart told my head a different story, which was that this was support. I complied once again, making sure he got settled. I stayed the weekend, helping unload furniture, getting groceries, unpacking and, once finished, relaxing and watching a movie. I cherished these moments as they were few and far between, being with the brother I knew, laughing and joking. Never quiet, always with something to say to me.

As I went to leave the next morning, he said, "Hey, I forgot to tell ya, when I stopped at the rental company to pick up my damage deposit, they told me I was one of the best tenants they ever had. If I'm ever lookin' for a place in Sylvan again to give them a call." And he gave a warm smile.

As I drove the long, straight highway home, I had a long time to think. My thoughts were jumbled and then quickly aligned like a car speeding down the highway, losing control, and then hitting a brick wall. He was so confident, so self-assured. He absolutely, with every bone in his body, believed what he just told me. He was a fabulous tenant. Oh, my God, a fabulous tenant? We had done this, not Brett; *us*. My mother, sister, and I.

I had been conscious, at least I thought so anyway, that I was never enabling. I had been so careful not to be like our mother and sister. I would never give him money, call in sick for him, make excuses blaming everyone else. I really believed that the things I was doing, like cleaning his house, packing his belongings, or helping him move were ways of being supportive. I instantly saw it in a completely different light. I grasp what all the professionals in some form or another may have been trying to say.

I had spent another three days away from my own family, even going so far as to rent a steam cleaner for that putrid couch! I physically gagged as I did the work; the hot soapy water brought the smell of vomit and urine to the surface. I thought of our regular *love u's*, a hug and kiss goodbye, then driving away from an adorable little character home, in a town far away, to a career that's bad for his recovery. Now, he faced even more seclusion, loneliness, and boredom. I had not only just told him without any words at all that I was in support of this, but I actually helped him! I instantly felt sick.

Like a crazy, desperate madman, I once again began researching anything and everything that mentions "enabling," this time seeing it from a completely different perspective. Many times when loved ones try to "help" an addict, they are actually making it easier for the addict to continue in the progression of their disease.

To put it in simple terms, "enabling" creates an atmosphere in which the alcoholic can comfortably continue his unacceptable behavior. I think all three of us women have continued to rationalize Brett's behavior, sheltering him in different ways.

And then I remembered something my brother told me so long ago— *CONSEQUENCE HAS NO BEARING ON ME* .

No wonder he believed this. I don't think anyone has held him accountable for any actions his whole life. And that is where life lesson's come from, learning from our mistakes. Oh, my God, what have I done?

I believe everything I have read on alcoholism; all the help from the doctors, therapists, and people who know so much more than I ever possibly could. And if I am being honest with myself, I know why I did some of these things—it is much easier to enable a loved one, in order to know he is safe, to know he is alive, than to face the alternative of letting him fend for himself in his less-than-functioning state.

I was making poor decision after poor decision. What I see now is that I was eliminating incentives for him to change. We are warned against enabling, because of how detrimental it is to the recovery of our addicted loved ones. Enabling takes away their motivation and personal responsibility and it allows their addiction to flourish, grow, and progress. Although unintentional, if someone is doing everything for you, that has a huge impact on self-esteem; unconsciously the person believes they can't do it for themself.

At the time enabling feels like love. But it isn't love and that's the painful truth.

As hard as I had tried, I know I had let my heart lead me; and I was not going to do that anymore.

I too had been so completely lost in a world that I did not understand. Which is why I was glad that I had continued my own therapy with Terry occasionally over the last couple of years. Besides my husband, Terry knew more about my childhood and family dynamics than anyone else in the world. That would include my brother's version, although I have no idea exactly what they talked about as that was between them. My equilibrium was off. It had been for a long time, and I looked for guidance on how to balance what was good for me and my family, as well as for my brother.

"Maybe it's time you start to worry more about your own wellbeing, and let Brett know it's unacceptable to clean up whatever mess he has left behind," he said. "Boundaries get blurred all the time, keeping the chaos going on."

This time I found courage. I set a healthy boundary when it came to my brother. When things started inevitably going south in the little town far away, for the first time in my whole life, I said no to the ones I love. I refused to get involved and listen to any of the gruesome details when my mother, brother, or sister called me. I am not sure what caused more pain: knowing all the specifics or knowing nothing at all. But I knew I couldn't keep going on as I had been doing. I continued to try and do the right thing and stay strong.

Not surprisingly, it ended very badly again for Brett and his new start. And I didn't need to see it with my own two eyes to know what happened.

I heard that he had moved back to Calgary and was living with Mom. Brett called me a couple of times. He seemed happier and more content, and he assured me that he was once again doing well. He had been seeing a girl, Marie, whom he met at the center in Montreal. He said he had been sober for about seven weeks. I could tell when he mentioned Marie that this wasn't one of those girls who hung around for a couple of days when he was in dire straits. When he was sober, he had so much love to give. And this was different. She too was leading a life of sobriety and he cared about her deeply.

It had been many months since I last saw him and I was so happy that he was on the right track. While I'd done my best to resist seeing him for fear of getting my heart broken, I was proud of his sobriety. I called him a couple of days later to see if he wanted to go on an overnight trip, whitewater rafting with Ryan and me in Banff.

"Ya, sure," he said in an instant.

My heart ached for my children. They had been robbed of loving relationships that most in this world take for granted. For reasons I will explain later, none of us see my husband's side of the family, which would help explain why it bothered me so much that my own mother and sister never showed my sons the love and attention that they deserve. I spent most of their childhood apologizing when birthdays and events went unnoticed. "It's fine, Mom," is what they would say. But it wasn't fine. It hurt my heart for my little boys who were growing into men. This is NOT how families are supposed to be.

But Brett was different from Mom and Nicole. My brother used to be the type of uncle who was always there, doting on his nephews, being genuinely interested in their lives from the very beginning. They had always known how much he loved them. Doing all the things that good uncles do, taking their needs into consideration, and making them feel so special. It is how I feel every time I think of my Auntie Sharon—how much she showered us with love as kids and how she treated Ricky and Ryan. Always making them the center of her universe when she came to visit. That is how my brother used to be, before the drinking, but that changed a long time ago.

It filled my heart with happiness to watch Brett and Ryan together, coming out of the tiny log cabin, both in skin-tight latex suits, posing for a quick pic. While Rick looks more like his dad, Ryan has more of the features from my side of the family, so he looks much like a younger version of his Uncle Brett.

An hour later, we were all side by side, hanging on for dear life, bouncing around on an inflatable black-and-yellow rubber boat, down the frigid, briskly rippling river, trying not to fall overboard. It couldn't have been a more beautiful day in July.

It is very strange, call it intuition, but when I invited Brett to see if he wanted to come with us, I had an uneasy feeling that something was wrong. Not for any other reason than he said yes. I have witnessed short bouts of sobriety over these years and it was against what he normally did at this stage of the game. It was just the opposite of what I thought should happen. When he was doing well, that's when I *didn't* hear from him. He had become more of a loner in the last few years. He didn't call often and when I invited him to do things he almost always said no. When he had to work, he was up and out the door. But on days off, he was never much motivated to do anything fun. I knew he struggled with the fun part, he'd told me as much. He always "enjoyed a few" while he did many of the fun activities in life. He had a hard time enjoying them sober, so he eventually just avoided doing them at all. I imagine it felt like a whole new world. I wasn't sure how to make it better. I was just confident that it would take some time.

I knew he was sober, there was no doubt, but something wasn't right. He was just too quiet; and he and I never had uncomfortable silences. I must have asked him twenty times over that two days, "Is something wrong?"

"No," he answered each and every time.

After a memorable and amazing weekend, we were driving down the highway together, and I was chatting constantly like I always did. Suddenly, Brett snapped abruptly, raising his voice, "Can you stop talking for a while?"

Neither Brett nor Ry in the backseat could tell, but instantly the flood gates opened in my eyes. Something was wrong; he would never talk to me like that, *not ever*.

I dropped Brett off, asking him one last time if he was sure he was alright. I really wanted this time to be special for Ryan, with nothing negative about his uncle to disrupt that, hiding the sickly feeling in my gut. Ryan and I continued on our journey as we were going to look at some puppies on our way home. They were the cutest little balls of fur we'd had ever seen. Ryan's excitement was undeniable. I picked the one that I loved, a little girl, and then looked in Ry's direction. In the palm of his hand lay a white fluffy male Morkie (a cross between a Maltese and a Yorkshire Terrier), his little paws gripping Ryan's fingers like they were meant to be together.

"Mom, please," he pleaded. "This is the one."

We drove home after a beautiful day in the Rocky Mountains with our new addition, Chevy, a little brother for our other dog Cole. A perfect ending for the day, despite the ripple of Brett's outburst that lingered in my mind.

Two days later, I was off again on another trip with Ryan and his best friend to California. Jim and I had been concerned about Ryan spending far too much time in front of the television playing video games, so we thought this would be a great way to get him out of the house and it would be a fun mom-son adventure. Jim was staying back for work. Rick was too as he was getting older and had a job working at the neighborhood boat dealership. He decided he would rather stay home and make some money.

Rick and Ry were always complete opposites. I watched Ryan like a hawk and kept him close at all times. I think back now, I hope that wasn't perceived as special treatment, as that couldn't be farther from the truth. Ryan had so many traits that mimicked my brother, from the time he was born: sweet, quiet, sensitive and, of course, anxiety that I did go over and above to make sure that nothing was going to go wrong. Ricky on the other hand was loud, boisterous, fun, opinionated, and able to take on the world from an early age. We were so proud of him and Jim and I were certain he was going to do just fine.

The three of us were flying to Los Angeles, going to Disneyland, then renting a car and driving through the desert to Las Vegas for a few days. I wasn't sure what we would do when we got there, probably hang at the pool, go to Circus Circus, and I promised to take them to the roller coaster at New York New York on the strip.

Our trip had been planned for a while, but the truth was I needed to get away. I was beyond overwhelmed and anxious again about my brother. My instincts were right. The minute I had dropped Brett off after the whitewater rafting, he went missing again.

When we arrived at the airport, while Jim was unloading our suitcases from the back of the truck, I kissed him goodbye, and whispered softly so the kids couldn't hear, "Please, promise me. If anything happens to Brett while I am away, *do not* tell me on the phone. I just couldn't bear it. Fly to California to give me the news."

I was no longer in denial as to the complexities of what was going on. I believed that unless our whole family, Brett, and his support systems changed, this was going to end badly. Very badly.

"Jodee, your brother is not going to die," he said.

"Yes, he is," I replied.

I was absolutely sure of it.

"AU REVOIR (GOODBYE)"

I did much soul searching while I was away and was not the same person I had been when I left for Disneyland just a week before. I made a conscious decision never to speak loudly or harshly to my brother again. I didn't think my brother was going to make it and I wouldn't be able to live with myself if the last thing I ever said to him was brutal. My approach would be that of only love and compassion, praying that he would find the strength to do what he needed to do to break free, stay sober, and live the beautiful life we all long for and I know he wants.

It had been two months of sheer agony. I had completely backed off, trying to do what I felt was right. This was the total opposite of what my heart was begging me to do. Our mother and sister dropped little details on me, making sure they crept into my life, but I refused to react. To say they were annoyed at me would be an understatement; their distaste and resentment for me was evident each time they called, which didn't make things any easier for me.

Still not knowing what to say, I had to try and explain as I still held out hope that this one time, maybe just this one time, something would click in my brother's mind.

I began typing on my keyboard, inserted a single sheet of white paper, hit "print," and then I folded it neatly, and slipped it into a touching card, just like the ones we had exchanged so many times before. But I couldn't mail it to him, since I didn't know where he was, only that he was alive. So, I sent it to our mother and asked that she made sure he got it.

Brett,

Don't want to say much 'cause it's your birthday & wanting you to know I am thinking of you.

It breaks my heart not to see you & talk to you but either things have to change or I need to say good bye. I cannot watch you kill yourself (perhaps by accident one of these times but that won't make it any easier).

I am haunted by your words, "Why won't a guy learn" when things are so very clear to me (and every counselor, therapist, friend, family member). Because you don't make any of the changes in your life that are recommended to you, you seem to each and every time make the same choices ... thus the same outcome.

I am not going to lecture as it does no good, but please know after this last time I so much hoped you would once again go to Montreal & finish the 90-day program that you started. (I had made the arrangements). From what I understand now, they told you you were not ready to leave the program.

I only hope you know two things:

1) I beg of you ... take the hard road. Treat yourself like any addict on the planet; you are no different. Follow the advice of the counselors & professionals; do as they say, please.

2) You joked (maybe not a joke) that I thought you were the worst alcoholic on the planet ... well, I don't know about that, but I do know one thing ... "I think you are loved more than any alcoholic on the planet."

I will hold dear in my heart the time we spent making candles, mixing "blue" crystals & putting out fires! I saw such a change in you then, laughing, talking. I try so hard to think of those kinds of times instead of the horrors I hear.

I love you with all of my heart, please make the right choices, please change the choices that you make.

xoxoxoxox me

Weeks later, my sister was beyond frantic, as Brett was once again at death's door. I had taken her calls the previous week or so, though I didn't have any of the answers and could only think of the one thing I knew how to say at the time: "He needs to go back to rehab." But of course, he refused.

"Jodee, please," she begged. "We don't know what to do, he won't go," Nicole said, her voice cracking in hysterics while he hid away in some dingy hotel somewhere.

I relented. "Call him. Tell him if he agrees to go, I will pick him up from detox."

And that was all it took for him to say yes. The promise I made was that I would be there five days later once he got the alcohol out of his system and be clean enough to go back to rehab.

I drove the hour and a half to Calgary, turned off the busy street, and waited impatiently in the parking lot of the Renfrew Recovery Centre. I had never been there, although I know he had been there plenty of times. It was a large, grey, boxy building, nondescript, and innocuous. You could easily drive past it without even realizing it existed, let alone wondering what takes place inside.

I could tell the door was locked as there was a small buzzer with a large white sign: "Dispose of all used needles before gaining entry." That sign was much more obvious; a harsh reminder to what our lives had become. I still got a sense of such appreciation that help was offered to him and so many others each and every time. And free of charge, thanks to donations and our national health care system.

I hadn't seen my brother since our rafting trip over two months earlier. His face lit up when he spotted me as he exited the door, clean, and somewhat clear after his five days of withdrawal.

"Hey," he said with a very short pause. "I didn't know if you would be here."

"Of course I'd be here. I promised I would," I said.

We talked for a bit, wandering around the empty parking lot. I am never at a loss for words, but that day I didn't know what to say to him.

I took a deep breath and tried to explain the reality. The cold hard truth. "Brett, you are out of chances. This is it. You need to know I am not going to spend my life doing this. You know I think back to Uncle Ed, how he lived. How everyone just seemed to accept how it was, and made sure all his bills were looked after. I get it. Dad, Auntie Myrna, Auntie Mary, Uncle Les, and even Grandma. How much they loved him, they didn't know what else to do."

As usual, Brett just continued listening, "Aside from the fact that that is not what you are supposed to do today, I could never watch that for the rest of my life. Force you to shower, get you dressed so you could come for dinner. I just couldn't do it. You need to know that."

"I don't blame ya," he said.

We drove down the street to Mom's house, since she had agreed to get him to Montreal. I would not go in; I was just not up to seeing her that day.

Brett was wrestling with his small bag of clothes from the backseat.

"Hey, I have something for you." And I handed him a CD by Martina McBride.

"In case you were wondering, this is how *I* feel. Play the last song 'When You Are Old' when you can." Brett loves his music; I can still hear the songs when I close my eyes. I had told him I loved him so many times throughout our lifetime, but I just wanted him to really *feel* it. That song sung in her sweet voice represents everything he means to me. I never asked for much from my family, but I did need something from my brother. He had to make it.

I prayed that he would listen, really listen, and understand. And, I hugged him goodbye.

On, September 26, 2006, my brother was back on a plane heading back to Clear Haven. He had been there less than a year earlier. This was no free card, not by a long shot. It would cost another twenty-five thousand.

Our mother put October's fee on her credit card, both of us knowing full well that she just couldn't afford to pay this, nor November or December either. Brett had no money, no assets, and so I was trying to think of something creative, anything at all. There is no explanation why I would ever know who to call. I suppose it was maybe a survival instinct, as after all I have always been very street smart. Brett's pension was the only thing I could think of that might have a little value. In Canada, we are not entitled to cash out our pension plan until we are sixty-five. I maneuvered my way through the rules and managed to find a loophole that if a person has some sort of "extraordinary circumstances," this pension fund could be unlocked. After much begging and pleading, I put the details in writing and faxed it to Georgina at the Revenue Agency. I explained that this was a life and death situation and my brother needed the money to pay for treatment. I respectfully requested that they give him access to his full amount of $27,000. After all, he wouldn't need to worry about his retirement if this didn't work.

When Brett signed the paperwork I faxed him, he wasn't really appreciative of the lengths I had gone to arrange this, nor thankful at all for them doing it.

"It's my fucking money, they have to give it to me," he snapped.

I was still taken aback when he acted a little pissy, after all he used not to be that way, but his sense of entitlement shocked me that day. He did not see himself like the rest of the world and it didn't even occur to him that everyone else has to wait until their sixties. My brother felt justified that he should get it handed to him today.

"Entitled." I had never used that word to describe my brother before, and it frightened me.

After years on this rollercoaster ride of addiction, Brett had a twisted view of what the world owed him. He was wallowing in his own self-pity. His life entitled him to act in ways that were immature and emotionally irresponsible. As this progressed, he demanded more of the world and expected less from himself. Through the fogged glass of addiction, and without the ability for self-reflection, he just couldn't see his true self. He could not see that his life was the result of how he was living it. And I continued to feel so completely helpless.

Within two weeks, a letter arrived on bright orange paper telling me that he knew he should have said something when we went whitewater rafting; that everything he had learned was to speak up about his feelings when "he knew a drink was in the distance." He knew that he fell into isolation and depression and felt too proud to say anything; how much work everyone had put into the last upswing and he didn't want to disappoint us again. He felt so happy at the candle shop, then BOOM. Something broke his spirit and he just didn't know what to say. He promised once again that he now knew what he needed to do to get healthy and once back on track, he could give back to me for all I had done. As always, he signed, "love Brett."

I had asked him once a while ago, "What goes on in your head when you want to take that first drink?"

"I don't know," he replied and this was well after many attempts at rehab, doctors, and therapy sessions.

"Well, don't you think that is the most important thing you need to figure out?"

This time I needed to know more, so when we chatted on the phone, I pressed a little. Or maybe it was a lot. What exactly had been going on the weekend of our rafting trip when he had been doing so well, then once again disappeared, and back to the bottle.

"I had been unpacking some things, looking through old albums and I found a teeny bluish-green pill in the corner of one of the boxes. I didn't know what it was, so I took it." As it turned out, it wasn't quite the same story as he conveyed in his letter to me. His motivation wasn't really that he was in a deep, dark depression when we were in Banff; he was coming off a high. The little pill was Ativan, which is used for anxiety. It acts on the brain and nerves to produce a calming effect.

I know how it makes me feel. It was the only time I ever took medication. I had to take two to be able to step on a plane as back then I had a phobia of flying. Just another unrealistic fear my anxiety was telling my head. The plane could go down and my heart wouldn't even skip a beat.

And so, when that bluish-green pill wears off, that is all it takes for an addict to want and need something more.

A month later, another letter arrived in my mailbox.

He said there was nothing more to say or promise, but the pain and guilt he was feeling was beyond what he could have imagined. He also said that we had given him a glimmer of hope. There was "no fucking way" he was going to live like this. He said the demons kept lingering and he had to find a way to leave them writhing in the sand for longer than six months. Or perhaps they were a collection of demons that he would have to purge in time. He promised himself this.

It made him sick that he was there in rehab after a beautiful rafting trip, walking Indie, and missing Kaddi's birthday. He had made a promise to himself that he would be healthy on his birthday on September 15, but of course that promise fell through like all the others.

He would share that no words could describe how much he missed me; how empty he felt not seeing me the last two months. He reiterated how we three have created a true, beautiful bond and we were going to grow old with it, with new grandkids one day. "I'M NOT DONE WITH MY DREAMS."

He ended his letter with a quote from his favorite book, *Hardcore Troubadour; The Life and Near Death of Steve Earle*. Something along the lines of being bone tired, exhausted from his self-indulgent life, and feeling wretched about putting his family through such pain.

My brother felt so much shame and guilt for everything that he was doing. We loved and forgave him but I don't think he forgave himself. I think he was doing a good job of trying to convince himself that he did when he was sober, but when he started drinking the shame would take over. Or maybe it took over and he started drinking. I don't know. That is just another part of this complex puzzle and why at times he was so disgusted he couldn't look at himself in the mirror. Both literally and figuratively as I learned later he actually removed the mirrors off his walls. Like many of the things that happened, I had never even heard of such a thing.

Together, once again, our Mom and Brett came up with a viable plan. He had no job, no money, no home, and extensive bills, so he felt it was better to come home thirty days early. He could use the money saved from the last month of treatment to get the valuable help that he needed. My brother had already arranged an appointment with Dr. Dimirsky, and promised to go to AA and see an AADAC counselor as soon as he got home. He would stay with Mom again, and when he was steady and on track, then and only then would he look for a job.

"It's a great plan, Jode. Don't worry."

There wasn't much money left from the release of his early pension fund. The taxes came off the check from the government instantly and although I didn't know the exact amount, I thought he would have received sixteen or seventeen thousand. Maybe. Montreal would have cost at least sixteen grand for the two months, so what money would be left? Before I agreed to get involved, I made Mom absolutely swear he had to use every cent of that money to pay for his treatment. There was to be no helping or bailing him out. So now I didn't know if that happened or not, but I was not going to ask.

Mom did mention to me, although briefly, that she'd found a "dual diagnosis" treatment center in Vancouver that she offered to send him to for the last thirty days. Sadly, I admit it flew right over my head as, at the time, I still had no knowledge of concurrent disorders, that there was a mental health issue that needed exploring, not just rehab to stop drinking. If our mother had learned something new, she didn't fill me in on it.

Brett declined Mum's offer, hopped back on a plane home sixty days into a ninety-day program from his seventh attempt at rehab. He had been back for only five days when I already began feeling uneasy. I knew he hadn't fulfilled his promises and he had made no attempt at any therapy, support, or help at all in those short few days. He wanted to pick up a few of his larger things from storage and so he called to borrow Jim's truck. We loaned it to him. And when night fell and we expected him back, he was a no show. And then day, night, day, night.

I didn't know what to say to my husband as I wasn't even sure what to say to myself. In my heart, I wanted so much for things to be different, and I believe it's possible, because the alternative is too painful to bear. But I know it is not possible. My reality is not because I am "on a high horse," being judgmental, or thinking I am better than everyone else like our mother always likes to say to me. It is my reality because everything and everyone is *exactly* the same. It is what the addictions community calls "The Definition of Insanity": doing the same thing over and over again and expecting a different result. I have no idea what our mother tells herself.

Brett had been missing for five days and my calls to him went unanswered. They went instantly to voice mail. And then finally he called.

"Hey," he said simply. Not his regular voice but yet the one I absolutely recognized.

"Jesus Christ, Brett, where are you? We are absolutely worried sick and Jim needs his truck for work," I said, trying hard not to freak out.

"I know. I am sorry."

Sorry, oh God, how I know. He was always so sorry.

"Where are you?" I repeated.

"I'm in Sylvan, downtown at Inn at the Lake." I knew exactly where that was. Not because this was a tiny town, but more because we have joked about this place many times. Inn at the Lake. It sounds so beautiful, peaceful, and its advertisement in the yellow pages describes it perfectly "just steps away from the sandy beaches of Sylvan Lake." It sounds blissful, exactly where you would book to bring your family for summer vacation, right? That is until you got there and then it would be a helluva surprise. It was one of those neglected, run down, incredibly cheap hotels and, since people aren't lining up to stay there, a perfect hideaway for those who are down and out, with no place to call home.

"I will be right there. Brett, you get me the keys to that truck."

"I'll leave them under the mat," he said.

Jim drove me and we sat in complete silence through town, passing the waterslides, ice cream parlor downtown, and the cabins on the lakeshore before turning around the bend. As he hit the signal to turn right into the hotel parking lot, we both spotted Jim's Chevy truck, the windshield completely smashed. My husband looked at me, yet didn't say a word, although I knew what he was thinking as I continued to expect so much of him. He pulled up beside the driver's door and I got out.

"I'll see you at home," he said.

I opened the door to the truck, flipped back the mat, grabbed the keys, and started the ignition. I was startled by Brett's *Soul Asylum* CD bursting through the speakers, and so I reached over and turned it down. I sat for a couple of minutes alone with my thoughts, then I picked up my cell phone and called Brett.

"You need to come out here. I want to talk to you," I said, surprised that he answered and hanging up without giving him a chance to respond.

As he emerged from his hell hole, many thoughts swirled in my mind. He shuffled across the parking lot looking like shit. I unrolled the window and we both were silent for a few seconds. And I took a deep breath.

"Brett, I can't do this anymore. I'm sorry. I refuse to help you in this life that you have created for yourself any longer."

He said nothing, just looked blankly at me.

"When you are ready, when you are really ready to make changes and embrace recovery, I will be here," I said stoically.

He looked down at the ground.

"Did you hear me?"

He nodded slightly.

"Brett, look at me." And he looked up with sad eyes. "I need you to hear me, to really hear me, this is important. If you are stuck, if you have nowhere to go, if you need help, please go to AA. They will know what to do." I paused for just a couple of seconds, to gather just a little more strength. "And Brett, no matter what, I need you to always remember, don't ever forget it, how much I love you."

"Jodee, don't worry, I don't even want to drink when I go back in there," he said so confidently.

"The thing is, Brett, the scary thing is I believe that you believe that," I replied.

And that was the last word said as I pulled away, watching through my rearview mirror as he went back inside. The warm tears began to roll down my cheeks and I cried. And cried. And cried.

I loved my brother above all others for almost half my life. I had tried to protect him from the effects of alcohol since he was two years old.

My world was crumbling around me. I couldn't save him. I finally had realized, only he could do that. I pray he forgives me. I had to save myself.

"RUNAWAY TRAIN "

The constant heartbreaking phone calls continued for a couple of weeks. And not just from my brother. I had made it perfectly clear to our mother and Nicole about my new position—"I don't want to hear it"—cutting them off mid-sentence over and over again. To them, that meant I didn't care about my brother or my family.

I was still haunted by the ringing telephone. I no longer had any relationship or physical contact with our dad. I hadn't for quite some time. Over the years, I had let so many things go, turned the other cheek because he's my father after all and I love him. But what I couldn't handle were Dad's continued drunken calls. Of course, Brett did it too.

There was one big difference between the phone calls from my father and my brother: Dad became an ass hole when he was drunk and Brett, if possible, became sweeter (although I am not sure which of these calls was worse).

I refused to listen to the negative things Dad would say about Brett, like why the hell he wasn't working. And I did resent that he was nowhere around to encourage or help his son. When it happened, I wouldn't react; my magic hang-ups eventually worked and the calls stopped.

But Brett was still dialing my number over and over. I never knew whether it would be a sad voice just wanting to talk or hysterical wails of someone in need and I just couldn't take it anymore. "Brett, you listen to me, and I mean it. You are never under any circumstances to call me when you are drunk again. Never."

My bath and body company was flourishing beyond my wildest expectations and it was certainly not an option to neglect my company this time round, especially during the busiest weeks of the year.

But, I was not about to take any chances. On December 26, 2006 after celebrating Christmas with my own family, my business responsibilities lightened and I had time to regroup. I called and changed my cell number.

It didn't change anything or remove any of the pain but in a small way I had a sense of peace as I knew, if it rang, it was only Jim or one of the boys as I didn't give anyone else the number. I didn't know what else to do; moving to Siberia was not an option.

It had been over six years—six long painful years—since I recognized a problem and I had asked Brett to live with us when we moved to Sylvan Lake in 2000. I am five foot seven; I was down to 108 lbs. I was struggling each morning just to get out of bed, and my husband was worried about my health, telling me my eyes were sunk deep into my head. In every sense, I felt like I was not going to survive this.

I needed to see my therapist Terry.

As I sat on the black leather couch, I began to speak.

"You know, I think back to when Jim and I first met and we weren't even married yet. My nana had a little dog named Benji when she died. Our mom took him for a while then she called us to take him as she felt it was too hard to look after him. She said she had a demanding job; somehow to her the rest of us didn't. Of course, without question, I said yes. Here we had this dog; he couldn't even walk up the stairs as he had such bad arthritis."

Terry just listened.

"Oh, and this story gets better," I said. "He was so old that he had trouble going to the bathroom, so here was this twenty-two-year-old guy in his robe on the back lawn, with a little piece of bathroom tissue, struggling to wipe a dog's ass." I smirked just a little, trapped in what was funny and twisted both at the same time. "Finally, Jim realized that this wasn't fair to the dog so he told me he was taking him for a walk but actually had him put down. And my mother's reaction? She was absolutely furious at us."

I started to cry.

"I am trying to finally do the right thing, for me, for Brett, for my own family, and they just won't leave me alone. This isn't just about Brett. Not everything that happens is his fault. So much of this started long ago and it just never ends. Our mom, my sister, and my brother completely suck the life out of me! Alcoholism aside, they call me to fix their problems. I don't hear from them at any other time unless they want something. 'Give me money, give me a job, look after Nana, take my teenage daughter, fix this dilemma.' It never ends—and neither me, nor my own family, get anything. Absolutely nothing in return! My God, my own mother has a birthday party for Brett's dog, but she doesn't even know her own grandsons' birthdays."

The weight of loss and shame was so heavy that it pulled the tears from my eyes and put a deep ache in my heart.

"It was different with Brett; he was always there for me, *always*. Through good and bad. We were there for each other; from the minute he was born. He gave, I gave. He wasn't selfish; he wasn't self-centered. Besides my husband, he is the greatest person I have ever known. And that's gone; he's gone."

I tried hard to swallow back the tears.

"What have I done to my own family? What kind of mother allows for this to go on? Let's someone cut their wrists or swallow pills in front of young children, and doesn't put a stop to it? What kind of mother does that!?"

Terry didn't answer, rather he just allowed me to keep talking.

"I don't know about the three of them—Mom, Nicole, and Brett—but I knew better! I have always known better. What damage might I have done to those little boys?"

I was now crying so hard, barely able to breathe, as Terry leaned over, struggling to grab some Kleenex for me. I felt like a failure; to my husband, my brother, and especially to my own children. I never wanted to say it out loud, that somehow it would disrespect and hurt Ricky and Ryan to know how I really felt. That I had enough love in my heart for all of them but to tell them the reason why I sacrificed their needs over someone else's. I was so wounded and broken from childhood and the responsibility that was put upon me so long ago and I couldn't find the strength to come to grips with all I had ever known. I loved my brother like he was my own son.

As I continued to sob, I was not faced with the reality of Brett's life. I was faced with the reality of my own.

"You know, Jodee, your mother, sister, and Brett have perhaps come to rely on you as the stable one who fixes things in the family. But I can see that you are getting tired and run down. You have enough on your plate with your own family, so I think it's okay for you to not always be the fixer in the family," Terry concluded.

The guilt and shame was overwhelming and the tears kept flowing. I was stuck between the two family groups and I was drowning.

"Jodee, you are not responsible for their lives," Terry said.

I did not reply.

"Jodee, did you hear me?" he repeated.

And I did hear him, loud and clear. But I know my brother, sister, and mother, so we sat silently for the longest time.

"They will never understand," I finally replied. I was thirty-nine years old.

"SLEEPYHOUSE "

I tried so hard to stick to what I had told Brett, staying firm with my boundaries. Six months sober and I would see him, not before. But, I loved and missed him so much that I couldn't quite make it that long.

Even though he had sold his house almost two years earlier, I was still paying for the storage unit—about $79 a month. I had asked so many times for him to pay me back, anything; any attempt at all or even to get my name off the lease would have helped. Yet, my requests had been avoided.

Tired of just being ignored, I took my key, opened the door of the small storage shed, and sold off the front-load washer and dryer that Mom had bought for him years before. I could only get a thousand, enough to cover about half the debt, but I didn't do it for the money anyway. I could tell from both Mom and Brett, each and every time I had mentioned it to them, it was almost annoyance that I was bringing it up. *She can afford it. What's the big deal?* And they didn't have to say it for me to know that was how they felt. It was just another expectation that they had of me. I promised myself in this new life of mine that I would hold Brett to the same standards and responsibilities as I held everyone else in this world. I wasn't doing him any favors treating him any other way. In fact, I believe my previous behavior was crippling him and his ability to be a functioning adult.

When I told them what I had done, my brother said nothing and our mother was absolutely infuriated at me.

Brett had been sober for three full months so I was incredibly excited and proud that he was coming to see me. He was finally going to pick up his belongings, so I was meeting him at my shop, which was just across the road from the storage facility. He called the house to say he was running behind and would be about two hours late and that I should meet him at the unit.

"No worries," I said. "But do you have a big flashlight? It is getting dark and there are no lights at the storage unit."

"Yup," he said simply.

"Okay, see ya in a bit."

As I put on my jacket, Jim asked again if I was sure that I didn't want him to come along. It had been so hard not to see my brother all this time that I was really exhilarated and full of happiness. I preferred to go on my own. I drove the five or so minutes through town, down the highway, then turned right into the industrial part of town.

I expected Brett any minute so I backed up, parked, rolled down the window, and anxiously waited for him to arrive.

About ten minutes later, he turned into the small parking lot. I turned off the ignition and jumped out, both of us getting out of our trucks at the same time. He tripped slightly over his own two feet, then stood up straight and walked towards me. Instantly, I knew and my heart began to race.

"Brett, oh, my God, you are drinking," I blurted out.

"Jeez, I am not drinking, Jodee." I knew he was and he began to yell. "I need you to explain some things to me. Why do you treat me like dog shit!? You know, perfect strangers treat me better than you do. Do you think that's right!?"

This wasn't the sweet, kind, passive drunk man that he usually was. He was fuming mad and tonight everything was my fault. I was filled with overwhelming emotions—sadness, disappointment, and shock. As he got closer to me, hurling these hurtful insults, for the first time I also had a sense of fear. Immediately, I was very aware that I was very much alone, no one was around that area at that time of night and I turned to take the ten or so steps back into my truck. One step, two, a few more, then he grabbed my shoulder and I struggled to open the door, terrified of what he might do! I managed to get inside with Brett reaching through the window, trying to grab my keys, my hands shaking so hard I was having trouble getting them into the ignition.

"That was my fucking washer and dryer, not yours. WHAT THE FUCK IS WRONG WITH YOU?!!"

I turned the key and the truck started. I threw it into drive and peeled out of the parking lot with gravel flying behind me. I had never witnessed him like this before. I didn't know who that person was.

When I got home and Jim saw me, I was frightened, shaking, and beyond hysterical. After consoling me for a few minutes, he picked up his cell phone and dialed Brett's number. When he didn't answer, Jim left a message, quick and to the point.

"You had better get out of town. If I find you, I will fucking kill you!!" he warned my brother.

My husband rarely snaps. His protective instincts had kicked in and he had finally had enough.

I didn't know if Brett had really been sober for three months. At this point, I didn't know anything at all. I called Mom the next day to go over the events and she was incensed.

"How dare Jim talk to Brett like that" was her reaction.

I was fighting with all of them, my sister, mother, brother. I was so exhausted. After yelling for a couple minutes and getting nowhere I simply hung up the phone.

I had had to live with so many realities these last few months, all the wrongs that I had done. The mistakes I had made with Brett, what I had asked of my own husband and, worst of all, of my own children. I know now that we don't do anyone any good when we sacrifice our own needs for those of someone else, regardless of who they are. But we just don't see it at the time.

I had to start worrying about my own family—putting them first—because we are not impervious to life's same problems as everyone else.

Ry had taken off on his scooter and was back a short time later. When I asked where he had been, he got the strangest look on his face—like he was lying. He said he was having a sleepover and get-together at his buddy's, and although he was still acting strangely and I was suspicious, I trusted him. So off he went.

Early the next morning, we realized that there was a big white lie, as I found an empty paper bag in his laundry basket that had big, bold, red writing, "DON'T DRINK AND DRIVE." Soon Ricky came to tell us that a kid in the neighborhood had caught Ryan hiding a bottle of booze in the trees the day before. I suppose Rick knew in his gut that at only fourteen years of age, his little brother was too young for this. When Ry got home, we sat him down, and asked for the truth. He admitted one of his buddy's older brothers got him a bottle for the party last night. We sat as a family and talked logically and openly about alcohol like we had before, reminding our sons about our family tree, which includes their Uncle Brett.

The boys knew I was no angel, although they didn't know everything.

That's how it all started with Brett and me, innocently partying in high school like everyone does. But there is one detail that is not the same. I used to drink, it never became a problem for me, but I chose to stop. Brett drank and eventually became "addicted" to alcohol. That is a huge difference. Why can some people occasionally drink without ever developing a problem? Yet someone else deteriorates right before your eyes. Some people go to unfathomable lengths just to get high with the promise of death not being able to stop them. I do think the term "alcoholism" is grossly misused, labelled, or misdiagnosed. Not everyone whose lives unravel has an actual addiction, but rather a problem with alcohol. All the scientists and medical professionals in the world may have differing opinions, about the cause and the cure, and what you believe certainly will take you on different paths. Whatever the reason is for people to become alcoholics, I was trying my best not to take any chances with my own children.

My husband and I, although frightened, were realistic about young people experimenting with alcohol and remember what it was like to be young. Jim and I sat and talked to Ry and Ricky for the longest while about Ryan sneakily hiding a bottle of booze. "Ryan, you are grounded for the whole summer. Not because of the drinking, we understand that will happen, but you are being grounded for the lying and excessive measures you took to do it."

As we had many times before, we reminded our sons that we have nothing against drinking alcohol; we understood that both of them would likely do that. What we were against is staying out late at night at the bar rather than being home with their family when they got older. And since we have a history of alcoholism on both sides of our family, we had always tried to teach them to respect alcohol. A beer on a hot summer day after you mow the lawn is totally acceptable, but coming home after work every day and having a few, is not, as that can grow into an addiction.

"What your Dad and I have decided is that for the next two months, you may go to work at the ice cream shop and then you have to come home. You can still do all the things you want to do, except staying over at a friend's house. But whatever those things are, I will be with you."

To most people, it wouldn't seem like grounding, not in the typical sense anyhow. But, I spent the next eight weeks with Ryan and his friends going to the pool, movies, the beach, and boating. Holding him hostage in our home wasn't the lesson we were going for.

From the time my brother was a teenager going snowmobiling, skiing, camping, fishing, hanging out with many of his friends or with his father, drinking was always involved. He had never done those things sober and when he tried he just couldn't find the joy. "Fucking boring," is an exact quote. So instead of working through it, he just stopped doing those things all together. We wanted to show Ry that you didn't need to be boozing it up to enjoy activities in life.

Meanwhile, my relationship with Nicole could be characterized as sketchy at best. She was divorced now from Adam. He was a nice, stable, hard-working man and in my opinion that was boring for my sister. I imagine it was painfully hard for him, as I am very aware how my sister talks to people; it wouldn't matter if it was her husband. The new "me" refused to give in when she asked for something and, as usual, she was sweet as cherry pie, until I said NO. Then came the fallout—screams, shouts, obscenity laced emails, and phone messages. That almost always ended with Jim and me not being able to see our nieces. That is until she calmed down weeks later, or needed a babysitter, whichever came first. But I loved her, so I continued to turn a blind eye.

I had no relationship at all with our mother. I had not seen or heard from her or Brett since that disastrous evening at the storage shed. Through Nicole, I reiterated to our mother my same message each and every time: "I will only see Mom if she agrees to meet me at a therapist's office."

I admit it took me a long time to realize that the relationship we had was not healthy and I thought we needed help to work on that. My biggest desire was that we could finally be united as a family when it came to Brett. But, my requests went denied, and months and months and months went by.

I know Mom believed I abandoned Brett, that I turned my back on him. She has no conscious thought that when I did absolutely everything to look after my brother and when I did absolutely nothing; it all *stayed exactly* the same. Luckily for me, what our mother thinks has never worn away my self-confidence or broken my spirit. I made a conscious decision many years ago to surround myself with people who build me up, not tear me down. That includes my husband, our friends, the family members we do see, and my wonderful, supportive girlfriends at work. However, the part that does rip through my soul and is hard to live with is I fear she made Brett believe I had abandoned him, too.

"BACK TO THE WALL"

It had been close to a year since I'd had any contact with Mom, but in the spring of 2008, the ice seemed to have melted. With my sister's help, Mom finally agreed to attend a therapy session with me. I never imagined it would be awkward to see our mother, but when she walked into the waiting room, she felt to me like a stranger.

Terry knew why I wanted to meet her there. I just felt we needed to find a common ground, and in the worst case scenario, a referee. I just wanted to try to make her understand my viewpoint. This whole situation was killing me and my family, not to mention Brett as well. And, based on what I'd recently learned, I was worried sick about another child, not just my own. Now, my young niece.

I knew things could get dicey, so I wanted to be aligned in my thoughts and began the session by reading a letter aloud to her:

Mom,

I have wanted you to come here for so long—our family is broken and we all need to work together to fix it. We need to listen to these professionals, and do what they say. Exactly what they say; this is not working, mother.

It just seems like you are blaming everyone else, like no one else is allowed to be hurt, or have feelings or opinions. Mom, you have never even asked if my own kids are ok. You divorced two men, both of them because of drinking and it was nowhere near this bad. Not even remotely close to this bad. Why was that ok for you?

She started squirming in her chair.

These horrors are not ending. The drinking and crazy things Brett is doing, barely hanging on, back in the hospital for whatever has happened this time. Then I learn the next weekend he is taking Payton. Mom, this continues to make him believe that once he sobers up for a few days things are alright, and they are not alright. So far from alright that I don't even know what to say anymore. Not to mention something bad could happen to Payton.

"Brett would never drink with Payton, Jodee," she snapped, interrupting me.

I didn't even acknowledge she just said that, after all that had been the tipping point of losing Dawn-Marie when he drank when looking after Matthew. Wouldn't all of our lives be different if love was enough? If love could keep him sober. Her comment bordered on insanity to me, so I brushed off those thoughts and kept reading.

When I reminded her again about what happened the storage unit evening, she got agitated and irate and couldn't control herself any longer.

"When Brett got home that night, he played me the voice mail message that Jim left him. How dare Jim talk to Brett like that. That's how people get hurt, Jodee!"

A full year had gone by, yet she was still livid. I agreed with her, someone could have gotten hurt, although I knew she didn't mean it could have been me. And in her mind, my brother still couldn't, or wasn't, doing anything wrong. She inferred that somehow my husband was to blame.

I retreated as no one was ever going to change her point of view, so I didn't even get to the part about the issues within *our* relationship. I bit my tongue once again as I knew, if I was going to have a relationship at all with our mother, I needed to remain silent. Since my family tree was losing limbs, I was trying desperately to hold on as long as I could. And it would be an impossible task for Terry, or any therapist, to help someone who has no flexibility at all.

By the end of May, Ricky was celebrating his high school graduation and we were so proud of him. The kid's as smart as a whip, and loves to work, but he hated school, it had always bored him as he is more of a hands-on type guy. Since neither Jim nor I graduated, we were over the top thrilled that he got his diploma. There was to be a big get together with speeches and a ceremony in our arena that afternoon. Later in the evening there would be a dinner banquet. In between the events, the graduating class was planning to go downtown in their caps and gowns to get their pictures taken at the lake. Graduation weekend is a very big deal in this small community.

Mom would be arriving within a couple of hours and I was just finishing up at work. In the same moment that I hung up the phone with a customer, my computer beeped with an email. It was my sister letting me know that she was coming to the ceremony, but wasn't going to come to the dinner celebration this evening as her new boyfriend was coming home from being away at work.

Instantly, I was furious, and I will take full responsibility for part of this. Ricky had told me he didn't want her there, but I had done it again. I didn't listen to what *he* wanted; I didn't put his needs first. I knew she didn't belong there; she didn't have any relationship with her nephews. "She's family, she should come," I told him. So, I bought her a ticket.

I called to let her know she needed to decide. "If you aren't at that grad dinner tonight, Nicole, our relationship is over."

We put on our best clothes, looked at both of our handsome sons dressed to the nines, Ricky in a tuxedo, and we ate and danced, celebrating his achievement. We had a table of eight—one seat remained empty.

This was not an overreaction on my part; this had been going on since my sister had been a teenager and getting progressively worse. I was not going to do this forever; hurting me was one thing, but not my family. I wouldn't put up with it anymore. A little normalcy, someone to care about my children, even for a couple hours. Is that too much to want? What's the saying? The straw that breaks the camel's back. This was a goddamn bushel of straw, I was done.

When I stopped at the mailbox in early December, I found a small white, bubble envelope. I knew the handwriting well although I hadn't seen it for a while. I undid the sticky tape and pulled out a five by seven inch photo that my brother had taken. It was in the woods, with big pine trees, a green tee-pee style tent, and next to it a black bear. On orange paper, in red pen:

HAPPY "B" DAY

My first Released Photo

"Searching"

♥ *Brett*

I didn't even show it to Jim; instead I just went downtown and when I got home carefully placed both the handwritten note and the camping photo in a designer wooden frame that I had bought at the store. I grabbed a nail from the garage; pounded a little hole in the wall next to the bedside table in our spare room just above the wooden ornaments that spelled "B-E-A-C-H." I ended up there once or twice a week as Jim's snoring was sometimes unbearable, so there it would hang and make me feel close to the brother I barely saw.

I cried there often in that room down the hall, while pretending every day that I was okay. Sometimes that was the truth and sometimes it was the lie I let my husband and children believe; after all there was nothing they could do to help me. I prayed there too, asking God to make something bad happen. No one should get hurt, just bad enough to make things change. Maybe he could let my brother get so desperate that he robbed a bank, so finally he would have the consequence he needed and be forced into months or years of sobriety in jail. I knew I should have asked for a miracle that he would just get well, but I had stopped asking for that a long time ago. I knew even God would need to go to more extraordinary measures.

"SLIVER"

I grabbed my favorite mug, filled it up, then turned on my computer bright and early before work. I could see an email from our mother, with the ominous heading: "CHANGE OF PLANS."

February 15, 2009

In just a few sentences, Mom let me know that she was changing her will; she wanted to do it while she was healthy enough to do so. She said she was not confident that her children would have "my best interest at heart."

And she would let me know once it was complete.

And in an instant our relationship was over.

She had finally broken me. And this wasn't about money. Quite frankly, I thought, my brother and sister were going to spend all her money. Me? I would not do what would be in her best interest? Didn't she think we had enough drama? This email was my tipping point; nothing I ever did would be enough for my mother.

I love her but I couldn't keep doing this; it was always something, a NEVER-ENDING BATTLE. I was completely beaten down. Every day it seemed to be something and then something else and something after that. By the time Jim got up, I had already replied, something along the lines of: "No matter what I do, it is not good enough for my mother. I have decided I am done trying."

"She'll call and apologize," Jim said, after I shared the story.

"Oh, okay. Then I will say, 'No problem.' Maybe she just went crazy for a few minutes, I get it."

We moved on to other subjects, enjoying our coffees together until it was time to go to work. I leaned in and kissed my husband goodbye, "Have a great day. Oh, by the way, Annie is *never* going to call and apologize."

After all, I know my mother.

I have lost other branches from my immediate family tree and I tried desperately to hold on. And now another branch was lying on the ground. Broken relationships with my father, my sister, and now my mother. I am grateful that my marriage to Jim is so rock solid; I could have lost that too. My family members were never strong enough to withstand the pressures of this journey through addiction, certainly when all of the characters (myself included) had issues of their own. My brother wasn't the only one who needed to look in the mirror.

I had been paying for my brother's therapy for so long that I'd paid probably close to three thousand dollars by then. I hadn't seen him, just the occasional email from him here and there. He had lost so many jobs due to his inability to stay sober and he didn't have benefits, so I felt at least this was a way for him to know I continued to believe in him and to encourage his sobriety. I hadn't even told my own husband; with everything that had happened I feared he would not understand how I was continuing to spend our hard-earned money on Brett. Was this enabling? I didn't think so at the time.

On, July 9, 2009, I arrived at a Starbucks in Calgary to meet Brett. He quickly jumped out of his car and came to my window to see what I wanted to order. He returned holding a huge cup of coffee for himself and passed me a pink, slushy smoothie through my driver's side window. "Hey, follow me to the park," he said.

We pulled off to the side of the road, he parked, and I parked right behind him. Indie jumped out the door as Brett got out. My brother still took my breath away when I saw him. When he was doing well, he is as handsome as any movie star.

"Oh, my God!!" I squealed so loudly that a couple of people walking nearby stopped in their tracks to stare. "Where did you get that?" I asked completely shocked and blown-away.

My brother was cradling a brown, wooden jewelry box with brass buttons. It resembled a smaller version of a pirate's chest, with small gold chains hanging from the side.

"I got it for ya." He handed me the treasure chest. "I found it at a pawn shop. I remember when we were young, I was sitting on your bed talking to you when you would be getting ready to go out with your friends. Your Rob

Lowe poster was hanging on the wall and just below it was your jewelry box. You know, just like this, the one that Auntie Sharon had bought for you one Christmas."

It didn't just *look* like my childhood jewelry box—it was an *exact* replica. The part that stunned me, the part that warmed my heart, was that back then he would have been only twelve years old. Why would a young boy even remember that? So completely thoughtful and sweet.

We walked and talked and talked some more. He had been sober for a couple of months and had been working close by at a job he absolutely hated. I don't want to give the impression we actually had a deep conversation about sobriety, or any conversation at all about it, because we didn't. But when I saw his physical transformation and he told me about his job and how long he'd been there, I could figure out the timeline. The job was in his field of power engineering, but not in a gas plant environment, so it was not like what he was used to. It was "shit pay" as he put it, only thirty dollars per hour, half of what he used to make. He had regular job hours, only two days off a week, no benefits, no sick time for three months, and no overtime.

After he finished telling me all about it, I gave a little giggle, leaned in, and kissed him on the cheek. "You hate it there, Brett, but you are sober. Sorry if I don't feel bad for you."

We kept walking for a while. Indie was quite a bit ahead of us, roaming around some trees.

"Brett, don't you worry that you'll get a ticket? Isn't he supposed to be on a leash?" I asked, Chevy right by my side.

"Fuck that," he replied. And that too was typical of how different he had become; my brother refused to follow even the simplest of life's rules.

"Hey, how's that movie coming along?" he asked.

I spun around quickly as I was about six or seven steps ahead of him, "What did you say?"

"You know, the movie. The one you are writing about me."

I couldn't believe it. In 2005, our lives had become such a crazy, complicated, out-of-control story that I started keeping notes. I told Brett back then I was going to write a movie about his life, because I didn't think anyone would ever possibly believe that this could happen from just alcohol. I thought it could be a powerful lesson; since almost everyone in the world has children who will one day enter high school or go off to college and start drinking. And to make people be even more aware if alcoholism runs in their family. He had not acknowledged or replied at the time; I didn't even think he had been listening to me.

"I stopped writing quite a while ago."

"Why?" he asked, looking stunned.

"Brett, no one wants a lesson. They want an inspiration."

"Don't worry Jodee. *I will* be an inspiration," he said positively. "You gotta keep writing."

When I didn't answer fast enough, he repeated, "Jodee."

"Okay, I'll keep writing."

It really was a beautiful summer day, the sun beaming, the dogs were barking, and I could smell the fresh flowers in the air.

"Hey, did you get that bear pic I mailed you for your birthday?" Brett asked.

"Yes, I did, thanks," I replied. That was over seven months ago, but of course I hadn't seen him since then.

"You should have seen it. If that was rock bottom, I fucking loved it. 79 ford, 77 camper, 72 pilot. An attainable fantasy come true. A new Dodge, a fifth wheel, a big house, and a line of credit, they can have it. I'll take a woodpecker as an alarm clock, a lynx in my yard, and a heavy river to slow the world down. On the other side of this newfound serenity, I had to learn to feel the pain, stinging me every time. Two baby bears, so cute, fuck. They seemed so strong together, no MAMA, just brother and sister. I left them berries and homo milk, just like Trevor drinks. They liked me, I knew it."

Brett and cousin Trevor had seen each other a lot, since both of them lived in Calgary. It was amazing how similar Trevor and Brett were, well, minus the addicted part. Trevor is the kindest soul, introverted, quiet, sensitive, and would give the shirt off his back to anyone in need. Just like Brett had become, Trevor was a lone wolf, spending much time alone, loving nothing more than enjoying the beauty of the outdoors with his dog, Jack (who happens to be half wolf).

I didn't comment, I just listened intently to Brett's story, trying to absorb everything he had said. When that picture had arrived in my mailbox, I didn't realize where it was taken or what it meant. Now I had the true meaning of what appeared in the photo in play-by-play action. As I began to try to understand, even I couldn't believe it had been two years since I had seen him. Our infamous family and friends grapevine over these last few months told me at least part of the story, although my interpretation would not be quite the same as my brother's.

What most of us would consider to be "rock bottom" situations that would propel us to change—drunk, few worldly possessions, jobless, broke, tired, and alone—were not "rock bottom" for my brother. Describing this beautiful bear story, so tranquil and serene. The fact is he was actually HOMELESS, living in a camper somewhere deep in the woods. Not only was Brett further into his denial about how bad things really were; he was having the time of his life. How do you compete with the version in his mind? I am not sure you can.

With Brett still making no formal commitment to recovery, I believed it was only a matter of time before he took a drink and destruction and his potential death would happen again. My heart just could not take the pain so I did not keep in touch.

I moved on with my life with my own family. I tried to shelter myself from the stories I heard. Mom bought Brett a house; well, not a house exactly. She bought a house and rented it to Brett. She became his landlord.

"You have mail!" echoed through my office when I turned on my computer.

From my sister

Sun, Oct 25, 2009

As hard as I tried to concentrate on my own life with my husband and the wellbeing of my sons, none of this would go away. I wasn't even safe at work.

Nicole accused me once again of not caring, and told me that things were bad again. She told me that I hadn't been part of the family, or at least her life, for two years. And with everything in her she could not understand how I could "pretend" that I didn't have a sister or nieces. She said she used to be sad not seeing or talking to me, but that feeling was now gone and she was ashamed I was her sister.

She proceeded to let me know she was also ashamed at how I treated our mother after all she had done and had been through, NOTHING that I had been around for. And that I had stopped talking to Mom AGAIN over a fucking email.

She then accused me of hurting her so badly, on purpose, when I told her about her childhood. And that unlike me, she wanted MOM in her life.

I don't expect this to make an impact—I am sending this to someone that doesn't give a fuck about ANYONE but herself—but I am telling you how I feel

Have a great life

I was used to these emails by now; they had arrived many times, blaming me for not caring, deserting my family, and abandoning Brett. I do care and I know I have a sister. Deep down maybe that is the reason why I never mentioned our early childhood to my brother. I thought maybe he would resent me, just as Nicole did. There was no reason in my mind for my brother to ever know. I had never told my sister about *her* childhood. That is crazy. I told her about mine when she was struggling with abandonment issues. As usual; nothing I did seemed to be right. I was the family traitor for daring to question all of this.

I was not the solution, but I wouldn't be part of the problem either. I was gaining strength and I felt if the worst happened I could only live with myself knowing that I gave Brett no other option than sobriety. If I had given him money for food or for rent, allowing him the means to use his money to buy booze and he died, I would never forgive myself. It was the line I drew for my own survival and I do believe it is what he needed a long time ago.

In the end, I wouldn't let the negative insults my sister said get to me. And besides it isn't true. I do care about my family. I have proved that to them again and again. I could run from the odd rumor, but what brought me to my knees, each and every time, what I couldn't ignore, implanted in these heinous sentences from my sister was that MY BROTHER WAS IN TROUBLE AGAIN.

"MISERY "

I received a quick email from my brother asking if it was alright if he saw Terry on Friday.

Wed, Dec 2, 2009 12:25 pm

Subject: friday

My head's clear now and Indie is sick of listening to me I think.

I knew what he meant by telling me his head was clear: he had been through another five-week episode with the finale being another job loss and probable ambulance call. I didn't need to be there to witness it; after all, this was never going to go miraculously away. After all, alcoholism is a progressive brain disease. What that means is if you don't stop drinking, the symptoms will get worse with time. I would continue to hide this from my husband and I agreed to keep paying for therapy.

It is a slippery slope when a person's heart is much stronger than their head. I was paying for therapy as a positive, supportive sister. I felt like someone in one of the many families who are in crisis on *Dr. Phil*. The mom is adamant: "Well, I can't let my son or daughter be out on the street!" Meanwhile, her marriage is falling apart from the stress and conflict, there's arguing and tears and more often than not the other siblings are sitting on opposite sides of the stage. We justify the things we do, make excuses, yet we do them anyway. At this stage, should I have been paying over a hundred dollars an hour of my hard-earned money for someone else's therapy? I doubt it. But we need help with that line between helping and enabling; and I am not the expert to draw it. All I know is I would tell that mother to listen carefully to Dr. Phil, or any professional. YES, you can let the one you love be homeless. And if you *all* get help from the beginning; stay aligned as a family, agree to disagree, change the unhealthy patterns and responses maybe it would never get as far as it did for us.

All of this constant pain and torture felt like it was going to go on forever and never end. I suppose that is the point; it does and will go on forever until the addict finds recovery. Or dies. And in the meantime, all anyone can do is try to survive it.

I was excited although apprehensive when Brett wanted to stop by a couple weeks later in the middle of December. The love I feel for my brother is forever; there is *nothing* he could ever do to change that. I would never deny seeing him when he was sober, even if my husband was worried about me, remembering the storage unit evening.

I tried to be prepared for any and all scenarios when it came to seeing Brett. It was the only way I could protect myself from the debilitating pain that I would feel if I saw him intoxicated, because if he was, I would send him away. And if that happened, I would be left imagining how it would end. For my own wellbeing, I had learned to detach. That was another one of the things that I learned on this journey about recovery; I learned that from books I continued to read as well as from the professionals. "Detaching" means loving others so much that you are finally willing to let go of your false sense of control over your loved one's behavior and not allow their addiction to control your own life. It's also knowing that we can't solve problems that aren't ours to solve, keeping in mind that I am still a work in progress. After all, I had been looking after others' problems for far too long and it is a hard habit to break.

When the knock at the door finally came that December day, I was hit with a powerful wave of relief. He wasn't drinking and we had a beautiful weekend together, going for dinner then watching *Inglorious Basterds* on our big screen. Sadly, each time I saw him he became even less of the person he was before. I was not trapped in the past; my comparison was between him then and the alcoholic I had known three years earlier. My wonderful brother was overconfident, arrogant actually, bragging about how amazing he was and how well he was doing. And he seemed to be pissed off at everything and everyone; his sweet demeanor seemed to be gone. I was prepared as well as I could be for what happens when Brett is intoxicated. But I became scared of this altered reality. After all, he was absolutely, one hundred percent, stone-cold, sober. Was this distorted thinking brain damage from years of severe substance abuse? I still don't know.

"Can I tell you something I have never told anyone?" he asked as he stood in my laundry room putting on his shoes.

"Of course," I replied.

"I always felt safe with you. You make me feel better. I thought you should know that," he said.

I smiled just a little. "I know," I said as I gave him a huge hug goodbye.

Sent: Sat, Jan 2, 2010 7:43 pm

Subject: NO RAIN

His email made me smile and reminded me how much he loves his music. Brett said if I am bored I should check out Blind Melon's *Behind the Music* on YouTube.

had fun, thanks

lv Brett

The next few months of winter into spring passed by. I still hadn't heard a peep from our mother and it had been over a year since she sent me the email about changing her will. I learned later she didn't change it, so all of that was completely unnecessary. I wasn't refusing to call her to be stubborn, unreasonable, or difficult; I was trying in some small way to let her know it wasn't alright for her to treat me that way. The more I give, the more she wants. And I was not going to take responsibility for her behavior; after all, the only thing I was guilty of was turning on my computer. And all I really wanted was an apology.

I hadn't seen Brett again for almost nine months and then I received another quick email.

Sent: Thu, Aug 19, 2010 1:52

Just wonderin' if ya needed a hand this fall, wanna get ahead!!!

Instantly, I knew that something catastrophic had happened ending with another job loss, and he needed a job and money. I sent him a cordial "nice to hear from you," ignoring the question then I hit delete.

Another winter flew by. I was busy in my office and my computer beeped with the arrival of a new email.

April 15, 2011 From Brett Tisdale

I apologize for not keepin' in touch, making some changes, thought I would let ya know Indie passed away today.

Talk to ya sometime soon.

"Makin' some changes." Oh, how I wished that were true. But it wasn't true, although I knew he believed it.

I sprang into action and grabbed the brown leather book off the corner of my desk, flipped to W then picked up the phone. I dialed and it rang three times.

"Hello?"

"Hey, Auntie Sharon, it's Jodee."

"Oh, hi."

"Everything is okay, don't worry—Brett just emailed me. Indie died today. Auntie Sharon, you are going to need to call Mom; she'll be devastated."

"Jodee, I will call you back later. Thanks for calling me," she said.

It had been over two years since I heard from our mother. I do love her and my first instinct was to make sure she was alright; after all she had raised Indie most of his life and so she would be filled with so much pain.

I pulled into the garage from work a few days later and closed the electric door. Jim was standing by the deep freeze, just hanging up the phone. As he turned around, I could see the tears and I jumped out of the truck.

"Oh, my God, what has happened?!!" I shrieked, my heart beating wildly as my mind rushed through thoughts of my loved ones and what could have happened.

"I have been on the phone with Nicole. She called and just wouldn't let up. First, she started with saying we care about no one but ourselves. Then she told me she was ashamed that I walked her down the aisle…."

"Okay, this has happened a hundred times before. Who cares? Hang up."

"I did, she just kept calling back."

Unfortunately, that's how it continued; any reason at all for my sister to unload and we got the brunt of it. Today, it turned out she flew off the handle because neither of us had called Mom to console her because Brett's dog died.

"When I told her that no one called us six months ago when we had to put Cole down, she became even angrier," Jim explained. "But, Jode, that's not it."

And he paused before telling me everything.

"She yelled and screamed, blaming me for ruining this whole family. That because of me, it has all been torn apart. All because of what I did."

"What?!" I yelled, as I stood next to a grown forty-three-year-old man, doubled over and crying with shame.

Although it had been over sixteen years since we had separated, the mere mention of it instantly reduced him to tears. The power of shame is very real; it's not imagined. He has loved me, been by my side through a whole lifetime, helping my family over and over again, yet asking nothing in return. All while raising two magnificent boys. Tears continued rolling down his face.

I said, "Look at me," staring into his blue eyes. "You shouldn't feel anything other than pride in the life we have built. I mean it. What happened between us back then has nothing to do with all of this. You are the one person that did the work and changed. We can't change our story of the past; it's the story we have. Here's what I know for sure. This would not be our life if that night had not happened. DO NOT give her that power, do not let my sister get to you."

I was so furious at Nicole; tired of her sharp tongue and unacceptable nastiness. Jim and I have been on the receiving end of blame for so long, remaining silent, taking the high road, but she had finally pushed me beyond my limit. For Nicole to cause my husband intentional harm through blaming him unwarrantedly I could not take. I began writing a scathing email to my sister, years of frustration in four paragraphs, ending with, *Fuck you, Nicole.*

Get a job! Get help! Lose my number! In any order.

I was not proud of this email, filled with foul language and how differently I saw things. I am not proud this is how I felt. I would do anything to put my broken family back together, but I had no control over that, any more than I had control over my brother.

Addiction affects *everyone* in a family; rips relationships to shreds, destroys marriages, changes children, makes us do and say things we would never normally do, and affects everything about our lives. Everyone is so lost and hurt that they sometimes turn the blame to each other. But deflecting blame, losing sight of the issue at hand—which for us is alcohol—is a grave mistake. We *all* suffer but the one who suffers the most, and has the most to lose, is the addict.

I finished typing, scrolled up, and my arrow hovered perfectly over the send key. I took a deep breath, but as furious as I was, I just couldn't do it. It is not who I am, no matter how angry and frustrated I get. I was not going to engage with my sister; that would make things worse.

After all, if I pushed that button, this wouldn't blow over in a couple of months and we would truly never be able to see our beautiful nieces again. So my husband and I would continue to take it, and take it and take it some more.

"FOR MY FRIENDS "

As usual, in a couple of days, my heart stopped racing, my anxiety lightened, and I could begin to focus again.

After more than two years of silence, I made the first move to call our mother and tell her how sorry I was to hear about Indie. I agreed to see her and knew exactly what I was going to say. Or not say.

On a nice sunny day at the beginning of May, I made the hour-and-a-half drive to Calgary. Our mother, although still beautiful, was showing signs of age. It was another harsh reminder to me of how life continues to go by.

I was glad I went. I could see she was in pain, as tears began to fill her eyes. After all, she was the one who had looked after Indie most of this time. We sat in her backyard, at her little garden table, and within minutes Mom started talking about Brett.

"I have already told Brett, there is no way I am doing this again. He is absolutely not to get another dog as I will not look after it." The word *not* was drawn and emphasized, making her point.

She began to tell me how her investment was going, the rental property she had bought just a couple of blocks away. She had a tenant living downstairs, and then my brother lived upstairs in the suite above.

"Since I retired, I thought this would be a good investment for me and motivation for Brett," Mom said. Unfortunately, she didn't think a home of his own, his sisters, my children, his nieces, Dawn-Marie, or a baby were motivation enough. She continued with her story, explaining that he hadn't paid any rent most of the time, and how broke she was. I just faked a smile and nodded, since no one could have seen that coming.

"Brett's doing great right now, but it has been so heartbreaking to watch the drinking the last few months. It has been so hard on me. You should see him. I would iron his white dress shirt for him to help him get ready to go for an interview. He looked so handsome."

I gave no response at all. Ironing the shirt for an almost forty-year-old man; that is so sad on so many levels. And it had actually been eleven years of drinking, not a few months, but I might have been the only one counting.

"Brett had been reading books and doing so well. He was frequenting the library and met a girl that worked there who he really liked. He took her on a date, and ordered a bottle of wine, I mean, what is he supposed to do? Tell every single person he meets his whole story? It is just so sad; I feel so bad for him."

My voice answered that question only in my head. *No, mother, actually I don't expect him to immediately tell someone this whole story.* But there's an entire world out there, full of sober people in recovery. A world full of alcoholics who have worked hard to come to terms with their own truth. They are courageous and brave and they have found the strength, in their own way, to say, "I am an alcoholic." And the point is that they aren't going to stay sober any other way.

I never did know what to call my mother's version of what was going on. There are lots of things he could have told his date. Or how about just taking her out for coffee instead? He could have told her he was on medication and couldn't drink that night; he's allergic; or he could tell her he was a goddamn Mormon. I didn't care.

So, to answer her question, what is he supposed to do? Anything. Anything other than ordering a bottle of wine if you couldn't stop yourself from drinking it.

None of this I said out loud, after all, I knew that it wasn't really a question.

I was about to burst and couldn't listen to this any longer. Our mother does not want to hear what I want to say, and there was no need to finish the wine story. We all know by now what happened after that first glass of red vino. I knew how it ended without being told, and that girl was long gone.

Mom kept talking, but I interrupted her mid-sentence. "Listen, Mom, if we are going to have a relationship, then the topic of Brett is off limits. If he and I do, or do not, have a relationship, that is between us. It really has nothing to do with you."

I went further than I normally do, telling her that she was going to live like this. I knew it and so did he. And that if she was broke, that was on her, not on Brett, so if she was making him feel guilty that wasn't fair, as he should never have been in that house to begin with.

Although she didn't ask, I told her about her grandchildren, what they had been up to. About Ricky, how hard he works and his great job and I shared some details about the brand new house he bought for himself. Quite an accomplishment as at the time he bought it he was only nineteen. I told her that Ry and Rebeca would be moving to Calgary that September as they were both going to school at SAIT Polytechnic (the Southern Alberta Institute of Technology).

"When they graduate, they both want to live back in Sylvan. It makes me so happy that both the kids want to settle where we are. Most of the Tisdales are around there and it is what I have always wanted. I dream of being surrounded by my family and of course someday by my grandchildren."

I am not sure what she heard during our visit, but the next thing I knew, she was selling both homes and moving to our small town of Sylvan Lake.

Received, June 16, 2011 from tizindie

Attached to this email were three pictures from my brother: A LITTLE BROWN LAB PUPPY. "Hey, here's little YUMA!"

Wow, I thought, another dog….

As usual, I wouldn't hear from Brett in months; he just checked in once in a while via email.

So, I replied, letting him know that I was in New York.

From: btisdale

Sent: Sat, Aug 13, 2011 9:23 pm

Cool, have a New York hot dog for me from some greasy vendor

I landed in Calgary after my week away. I needed to get home, but I was making an effort in my relationship with our mother so we were going for a quick dinner a little later. Auntie Sharon was visiting and I came bearing gifts.

I rolled in my pink leather carry-on bag, unzipped the silver zipper. "Here, Mom, I got you something," I said.

I handed her a gold-and-cream box, and set another one on the coffee table. She unfolded the cardboard and pulled out a three-wick Donald Trump candle. Her nose pressed close to the glass, she said, "Oh, my God, this smells fabulous, thank you."

"You're welcome" I told her. "The other one is for Auntie Sharon,"

I then pulled a black t-shirt out of my bag. There was a large image of a bridge in New York City with huge, bold writing: BROOKLYN.

"This is for Brett, Mom. Can you give it to him?" I asked, as I handed it to her, placing it in her arms.

It had been so many years since I had bought anything for him for a birthday or Christmas, which was against my nature. But I couldn't, or should I say, *wouldn't*. He had always been drinking on those occasions and I so wanted him to realize that he needed to change, to realize that these important milestones would pass him by otherwise. Today, I just wanted him to know that I was thinking about him. My brother would love New York.

"Hey, maybe you could call Brett, see if he wants to come for dinner with us?" I suggested.

Without any hesitation at all, "No, he can't, Jodee. He is drinking again."

I am not sure why she couldn't spare my feelings, even just once. "He is working, he's busy," or make up some other excuse. This news hit me like a freight train and left me struggling and breathless for days.

And it was too late to take the t-shirt back.

"HARD CORE TROUBADOUR "

I hadn't heard anything for a couple of months. It was Halloween 2011 and I saw our cousin Kelly. Normally, we didn't talk about Brett at all as it just caused pain for both of us. But I was worried, so I was just looking for reassurance that he was okay.

"Hey, have you heard from Brett?" I could tell he was hesitating. "It's okay," I assured our cousin. "You can tell me; I can take it."

"Well, he has lost his job again. They have sent him a demand letter; he's really worked up and stressed out. They want over twenty grand back from him."

There was never a lack of jobs, and this continued to compound the problem. Due to confidentiality and human rights, these employers could never share with the next the real reason why Brett no longer worked there. And this was dangerous. This wasn't a job where you were selling cheeseburgers. This was a gas plant where panels and gauges are monitored, twenty-four hours a day. If your head is cloudy or you don't have your wits about you, someone can get hurt. The safe and efficient operation of these gas plants is the responsibility of these ticketed power engineers, with alarms and whistles if there is a problem. One of them screws up, there could be an explosion, and someone could die.

Not only could he get over $67 an hour at the time, he sometimes got huge signing bonuses and relocation allowances. Multi-million dollar corporations at the end of the day are so scared to be sued for wrongful dismissal by someone with a disease that they make bad choices. One of the previous employers, a short time earlier, wrote Brett a check for over $11,000 as a "retiring allowance" for less than six months' work. That is so messed up, a huge lump sum of money is not what an addict needs. But they don't know what to do any more than we do.

Kelly didn't really say much more, and there was no need. He was protecting me and I love him for it. My heart breaks for him; he too has lost someone that he loves. His best friend, whom I knew he saw about as often as I did. Another painful boundary, forced to consider the wellbeing of yourself and your own family first. I backed off with any more questions, as I just didn't want to hear anymore. So, whether Brett had told him about being sued during a late night drunken phone call, or whether a collection agency had called Kelly's house again (Brett continued to put our cousin Kelly down as a reference), it didn't matter.

The point was that it had ended badly, again, likely with an ambulance call with no lesson learned.

My brother was confused on so many levels, yet a mastermind on others. From what I understand, Brett got a professional to write a letter saying that the job up north, secluded, far away from his support systems, was not good for his recovery as he was sick with an illness. Ultimately, they backed down on wanting the twenty thousand dollars repaid. He knew *exactly* how to make this life continue to work for him. In my opinion, my brother was not in recovery. I don't think he thought he even had a problem as he was in such complete denial. And so the same choices, the same path, and same the cycle would start all over again, getting the exact same type of job in a town far away.

In early December, I was working in Calgary and Ricky and Ryan came along to help. They were taking me out for dinner for my forty-third birthday, which was the next day, and I was picking them all up at Mom's. I was running a little late as the roads weren't the best. Our brutal winters typically start early in Alberta, slowing everything down. I was doing my best to hurry since we had a reservation at a nearby Italian restaurant at 6:30 p.m.

I pulled up to a big snowbank in front of Mom's house and honked the horn, once, twice and no one came. I jumped out and hurried through the front door, "Guys, c'mon, we're going to be late," I said.

"Surprise!!" they all yelled, Yuma barking his welcome and running over to the door. And from behind the couch popped Brett, holding a cup of coffee. "Surprise," he said.

Oh, we were not going out for dinner at all. I instantly saw a beautifully decorated room and a couple of bags of gifts and smelled the sweet aroma of dinner filling the air. Rick and Ryan looked like cats that had swallowed the canary, beaming as they had managed to keep the party a secret. Our Mom had very obviously taken a great deal of time to plan this evening, serving up salad and homemade lasagna. I was overwhelmed and grateful. This was one of the only times I can remember my mother ever doing anything nice for me.

After dinner, I sat on the floor and put on my party hat. Brett snapped a picture, then handed me a blue gift bag. Inside was a little rock.

"It is for peace and luck," he said. "The other thing is kind of a joke."

As I pushed back the tissue paper, I found a black coffee mug with the logo of a topless mermaid. I didn't know what exactly he meant by "joke." The fact that I would never buy an expensive coffee from somewhere when I have a free pot at home? A reminder of our beautiful walk that day when we met at Starbucks? Or a nod to all those daily coffees we used to share when we would sit and talk? Or was it just his funny way of letting me know that he knew that I hated that he kept drinking coffee late into the night but he did it anyway? Maybe it was all those things—I didn't care. My brother knew me and I knew him. How much joy you can get from such a simple gift; I loved that freakin' mug.

"Thanks," I said with a warm smile.

The only thing that could have made this amazing evening even better was if Jim and Ry's girlfriend Rebeca had been there, but they were away working together up north at a show. I reveled in seeing my sons, now almost nineteen and twenty-one, interacting with their uncle as the adults that they now were. Talking, laughing, and sharing what had been going on in their lives. Ryan was taking Power Engineering at college. Watching the two of them side by side warmed my heart. Past memories of our once-happy family filled my mind. How close Brett used to be with his nephews and I couldn't help but think back to the night of Ryan's birth when he had been part of his delivery.

I can't explain why some things happen in our life. A mere coincidence? Fate?

As I sat and watched them, I felt a complete sense of pride and love.

Ryan was following in the career path of his Uncle. Brett was telling Ry all about the different engineering plants, which ones are better, what they each have to offer. Clicking on the mouse, he showed him different websites. My heart melted for so many reasons. My brother had missed years of their lives. When I sorted through the pain, the destruction, and everything that we had been through, I realized it had not changed how much they loved my brother. I hope he knew that. And he loved them, too.

For the next couple of months I told everyone I knew that that wonderful evening was "my best birthday ever." It ended as usual—a hug, a kiss on the cheek. "I love you," I whispered in my brother's ear.

"I love you, too," Brett replied, like a thousand times before.

"BOTHER"

"Jodee, someone's here," Jim called, which startled me awake in the spare bedroom down the hall. He had been snoring so I had been there for only a couple of hours. I was dazed and confused, and I struggled to focus on the clock beside my bed. It was 3:15 a.m.

I wasn't sure what Jim meant: someone's in the yard, someone has broken in? Half asleep, I scurried down the hall to grab the telephone. I was high above at our bedroom landing and I looked down over the railing and I could see the front door, open about a foot. Jim was already there and through the blackness of night, I could see the glowing reflection of bright, bold yellow stripes on dark pant legs.

Jim said nothing but turned around and I began to feel lightheaded as if I was floating out of my body. I knew why they were there. It was not my children, as I had the sense to know that if it had been, he would have dropped to the ground. As I floated down the twenty or so stairs, Jim passed me, brushing my shoulder as he had started walking back in my direction. His eyes welled up with tears. As I got to the two men at the front door, I only heard four words: "The Cochrane RCMP called ...."

They took two steps onto my tile entrance and one reached out his arms. "Don't touch me," I said and I moved back quickly. My husband handed me some Kleenex and waited close by. He knew I would let him know when I needed him to hold me. I felt dizzy, my head in a spin, like it was disassembled from my body. I continued to stand at the front door, taking two steps, pressing my body against the dark beige walls. I had known this day would come yet that knowledge did not diminish or prepare me for the overwhelming pain, despair, shock, and sadness. The room was silent except for the occasional soft whimper, as I just stood in the corner and cried. And cried. And cried.

Lost in a nightmare, I dragged myself upstairs and put on a pair of old sweatpants, a hoodie, and tied my long hair into a pony. And Jim and I jumped into my SUV and headed a short distance across town. I hadn't seen my brother since my birthday, and that was over three-and-a-half months earlier. Mom had moved to Sylvan Lake less than three weeks before. We pulled up to the cute, white cabin that she was renting, just a block from the lake.

"Do you want me to come with you?" Jim asked, always with such support.

"No, I will do it." I replied.

I walked up the path and knocked on the small glass pane of the kitchen window and Yuma began to bark. "Hello? Hello?" I heard within, in a couple of minutes.

"It's me, Mom." I said loudly so she could hear me through the wall. She was used to me coming early. I was so busy at work that I had been getting up extra early, sometimes at 5:00 a.m., to have coffee with her each morning. That was not why I was there today.

I stood at the porch as the door creaked open. Yuma bolted out the door and Jim grabbed his collar. He waited outside with the two police officers.

"What's wrong? What's wrong?" My mother asked, the puzzle pieces coming together in her mind.

"I am sorry," I said calmly.

"What! What! What has happened?!" she yelled.

"He's gone, mom." I caught her in my arms and Jim told me later her wails and screams could be heard from the street.

Once I got her safely in bed, I told Jim that I needed to head to Red Deer to get Nicole, but he would not hear of it. "No, you stay with your mom. I will do it," he said. I did not want the RCMP to be the ones to break my sister's nor our father's heart. Jim drove down the highway to tell Nickie that her brother was gone. And together they would drive an hour and tell Peter.

"Jodee, do not let him lie there any longer then he has to. Please," my mother asked of me within the hour.

"I understand, Mom. Don't worry. I will look after it."

Just after noon, barely nine hours since this devastating news, I was at a funeral home in town with my sister. I made the arrangements for them to pick up Brett's body from the coroner's office and to bring him safely home.

Nicole left shortly after as she needed to somehow find the strength to tell Payton and Kaddi that their beloved Uncle Brett was gone.

I spent the night at Mom's house and, when she was finally asleep, I crawled into the spare bed, although I didn't feel like myself. I was confused and feeling fuzzy, as though my brain was floating in my head, bouncing around softly from side to side. This, I believed, was what insanity felt like. I placed my head gently on the pillow and the covers tightly over my head. I had shed a million tears over these years, and I had been strong all day. I began to cry, my body retching from the pain. For the first time in my whole life, I remember thinking, "I hope I don't wake up."

I came home early Tuesday. Jim was sitting quietly on the couch and we talked and cried together for a while.

"Jode, I don't want to upset you, but there's a drunken message on the answering machine from your dad," he said. "He wants to know when we are all going to go and clean out Brett's apartment."

Without hesitation I told my husband firmly, "I am a good person, but a saint I am not. There is no fucking way I will allow him to go rifle through Brett's belongings. He has not been here to help, not even once, since that first time at the Pine Park Hotel over six years ago. We *all* must live with the choices we make."

I sat silently for a few minutes.

"Can you do me a favor? I have so much to do first. Can you call Trevor, ask that he meet us there on Friday morning? I am sorry we have to ask him, but he is the only one who knows where Brett was living."

"Ya, I'll call him."

By late Tuesday, I knew I needed to make some decisions as our mother could barely get out of bed. I called a lawyer to get advice as I knew my brother would have no will. After explaining the details, the fact that there would be no money, just substantial debt and nothing of any real value to sell, I was not sure what to do. I realized that we could go to court, but for what? He believed that my mother would be the executor due to the circumstances, so she should take that role on. When I explained that I doubted she would be able to do that, he replied, "She certainly can give that authority to you."

"Okay," I said.

"And, Jodee, I am so sorry for the loss of your brother," David replied.

"Thank you. Me, too," I replied softly.

As I imagined, when I gently tried to talk to Mom about what she needed to do, her reply was one that I had heard so many times before, "Jodee, I can't handle this. You do it please."

I took control and did *everything* surrounding my brother's funeral. For the first time in my whole life, I was grateful my family was incapable. I booked a funeral home, wrote his obituary, put together the pictures for the video, and ordered the food. I did every single thing with meticulous detail.

I tried to spend every minute I could with Mom, to make sure she was okay. I was struggling at her kitchen table with a pencil and a piece of white scrap paper. I was conflicted with knowing what I was going to say for Brett's eulogy, to everyone who loved him, but I knew it needed to be the truth.

As I scribbled and erased, scribbled and erased, Mom walked behind me and sat down on the couch. "Don't you dare say he was an alcoholic. He hated that word."

I turned casually. My usual response of silence was not the case that day. "Don't you think that was the problem?" I replied.

And that was always a huge part of the problem—the shame, the inability to be confident enough to deal with the stigma that comes along with addiction. Society does not accept alcoholism. It doesn't accept sobriety, either; in fact, it discourages sobriety. I challenge anyone to go to a party or a wedding and not drink, and to watch the reaction of family, friends, and even strangers. I haven't had a drink in over twenty years and it still happens to me all the time—the rude comments, the stares, the disbelief.

"I can have just one. C'mon, c'mon, here," someone says, passing me a glass. Or, "You don't drink? Why, what is wrong with you?"

Wrong with me? Why would something have to be wrong with me?

My own brother couldn't find the courage to tell Dawn-Marie, someone he planned to marry, that he was an alcoholic, let alone to stand up to strangers, friends or sadly, even some members of his own family. His alternative was to drink. To fit in. To be normal. To be part of the crowd. The disease progressed and pretty soon he believed his own lies.

I took the pencil and wrote as part of my eulogy, *My brother would lose his battle with alcohol addiction.* I had a long way to go, but there was a start. Thanks, Mom.

There wasn't a lot of choice for a place for the family to pay respects after the funeral in this small town at the lake, and I thought the legion was highly inappropriate and therefore not an option. Instead, I found a beautiful room at a hotel downtown looking out onto the water. Jim took me to the dollar store later in the day and we bought about thirty different types of picture frames. I knew this would make my brother laugh. He loved the dollar store; he wasn't flashy or pretentious and the simpler, the better. He cherished his pictures, and I was going to fill the room with a lifetime of moments—random shots of all ages of him with friends and family for his celebration of life.

I met Dad and Leona at the hotel. Our mother detests Dad so badly she didn't even want him invited to the funeral. But I would never have that. And Brett would never want that either. To save any conflict, I made arrangements that our families would sit in two separate rooms before the service.

I at least wanted to make Dad and Leona feel like they were involved in the plans and, as I showed them around the banquet room, they seemed genuinely happy with the things I had done so far.

"Dad, I need you to know that when you watch the tribute video that the first half is Mom's side of the family, us growing up with Nana, Papa, Auntie Sharon. So, just wait. The second half is you and all the Tisdales."

"Okay," he said meekly.

"It would be really great if you guys could buy the candles, nothing fancy, for the tables, maybe twenty-five or so?" I asked.

"Um, there really aren't candles where we live, Jodee. Maybe you could just get them," Leona replied.

I hugged them goodbye, brushed off their question about going to his apartment, turned, and walked away. That's okay. I would rather get the candles myself anyway.

I acknowledge that Dad and Leona were paying for half the funeral. I had told my mother earlier in the week that I would pay for the other half.

"I understand, Mom, if you want to pay for the balance yourself. He's your son. But it would be my gift to him. I will do what you want." We agreed to split the other half.

I then did the hardest thing I have ever done in my whole life—ordered my brother's cremation. As I had done for the last few years, I got good at hiding away the grotesque images in my imagination, removing them from my conscious mind. There was one thing I refused to find out. I would run from the truth. I just did not want to know how long he had been there before they found him. I could not face the reality of the pictures that plagued my mind. Metamorphosis, a rope mark, decay, bones ....

Hiding those thoughts is how I survived. They would surface sometime soon, just as they always did and I would not have any choice but to deal with the reality and pain. But at least that was not that day.

For that reason, I tried, but I could not find the courage to go to the morgue to see him and say goodbye. I knew my own limits and that would have been more than I could take. I pray he forgives me.

"HEAVEN"

It was early Friday morning, a typical blizzardy day in Alberta. No one had any business being on the roads, as the wind was blowing fiercely and vehicles were in the ditch in every direction. Regardless of the dangers, there was no other choice. There are times when I needed to think of someone else's wellbeing over and above my own. I thought of the unimaginable trauma and grief for an eighty-plus-year-old couple, Brett's landlords who had found him in his apartment, the one he rented after Mom sold her house and moved to Sylvan Lake. I needed to remove some of their pain, help them forget.

Jim and I met up with Trevor about halfway there, following him another hour out west. We drove through the trees to Bragg Creek, a community of less than six hundred people tucked away from the main highway. Brett had only been in the area less than six weeks, accepting another gas plant job. We passed a couple of small stores and a gas station, then turned down a secluded road. We were just steps away from where *Legends of the Fall* was filmed. The views are still ones that I never quite get used to. The snow-covered mountains always take my breath away.

I was anxious but prepared as we pulled into an acreage lot about fifteen minutes from town. I could see Brett's much-loved old Ford truck parked next to a heaped-up snowbank as we turned right into the yard.

It had been four days since that knock at my door. This morning, I kissed my husband. I thanked him but said I needed to do this on my own. It was my final journey of the life I shared with my brother and I needed to do it alone.

As I walked up to where Brett had spent his final moments, I could see that his home was a separate building isolated from the main house. It had a loft above the garage made of dark brown cedar. I walked about thirty steps up the stairs, knowing my little brother probably would have been carried down them in a black body bag. As I approached the landing, the scenery was astonishing. I looked to the left and noticed this would be the view from his living room window—mounds of snow everywhere, large pine trees, and a rippling river only partially frozen. The water was so close I could almost reach out and touch it. I stopped for a couple of seconds, making sure I was ready. Then with a trembling hand, I gently turned the knob going to the place where Brett took his last breath. As I opened the door slowly, I saw my brother's hiking shoes lying on the welcome mat at the front door. The brown and beige striped laces were waiting, ready for him to put them on and take Yuma for a walk.

I took three steps and turned to the right. I saw a chair, a television, a book *In the Realm of Hungry Ghosts*, two bibles, a coffee table, a notepad, an open laptop, and, on the ground, a picture waiting to be hung.

I turned to the left—a kitchen, no table, a blackberry phone, his wallet at the edge of the window sill, and a half empty pack of Export A Gold cigarettes. Everything was perfectly clean and organized, except for a dirty pot on the stove, stuck with dried spaghetti noodles. I noticed a picture displayed proudly on the refrigerator—drawn by Kaddi. I kept walking, trying to assess, to make sense, to understand. I was okay, surprisingly okay. I passed the bathroom and saw an old wooden table at the end of the hallway, with a small papier mâché box on top. I opened the lid and it was filled with a few trinkets. There was a spare room on the left filled with boxes and then I took two steps into his bedroom on the right.

As I entered, I instantly gasped out loud. Lying on the very top of the overflowing wicker clothes hamper, on top of a pair of Levi's, was a black t-shirt. BROOKLYN. I walked over and took his shirt in my arms, held it up to my nose, took a deep breath, fell to the bare mattress in the corner, and sobbed uncontrollably. The gift I'd bought for him months ago to remind him that I was thinking of him when I returned from New York. It was the last thing he wore. Did he know I would come?

I spent the next few hours sorting things into piles, my loving husband and wonderful cousin Trevor following my every command. Keepsakes. Garbage. Trailer.

I entered the bathroom, holding a black garbage bag in my left hand. I saw his brown leather shaving kit. I started picking up each item and looking at each thing carefully. A toothbrush. Garbage. Toothpaste. Garbage. Fingernail clippers. Garbage. A nose hair trimmer.

What am I doing!? the voice inside me called out. I picked up the kit and threw the whole thing into the garbage; he was not going to need it anymore. As I took a closer look in the kitchen, I found a bag of empties and tied the plastic ends into a knot. In the stainless steel sink remained a wine glass, a few drops of burgundy liquid still in the bottom. This wasn't like all the vodka bottles I had seen before and I knew he didn't see anyone when he locked himself away. Why would a grown man be alone drinking bottles of wine? But it doesn't matter, beer, vodka, wine; it is all the same for an alcoholic.

When the future for all his belongings was settled, we, on our hands and knees, washed the floors, the fridge, and the stove, while acting like we were roommates moving onto the next chapter of our lives. But we weren't roommates and I wasn't sure how any of us could move on.

The funeral was the next day, and I still had so much more to do.

Jim closed the trailer door and walked around the side of the truck.

"You need to do one more thing for me, please," I said.

My husband looked into my eyes.

"When we get back, you need to tell my mother and sister that I have done here what needed to be done. I have kept for myself just a few meaningful things and set aside some keepsakes that I thought they would want. They can keep all that stuff in the trailer or give it all to charity. I don't care. But what needs to be made absolutely clear is I NEVER want to see those things again." Seeing these things later would just cause me heartache.

"I will tell them."

As we pulled out and drove down the beautiful snowy road, through the majestic pine trees and the pointy mountain peaks that my brother would never again see, I finally managed to gather enough strength to ask, "Where was he?"

After a short pause, Jim replied, "In his bedroom closet."

I laid my head on the side of the cold, passenger window, and tears began to stream down my cheeks.

"Okay," I whispered.

"HAVE YOU EVER REALLY LOVED A WOMAN?"

Something unforeseen.

In 2015, it was finally time to tell our adult sons the *whole* story. To try to make sense of everything that had happened and how we all got here. After all, I was writing a story about my brother's life. I would never share these painful memories and the intimate details of his journey if I wasn't prepared to be honest about mine. Jim and I had not spoken of a certain night to anyone for over twenty years. We could have kept it a secret forever, but there is no life's lesson in hiding the truth.

After weeks of heavy conversation and tears from both of us, my husband agreed that I could tell our children and then the world. Jim sobbed uncontrollably as we told each son the painful truth, the shame so real all these years later. He actually believed they would never speak to him again for a mistake made almost a lifetime ago.

Once again it was March 1995, and we were a normal, average, everyday family.

And the next day, we weren't.

We were driving home from an evening out—a bowling party for my work. I wasn't feeling well as I had a slight throat infection, but we didn't go out very often without the kids so it was a welcome treat. I couldn't drink alcohol with the medication for my throat; Jim on the other hand enjoyed more than a few.

Our marriage was already going through some bumps, plus I wasn't pleased that Jim had indulged in so many cocktails. We sat in complete silence during the thirty-minute drive home. When we arrived, we were surprised to find an empty house—Jim's Mom wasn't there with the kids, even though she had been babysitting them. A note on the kitchen table told the story.

Took the kids for a sleepover with Grandma.

Still annoyed that Jim had got so drunk, I got my pajamas on and crawled into bed. Jim was already there.

I was drifting off to sleep, safe and warm, when I felt his drunken hand grab my thigh. I could almost taste the rye when his warm, putrid breath traveled through my nostrils.

This was the last thing on my mind. I pushed his hand away. Seconds later, it was back.

I flung away his hand once more and I sat up. "I'm leaving," I said.

But before I could even react, he was standing over me on my side of the bed. With unimaginable force, he lifted me in the air by my arms, and in one powerful swoop, ripped off my pajamas like they were made of a thin sheet of paper. I was instantly cold, completely exposed, and caught in the moon rays shining through our cheap blinds. He jumped back, panic-stricken as to what he had just done.

There was no time to think. Before my conscious mind could comprehend, I was running naked down the hall. Away from the one I loved, the one who loved me, too. Twelve or fourteen quick steps, then a leap to the front door. I reached for the doorknob and then I stopped, breathless, realizing that I was completely bare. I turned around and saw Jim had somehow made his way to the kitchen at the top of the stairs. He said absolutely nothing, just looked at me expressionless as his hand reached up slowly to the butcher's block. My life instantly became slow motion. I was mesmerized by the long, sharp Henkel knife as he carefully set it on the wooden table in front of him. I froze, unable to move for a split instant. My mind was trying to formulate what that meant. Was it for him? For me?

My terror escalated in just a matter of moments and there was no time for an analysis of options or a conscious choice as my legs began to move me fast and furiously out the door. I was completely naked as I ran down the street into the cold, dark night. I saw the bright glare of headlights before I heard the car driving slowly down my street and I could hear the muffled echoes of a shrieking female in the background. The young female driver pulled over and let me in, feeling sympathy for the woman screaming in the dead of night. It took me a minute or two to realize that those shrill cries had been my own. I was trembling and hysterical, although I knew I was safe as we zoomed away and I didn't look back. But, the nightmare was just beginning.

At the police station, I removed the shirt someone had given me and stood in front of two officers, naked from the waist up. They took pictures of my badly bruised arms. Snap, snap, click, click. "Turn to the right, please." Snap, snap, click, click.

Within a few hours, my mom arrived and we followed behind a blue RCMP car. Jim was there, at his sister's. The police had already called to let them know what was going to happen next. I watched from the car as the front door opened, some of Jim's family members standing there beside him. Jim, the father of my children, took a couple of steps, turned around, was arrested, handcuffed, and led into the back of a police car. My children's daddy would be charged with "assault with a weapon."

They then pulled around the corner and parked slightly out of sight, and waited as his family went to wake the children. When I got to my front door, the boys greeted me with tired eyes and big smiles. And I left with my two beautiful sons.

I loved my husband; well, at least I did yesterday.

He then spent a couple of weeks in a jail downtown, while I told the kids that Daddy was at work. They were so young after all; they had no concept of time. I told only a couple of my close friends about that night. And both our families knew what happened. Only Jim and I knew the details of what actually had gone on behind the scenes. I have always been private; it's just not my style to share all my personal problems. After all, everyone has issues of their own.

I hid everything from everyone as I tried to figure out what the hell had happened and wondered what I was going to do. I put on a brave smile at work where I was a cosmetics manager. Missing work for any reason was not a financial option.

I visited Jim a few times during his incarceration. I had to go through metal detectors and searches before being able to go inside. It was surreal sitting on a stainless steel stool looking through a glass window at a thin man in an orange jumpsuit. He was barely recognizable to me. I was shocked, confused, lost, sad, scared, and mad.

I had always been the stable one, the one who made all the right choices. Well,

I thought I had, or I had tried to be. And yet, there I was, and I had no idea how I got there.

Upon his release, Jim had a "no contact order" to keep his distance from me, which was lifted a couple of weeks later. But there was no way I was letting him back into our house.

It was the most stable, loving, calm separation for the children; I made sure of that. I would stay at the house during the week, and then on the weekends I would leave, which allowed Jim a couple of days at home with the boys. Back then, showing nothing but love and support, I would sleep in a small sleeping bag on the floor of Brett and Bobbie's tiny apartment. My brother would be there for me, holding me when I cried. Without judgment, he would be there, whatever I decided.

The raw emotions brought up during counseling between Jim and me were very hard to hide when we made the switch off with the children every weekend, but we did it. I hated Jim for doing this to us, but I loved my children more. If we couldn't work it out, that was between us.

This was the most volatile, disruptive, and horrible few months of my life. So much so, I filed for divorce.

I was only twenty-six years old. I used to lie in bed, feeling tired, broken, and alone; four-year-old Ricky was sound asleep across the hall. Beside me, nestled close, sleeping, was our two-year-old Ryan. His white blond hair and round face were so peaceful and innocent. I decided that I was going to quit my job, leave this city, and move far away from my soon to be ex-husband and his family. The kids would see their dad only on some occasional weekends.

As I looked at Ryan's sweet little face, I realized their lives and who they would become were about to change forever. I would *never* stay together with Jim for the sake of the children; we deserved better and would not live this way. But, for them, I would try a thousand times harder to make our marriage work. If it were at all possible to keep their parents together, have a happy, healthy, and, most importantly to me, a home where they felt "safe," I would try.

So, I agreed to continue counseling with my husband and two weeks later I fired my lawyer.

"ALL THE THINGS WE'VE NEVER DONE"

My world became a place of unfamiliarity. I went with my husband to see a probation officer and I attended Jim's anger-management classes. We continued couple's therapy, which had almost been our breaking point weeks earlier as everything became too much to take. It brought up so many issues, individual flaws, our marriage, how we managed with problems and, yes, our childhoods.

We were still so young. Things had started changing and we hadn't even noticed. I had married at twenty-one and I didn't even realize that I was growing into the person who I would become. We had two little kids, the stresses of money, work, family interference and, let's be honest, we certainly weren't having sex every second of the day like we had when we were first dating. We felt all these pressures in our marriage, which caused ripples. We just didn't understand why or what to do about it. "Real life," I call it now. We combined all of this with an alcohol-fueled evening, which magnified the problems tenfold and, in an instant, everything changed forever.

I hear people sometimes say, "You can't blame your parents." Blame? This is not about blame; this is about some of the reasons "why" we make certain choices. What we have seen; where we get our values; the things that become our lessons of right, not our lessons of wrong.

Through therapy I came to realize, without ever knowing it before, that due to my childhood memories, I would never have sex with a drunken man. And, like my mother, I was going to sleep on the couch to get away from the unwanted advances.

Jim, the youngest child in his family, had witnessed countless Friday nights (and Saturdays to Thursdays, too) with weapons and brawls. It had been so much worse than I ever lived through. He always got so overwhelmed with anger when he drank rye, getting into bar fights on many occasions, and that had been his drink of choice on that particular evening. When he grabbed the knife, he thought it would make me just sit and talk. That reasoning made sense to him in his plastered mind. Alcohol by itself was not to blame.

But alcohol added to our early childhood memories, heredity, marital stress, trauma, and a fight created the perfect storm for disaster. None of that is an excuse for his actions; it does not make them any less wrong.

To add fuel to the fire, his support systems encouraged him to believe this wasn't so bad and that it was all my fault. In time, he found the strength to break free of that belief. My husband stood alone, distancing himself from his own family that he loved very much. He blamed no one, no one but himself. I eventually forgave this mistake of enormous proportions. Although my husband is not an "alcoholic" by definition, he is certainly someone with a problem with drinking. So, Jim chose to give up alcohol forever. In support, I decided to do the same. We both suffered the consequences of that fateful night, and we realized how our childhoods and alcohol had played a part in lighting the fuse.

We invited no one to the court date, except my one girlfriend. No family at all. We were putting our lives back together and we wanted to do that alone. Jim's Dad had put fifteen thousand dollars in a bank account for him to cover his lawyer and, although we were flat broke and in debt, that account went untouched. Even then, I was tough as nails when I didn't agree with something, and I bit back hard when Jim's lawyer (whom his family hired) asked me to change my story when I testified. "Not a fucking chance." I think he knew instantly he could be in trouble and he refused to see me again.

I am not sure how the system works in the USA, but in Canada the charges are laid by the police department and the prosecution asked for Jim to receive three years behind bars.

I do not recall exactly what I said, but it was the truth. "The truth, the whole truth, and nothing but the truth," as I lifted my right hand. I interrupted the prosecutor when he tried to cut short my story as to why I was there supporting my husband. "May I finish?" I asked, looking at the judge.

It was so long ago, I don't recall my exact words but I said something like I do know that I did the right thing by calling the police. I knew that Jim's actions were a grave mistake and both of us saw it as that. The prosecution was spinning the story, saying that Jim must have been abusive, that this had happened before, that this was a pattern. I would have agreed with all those things if they had been true and I would have been long gone. But they weren't true.

That didn't mean that what Jim did was right. No one should accept abuse on any level; it is wrong. I didn't talk in court about the things we had both witnessed all those years ago when we were children. After all, those were our private stories that we were still working through. I do remember that if my husband had been sent away for three years, we would have accepted that punishment.

A grade twelve law class was in the courtroom when I took the stand. When I finished speaking, many of the teenagers were crying.

Jim got freedom, except for weekends in jail. For the next couple of months, I would pack our young sons in my small Pontiac Sunfire on Friday nights and take their daddy to "work." We would have little camp outs in the tent in our basement, peaking through the open door, watching movies together on the television. And then we would drive back downtown and pick their dad up on Sunday nights.

From the time Jim and I first met, we always talked about where we had come from. We never promised ourselves we could be perfect. We just promised ourselves that we could do better.

And, though it may be hard for many to understand, I would not take back that night even if I could.

I don't believe this would be my life had that night never happened. How we saw each other and how we saw the world was never the same afterwards. I have been married to this man for twenty-six years now. He loves me deeply and makes me feel it every day. We still hold hands, we talk and communicate more than anyone I know; he is loved and respected by *all* who know him. After all these years when he looks at me, he still thinks I am the most beautiful girl in the world—we are madly, deeply, passionately in love. My husband inspires me every day.

We have raised our sons the right way. We know we can't control who or what they will become, but we have taught them proper values and lessons, and although we are not perfect, we have tried very hard to be good role models.

We became different people after that split-second of horror, and our children's lives are better because of it. Of course, they just didn't know it. They knew we had separated; they did recollect that. They knew about some of the influences of our family members, that we had to make some painful choices. They just didn't know the whole story.

I don't believe it is a coincidence that these patterns continue generation after generation. Coming from such chronic dysfunction, being raised in that environment, with alcohol at every turn, Jim and I had to acknowledge there was unhealthy behavior going on around us that wasn't good for our lives, our marriage, or our children. But when it is all you have ever known and they are the ones you love more than anything else in the world, it is very hard to break free.

Even Jim's own father, also an alcoholic, offered Jim some valuable advice, "Take your beautiful wife and those two little boys and move far away from here." He told Jim that right before passing away from cancer.

My husband chose us. Our marriage wouldn't have survived had we stayed in Edmonton. It took a little while, but as soon as we could, he moved us to Sylvan Lake. We tried to break the cycle of alcoholism in our family and we did that together.

And so there it is—a secret no more.

"THE DANCE"

I have not thought about that time in our lives in so long, and yet it still pains me greatly, knowing what we could have lost.

I never realized it until long after my brother was gone, but Brett's big surprise so long ago, the first AA meeting, and his realization of having a problem and this catastrophic event with my husband happened within months of each other. My brother and I made completely different life choices about alcohol. And our lives went in completely different directions.

How different things might be today if we all had talked about our feelings, trauma, and family histories, giving each other valuable insight. My brother might have made a different choice back then, when alcohol was just a problem and not an actual addiction. Before it had grabbed hold of him and just wouldn't let him go, before it was so far past the realm of what anyone could possibly imagine.

I wish I had talked openly and honestly with Brett about my relationship with Jim back then, so that my brother perhaps could relate. At the time you are so scared of being condemned and judged that you stay silent, even from close family members. I could have talked about our struggles and our separation, about how I viewed alcohol, about Jim's and my childhood experiences, and how they affected our lives.

The last thing I ever want to do in 2016 is rewrite history or tell a story that isn't one hundred percent true. My greater understanding of alcohol and drug addiction has left me shattered at times and rocked to my core. I always believed at the time that my brother was drinking based on simply being addicted and for a variety of reasons he wasn't willing or able to change. Science has progressed, or maybe this newfound knowledge that I have was available all along and I just didn't realize at the time how Brett's problems went so much deeper than alcoholism. I do believe that my brother's problems began with feelings he didn't understand, childhood trauma that—since he didn't totally remember—confused him. Childhood trauma and/or sexual abuse can lead to alcohol or drug addiction as way to cope with the feelings of emptiness.

I see so many things more clearly now after years of trying to educate myself and understand. I don't believe Brett's disturbing early childhood dreams and sleepwalking were simply dreams after all but rather night terrors caused by trauma; they of course started again in adulthood.

Perhaps his arrogance was actually a sign of low self-esteem; he was trying to hide his lack of self-worth. Survivors of early childhood trauma often suffer from low self-esteem, shame, self-blame, and guilt. They become out of touch with their feelings—confused by emotion or reactions they can't explain. We know now that trauma can even cause people to cut and to harm themselves out of a sense of despair.

Wonderful doctors like Dr. Gabor Maté, a Canadian physician who is a renowned speaker, bestselling author and a highly sought after expert on a range of topics including addiction, stress and childhood development. He brings attention to the impact of these experiences on the most severely addicted, claiming that the core of all addictions is trauma and that adverse childhood experiences have been shown to exponentially increase the risk of addiction later in life.

I doubt I would have ever known who Dr. Maté is except for the fact that my brother had one of his books sitting on his bible in his living room. I read that book—*In the Realm of Hungry Ghosts: Close Encounters with Addiction* —so Brett continued to help me on this journey long after he was gone.

I was always of the mindset that our past didn't affect my brother. I felt it certainly had nothing to do with his drinking. I was protecting him and my parents, too. I never wanted him to think less of them. After all, our mom and dad are not perfect and they loved us very much. So, I remained silent. And in the end, I wasn't protecting him at all.

I found something weeks after Brett had died, tucked neatly in between the pages of my brother's bible, the one of only a few sentimental items that I had wanted. Written in blue felt pen, *0->5, Mom's love, but the fights - 5 & up, scared without Jody.*

Nothing in the world made Brett and me who we are more than those

Friday nights. Even if one could not remember and one of us could never forget.

What is interesting, you see, is we had written letters, shared cards, communicated through emails and texts, and I had read probably over two hundred pages from his journals, always written the same way over the years, "Jodee." Not surprising as that is how I spell my name. But here, on a single piece of lined paper, it was written differently. I could tell he wrote it when he was an adult as there were a few words about missing Kaddi's birthday on September 15. And even more profound and enlightening, he wrote about "a couple years of emptiness" during his late teens, early twenties a few paragraphs down, which still makes me cry. Brett got it right when he wrote this note. I had changed the spelling when I was just a teenager, but when I was a little girl, when he and I were taking on the world, it was "J-o-d-y."

I hear people sometimes who are so mad and frustrated through their addiction journey that they blame the health care professionals. But I am not that girl. I appreciate greatly all the help offered to us by doctors, psychiatrists, psychologists, therapists, and AADAC counselors, especially Dr. Mark Dimirsky and Terry. Everyone went above and beyond and tried to help us; the list is long. The system itself is far from perfect, and I admit that. And that speaking out together, educating, and standing tall in a world of judgment will help make a difference in eliminating the stigma that surrounds addictions and bringing more awareness about the things that aren't working and evoke change. In the end though, none of these people or the help they can provide are going to offer an easy answer. And it is unfair to believe the solution lies solely on their shoulders.

So I am not going to focus on the things we missed or the secrets we kept, as none of us can go back; life is about going forward. If all the stars had aligned, if the signs had all been known, would knowing that adverse childhood experiences or trauma are precursors to addiction, anxiety, depression, PTSD and other mental illnesses have made a difference in my brother's recovery? Only if *he* had been prepared to be honest with his feelings, do all the hard work, make some difficult choices, and change. So, we will never know.

I think we—his family—did more harm to my brother than the system ever did. I can only take responsibility and regret for my part, some of the things I did helped progress this along. *Everything* we do matters.

I sometimes feel anxious and nervous, writing a book on addiction. After all, I am not in recovery, not in the typical sense anyway. But what is very real is that everyone involved needs to "recover." As much as I continue to work hard to educate myself and bring attention to what goes on in order to help the families, the truth is I don't know what it is like to be addicted to alcohol or to drugs. But I do know what it is like to feel powerless to something that takes control over your life. It is not easy to break patterns of all we have ever known, even when our choices hurt us or hurt the ones we love. I know that sometimes those behaviors are etched deep inside.

I continued to cause my own husband pain long after Brett was gone. He felt the hurt of watching his wife cry almost every day for two years in front of a laptop screen, as I was determined to tell my brother's story. Filling my black Starbucks mug that Brett gave me, early at 4 or 5 a.m., and playing his favorite songs over and over again. As usual, Jim put his own pain aside to support me and what I needed in order to come to terms with my brother's death. I wouldn't realize until about three quarters of the way through writing this book, in what Oprah would call an "aha" moment, that it was perhaps not his story after all, but mine—I have learned through this process so much about myself. I am grateful I didn't know that early on as I would never have even started writing. When I finished typing my first draft and had time to stand back, reading the story over and over again, I could feel how heartbreaking it was for all involved.

I commented to Jim, "I would have understood if you had finally had enough and forbade me to see my brother."

I meant that as a positive. To acknowledge that I wasn't making the best choices back then, for myself, my family, and even for my own brother. But my husband, knowing how much I loved Brett, was giving me the time to sort through that on my own. Some may think he did that because he loved me so much. Or that that is how much he loved Brett. After all, Jim had known my brother since he was sixteen years old. But I have been married to this man for a very long time; no one knows me better or loves me more. I have always known why he didn't put his foot down. And finally my husband had the courage to say it out loud.

"If I had made you choose back then, you would not have chosen me," Jim said.

And I began to cry as hard as on that fateful day, as I knew he was right. I would not have chosen Jim. I would have left my own children and husband back then to save the one I loved, the little boy with the round cheeks and big heart.

"HEADLIGHTS"

So much has happened in the last four years since my brother died. Sadly, my family did not change and I am estranged from my mother and my sister. I can no longer endure their continued insistence that I didn't do enough, or in fact anything during the last five years of my brother's life. I concede the story they tell themselves is not the same as mine.

I am much stronger and healthier now, more aware as to what I am and what I am not. As I will live the rest of my life filled with powerful emotions, having good days and bad, the emotion I do not carry is guilt. I know I did everything I could for my brother, making mistakes along the way. After all he was human and so am I. I wish I had gotten help for myself first, it is on the top of my list of many things I wish I had done differently. I wish that we could have stood beside each other as a family in a healthy, positive way because we are in this disease together. But when we lose ourselves in someone else's addiction, we are no good to anyone; not ourselves and certainly not the ones we love. In the end, we are not culpable for someone else's path. Just our own. It took me a long time to get here, finding my own voice where my mom is concerned. The little girl inside me still struggles, but I know that is just my heart playing with my head. I can say now with complete confidence. I am not responsible for their lives. I never was.

I will love my father, my mother, and my sister Nicole from a distance; this is for my own health and wellbeing. And I am sorry for their loss.

Since I was a little girl, my perception was that alcohol caused almost everything bad that has happened in my life. Either directly or indirectly. It took away my daddy. My mom. My sister. My brother. It almost cost me my marriage. It almost cost my sons their father.

Addiction affects us all and none of our lives are ever quite the same. I imagine this happens even when loved ones do find recovery. People stop talking to you as they take sides without knowing anything about your life. Just being neutral I guess isn't human nature. But no one really knows what goes on behind closed doors and in my case people confuse their relationship with my brother with that of mine. This journey and loss could have brought my family closer together; my brother would have wanted that.

I struggled for many weeks, not because of this story. I have no shame and I am exceptionally proud. This is a no-holds-barred, nothing-is-off-limits, unapologetic account of what it was really like as I know now that I am *not* alone.

Alone. That is what I felt for so long. It is how I believe my brother felt. Sharing these stories gives us power, it gives us strength. And it gives others hope when at times we all feel completely hopeless. Maybe it is a mistake to strictly concentrate on how many people are successful in recovery. Let us not only celebrate and learn from those who achieve sobriety but also let us learn from those who didn't. Let us not consider these to be lessons of failure—gloomy, dark, depressing tales of alcohol and drug addiction. But rather the opposite; let us consider that these lessons lived by someone else give others insight, courage, knowledge, and, yes, hope.

You know, someone Brett and I know well actually said right to me, "Your brother was a junkie and deserved to die; he had more than enough chances." Another person, a very close family member, warned me not to tell this story as it would "destroy his memory." I am not going to spend my life arguing, debating, letting people break my spirit for the truth I know and believe with all of my heart. What I remind myself when I speak of addiction or of Brett is that this way of thinking is not at all about my brother's character or who he was; it is about theirs.

Besides, I made a promise to my brother a long time ago to keep writing, and I have never broken a promise to him in my whole life. So, I thank him for giving me the courage to continue, when on most days I just wanted to forget.

Where I am conflicted is about summing up the moral, the "one big message" that I want to convey to the world. Is it the progression of alcoholism, the causes, shame, blame, denial, dysfunction, unhealthy family relationships, heredity, environment, codependency, trauma, mental illness, hope, love, forgiveness? And then I realize, I still do not have all the answers, none of us does. I know that addiction is complicated and there is no "one-size-fits-all" answer or approach for that, or for any of life's problems. I hope you take away from my pages what *you* need. I can't do that for you as I know that would be too much responsibility for a sister to bear.

I had finally finished our love story, my gift to my brother, the end of our journey and his voice for the very last time.

And then … some things happen in life that are unexplainable. Like many of the stories I have told, I wouldn't believe it unless I had been there. It is not possible; and it defies the voice of reason.

Due to bad weather in Alberta, my husband and I drove to British Columbia for our week's vacation. It was pouring rain in our favorite places—Sicamous and Penticton—so we continued driving south looking for sun and settled in Osoyoos, a place we had never been before not even as children. Out on the boat, enjoying our down time from work, we sailed into US waters quite by accident and found a unique resort community on the water. After our week of holiday, we drove the eleven hours home and we were so intrigued that Jim looked the resort up on google maps on the internet. It was just inside the border in Oroville, Washington, USA, a small town of less than 1,800 people. It has adorable fifties-style cottage homes, a pool, a diner, a gym, marina, and a beautiful beach. We live at the lake, the last thing in the world we were considering was purchasing another home. But the environment and setting were like nothing we had ever seen. We felt it was the lifestyle there that we wanted, that our friends could come, our nieces and nephews, our sons, their significant others, and where someday we will entertain our grandchildren. Loving them long before they are born. On a whim, we purchased a family vacation home.

Two weeks later, on August 18, 2016, I sat in the truck in a grocery store parking lot in Oroville for fifteen minutes waiting for Jim. He jumped in the vehicle and slammed the door.

"Turn off the truck," I said.

"What's wrong?" he asked startled, not noticing that I had been crying.

"Just turn it off for a second. You know how I have been working all week early in the morning on my final manuscript changes from my editor, Nina?"

"Ya," Jim replied.

I began to smile and my eyes filled with tears like they have so many times before.

"And less than two hours ago I had a conference call, trying to finalize the title I want to use."

He just stared at me.

"I am sitting here. In a different country. In a tiny town we shouldn't be in. At a grocery store we shouldn't be at, except for the fact that the other one down the street ran out of romaine lettuce. And you parked right here. You could have parked anywhere in this huge lot."

"Oh-kay." he said, with a bit of a drawl.

"I am sitting here, knowing I am so close. I am almost done. I was thinking of Brett. Can he see me? Is he happy? Is he proud of me? Did I get the story just right?"

My husband is now looking at me with concern and bewilderment. I turned to him and said simply, "Look up."

And he lifted his head.

Behind the store is a small mountain, and in white rocks, big and bold. No other names, just: JODY

"UNITY"

We are left sometimes, in this life, without all the answers we are looking for. I hope in my brother's last dark days he remembered how much I loved him. And then, once again, my eyes fill with tears as I think perhaps he did not. What I do know, with absolute certainty, is that my brother died of addiction. It took away everything, not at the beginning, but at the end. He didn't get to choose how he felt any longer and when using, alcohol became a requirement for him to live.

Alcohol took away my brother's ability to be a son, a brother, a husband, a father, and to ever grow old. We tell ourselves different truths; I suppose we do that as a way to survive the pain. But my truth is that this never had to end this way. Had my brother found sobriety, he would still be anxious and uncomfortable, have issues he would need to work on, struggles with family and all of life's difficulties that we all have. But he would be alive.

I realize now perhaps it was my brother who was right all along. I looked up "inspiration" in the dictionary: "A person, experience or place that gives you new ideas for something you do."

I hope you all find the strength and courage to make the changes you need, whatever those are, to live the beautiful life you have imagined. We are not promised that it is easy. What we are promised is that it is possible.

IN LOVING MEMORY

On Sunday, March 18, 2012 after at least eighteen days of consecutive drinking, my little brother hanged himself in his bedroom closet. He was thirty-nine. His name was Brett Tisdale.

SOME OF MY FAVORITE BOOKS

I continue to gravitate towards reading books on addiction and self-help, some clinical, some not. I find comfort in them, knowing that I am not alone and that help is available. Not everyone is blessed with being able to afford therapists and treatment centers; other resources are available. I hope I never stop learning.

Addiction and Self-Help

Not My Child: A Progressive and Proactive Approach for Healing Addicted Teenagers and Their Families by Dr. Frank Lawlis, PhD

In the Realm of Hungry Ghosts: Close Encounters with Addiction by Dr. Gabor Maté, MD

Beyond Addiction: How Science and Kindness Help People Change by Jeffrey Foote, PhD, Carrie Wilkens, PhD, and Nicole Kosanke, PhD, with Stephanie Higgs

Many Faces One Voice: Secrets from the Anonymous People by Bud Mikhitarian

Mothers Who Can't Love: A Healing Guide for Daughters by Susan Forward, PhD, with Donna Frazier Glynn

Toxic Parents: Overcoming Their Hurtful Legacy and Reclaiming Your Life by Susan Forward, PhD with Craig Buck

Conversations with a Rattlesnake: Raw and Honest Reflections on Healing and Trauma by Theo Fleury and Kim Barthel

Codependent No More: How to Stop Controlling Others and Start Caring For Yourself by Melody Beattie

Women & Shame: Reaching Out, Speaking Truths and Building Connection by Brene Brown PhD

Memoirs

Hardcore Troubadour: The Life and Near Death of Steve Earle by Lauren St. John.

Playing with Fire by Theo Fleury with Kirstie McLellan Day

Between Breaths: A Memoir of Panic and Addiction by Elizabeth Vargas
Symptoms of Withdrawal: A Memoir of Snapshots and Redemption
     by Christopher Kennedy Lawford
Beautiful Boy: A Father's Journey Through his Son's Addiction by David Sheff

Film/Documentary
The Anonymous People directed by Greg Williams

CONTACT INFORMATION

In April 2016, Jodee challenged herself, stepping outside her comfort zone and all she has known for close to twenty years. She sold her beauty company in order to follow her heart to dedicate herself to bringing attention, awareness, and compassion for families struggling with an addicted loved one. She encourages everyone to get help for themselves first. And to find the courage to speak openly and honestly, without shame.

Jodee has pledged 50% of all author profits from the sale of *The Sun is Gone* to organizations that benefit Alcohol, Drug Addiction and Mental Illness programs.

To contact Jodee for an interview or as a keynote speaker for an event supporting Addiction, Recovery, Mental Illness, or Suicide Awareness from a family perspective, you can visit www.jodeeprouse.com

ACKNOWLEDGMENTS

Thank you to the ones who supported, helped, and believed in me early on: Danny Baldassarre, Harley Richards, Mark Malatesta, Jon DeActis, Erika Armstrong, Jenna Swan, Mary-Ann Barr, and Julie and Greg Salisbury at Influence Publishing.

Huge hug and thanks to the beautiful, strong, supportive women at my company who allowed me the freedom to step-back and embark on this new "chapter" of my life: Jackie Savage, Trina Eddy, Dianne Vivian, Stacey Underwood, Christina Munz, Jillian Martin, Laura Gress, Nadine Becker, Aleesha Darago, Deanna Palechek, Amanda English, and Erin Hopfner.

To, Allan and Donnagay Birkbeck and Kristine Scott for your love and friendship. Kelly and Carolynn Tisdale, Trevor Duval, and my aunts, uncles, and other cousins, all of whom I love very much. And to, Dawn-Marie for your bravery, friendship, and support.

Thank you to my editor Nina Shoroplova for your guidance, patience, understanding, and open heart, and for taking me from a sister to a writer. You are amazing.

I'll be forever grateful to Terry, Dr. Mark Dimirsky, and the countless others who were there to help our family throughout this journey.

Thank you to the National Council on Alcoholism and Drug Dependence, Inc. (NCADD). As well, thanks to Dr. Gabor Maté, Dr. Frank Lawlis, Carrie Wilkins, PhD, Susan Forward, PhD, Bud Mikhitarian, Athena Bass, and Kim Barthel for your inspiration and powerful testimonials.

Words cannot express my gratitude to Siegfried and the late Ursula Beckedorf, for the love and care you gave my brother during the last few weeks of his life.

Ron Joel, for the positive influence you have had on my life and for your unconditional love.

Rebeca Engel, you are beautiful, inside and out. I could not love you more if you were my own daughter.

To my sons and nieces, Rick, Ryan, Payton, and Kaddi. Your Uncle Brett loved you all very much and I do too.

To my brother, Brett; I miss you every minute of every day. This love is forever and in my heart you will remain. Until we meet again.

And to Jim, thank you for my beautiful life. To you, I owe *everything*. xo

Author Biography

Jodee Prouse is a daughter, sister, wife, mother, aunt, friend, neighbor, co-worker.

She is an advocate and a voice for families surrounding alcohol, drug addiction, and mental illness.

She lives with her husband of 26 years, Jim. They split their time between Sylvan Lake, Alberta and their home in Oroville, Washington.

CPSIA information can be obtained
at www.ICGtesting.com
Printed in the USA
FSOW03n1814150417
33052FS